300

"In Business as in Life –
You Don't Get What You Deserve,
You Get What You Negotiate"

OTHER BOOKS BY CHESTER L. KARRASS

Give and Take

The Negotiating Game

Both Win Management*

Negotiating Effectively
Within Your Own Organization

* Coauthored with William Glasser M.D.

IN BUSINESS AS IN LIFE –
YOU DON'T GET WHAT
YOU DESERVE,
YOU GET WHAT YOU
NEGOTIATE

CHESTER L. KARRASS

Stanford St. Press
8370 Wilshire Boulevard
Beverly Hills, CA 90211-2333

"In Business As In Life –
You Don't Get What You Deserve, You Get What You Negotiate"

Writing this book required long periods of quiet thought and many hours of discussion with my dear wife, Erika. Without her help and patience it could not have been done. It was a long journey, jointly travelled and enjoyed. Thank you, Erika.

Acknowledgements

Writing a book on a subject as comprehensive as negotiation cannot be accomplished without help from many people. Most of all I wish to acknowledge the help of Frank Mobus, my friend and associate. Together we spent much time discussing the many aspects of this complex subject.

In addition, help was graciously provided by Pat Rodgers and Mel Klayman, with whom I exchanged many words and ideas. For the assistance it takes to change a manuscript into a finished product I owe much to Roy Gechter and Judith Orth, who carried me through draft after draft.

And finally, I wish to acknowledge the farsighted research support provided years ago by the Hughes organization and two of its executives, Theodore Kotsovolos and the late William A. Van Allen, without which none of this would have been possible.

From the Author to the Reader

In the old country my Uncle Tony learned to make wine in the bathtub. When he came to America he continued to do so. Some years the wine was pretty good; in others, it wasn't so good.

At Easter time he always brought a few bottles to the table, not more than two or three. Then he poured glasses and proudly asked the guests how it was. Most were very gracious in their comments, but one I remember didn't answer Uncle Tony right away.

After a few moments of slightly embarrassing silence the guest said, "It's just right Tony."

"What do you mean, just right?" asked Tony.

The man said, "If it was any better you wouldn't have given it to me. If it was any worse I couldn't have drunk it. It was just right."

Well, when I thought about it, that's the way most people seem to come out in negotiation: even professional buyers, sellers and executives who make big deals, or even diplomats on the world stage.

When asked by their managers or others how they came out, they usually say something like this: "If it was any better, they wouldn't have given it to us, and if it was any worse, we wouldn't have taken it. It was just right."

This book is about how we can make agreements in any negotiation, big or small, that are far better than "just right." Agreements that are better for ourselves and better for both sides.

Introduction

A FEW WORDS ABOUT WHAT WE GET AND WHAT WE DESERVE IN BUSINESS AND SOCIAL AFFAIRS

In business as in life, you don't get what you deserve, you get what you negotiate. I know there are many who disagree with this statement. They believe, as I do, that people are fundamentally fair and reasonable in their dealings. They govern their behavior by the Golden Rule: Do unto others as you would have them do unto you. That too is sound advice for living a meaningful and useful life. Yet, despite this almost universal assertion of goodwill, there is, all too often, a wide disparity between the satisfactions we deserve from our relationships and those we get.

Whenever two people do business or interact with one another, the likelihood is that they bring to the relationship differences in viewpoint that must be reconciled. They may hold dissimilar values or goals. They may bring to the relationship differing talents and means which serve to determine the balance of power and the influence each will exert on the other. Even if by some miracle their values, goals, means and talents coincide, they may still disagree on the best method to achieve what both desire. All these differences represent areas of legitimate conflict which must be settled if the two parties are to get along with a measure of mutual satisfaction.

Negotiation is the process that brings these diverse viewpoints together. We all negotiate: buyers and sellers, politicians and diplomats, executives and those who work for them. And, of course, husbands, wives, friends, and children negotiate every day but rarely call it that. Even those who say they hate to negotiate or won't do it negotiate whether they want to or not. That's why Newsweek called negotiation "The Game of Life."

What we deserve and what we get in business and social affairs can only be settled by give and take. The trouble is that those not skilled at it will get less than their due, perhaps a lot less. All we can do is learn what we can about negotiation and practice what we learn. Only with this heightened awareness can we be sure that we will get something close to what we deserve.

Contents

PART I

WIN-WIN STRATEGIES

CHAPTER 1
Learning to Negotiate from Other Cultures

The Chinese the French, The Japanese and the Middle East *1*

CHAPTER 2
Winning in Negotiation

Fourteen Time-tested Rules for Getting What You Want –
The Competitive Negotiation *21*

CHAPTER 3
The Super-Winners in Business Are Always
Win-Win Negotiators

What It Is and How to Do It – The Value Building Negotiation *55*

CHAPTER 4
Bargaining Power: Making the Most of
the Power You Have *71*

CHAPTER 5
New Insights: What Makes a Good Negotiator
and a Successful Team *101*

CHAPTER 6
The Strategy of Long-Lasting Relationships and Partnerships
Maximizing Win-Win Satisfactions for Both Parties 117

CHAPTER 7
Setting Reachable Targets – "Ready - Fire - Aim" 137

CHAPTER 8
The Strategy of Taking on a Firm Price
For Those Who Buy Anything as Consumers or in Business 149

CHAPTER 9
The Strategy of Defending Your Selling Price
For Those Who Sell Anything - Business or Personal 165

CHAPTER 10
The Strategy of Planning and Preparation
Including the Quick Planning Kit for Those with Little Time.....................187

PART II

NEGOTIATING TACTICS AND DEFENSES
Value Generating and Competitive Approaches That Get Results

CHAPTER 11
Powerful Demand and Offer Tactics 213

CHAPTER 12
Time Pressure Tactics and Defenses.............................257

CHAPTER 13
Authority and Lack of Authority Pressures 293

CHAPTER 14
Gaining and Maintaining the Initiative

Even When Things Are Not Going Well 321

CHAPTER 15
How Others May Try to Intimidate You
and What to Do About It 351

CHAPTER 16
Ten Borderline and Dirty Tricks to Watch Out For 375

CHAPTER 17
The Art of Breaking a Deadlock

Fourteen Ways to Bridge the Settlement Gap When Talks Break Down 405

CHAPTER 18
Closing Strategies and Tactics 429

CHAPTER 19
Dr. Karrass' Prescription for Success 459

PART I

WIN-WIN STRATEGIES

1

Learning to Negotiate from Other Cultures

THE CHINESE, THE JAPANESE, THE FRENCH, AND THE MIDDLE-EAST:

Ten Powerful but Low-Key Approaches that Work

In business as in life, you don't get what you deserve, you get what you negotiate. Those too timid or unskilled to negotiate well leave too much on the table and get far less than they deserve.

Negotiation is negotiation wherever it takes place. The psychological, emotional and tactical factors that determine who will do well apply to any bargaining situation, large or small. The high stakes, billion dollar deals we read about in the newspapers are much the same as those we encounter as consumers when buying a washing machine or selling a home. Dealing with your landlord has much in common with dealing with the Ayatollah in Iran. The rules leading to success are the same.

Nobody is born with a "good negotiator" gene. The art of negotiating can be learned. You don't have to be a Harvard graduate to understand how it works. Every good negotiator I know learned from their own mistakes or was lucky enough to be taught by someone who was good at it.

Whether you are as rich as Rockefeller or Bill Gates, or just like the rest of us, it is smart to learn about negotiating. Rich or poor, we all hate to be taken. We feel foolish leaving too many chips on the bargaining table. Sam Walton, the founder of Wal-Mart, certainly felt that way, even after he had accumulated enormous wealth.

I met Walton when I was invited to speak at Wal-Mart headquarters in the Arkansas foothills. Sam, in his battered old baseball cap, presided over the weekly Saturday morning executive meeting. To my surprise, over 400 executives showed up to find out what was going on at their 2000 stores and to hear something about the give and take of bargaining.

Wal-Mart buyers are described by those who sell to them as the toughest negotiators in the retail business. That's how they keep their prices low. These world-class negotiators were eager to discover what they could about a skill they were already experts at. To this day, I have never spoken to an audience who took as many notes or asked as many questions.

In addition to making the speech, I had arranged with Wal-Mart to videotape the talk for training purposes. During the speech, Mr. Walton sat to my right behind the podium. He was out of my line of sight as I spoke to the audience. Only after I viewed the video could I see Sam taking notes like a college kid getting ready for a final exam. As he listened, his head often nodded affirmatively to what was said. His mouth could be seen shaping itself soundlessly with words like, "That's right, that's right" and "Yes, yes." Sam Walton, the 73-year-old billionaire, was really involved in what was being said.

After the speech, we talked for a while. Sam told me he had developed a strong and enduring interest in negotiation from his father, who dealt in real estate mortgage lending. "Most of all," he said, "I learned from mistakes I made early in my career" – mistakes which lost him good store locations and valuable options. As he spoke it was easy to see that, even after all these many years, it still bothered him to have left so much on the table at those old negotiations. He was still as determined as ever to learn more about the subject and to make sure that his executives did the same. "That's why we are having you and your seminars here," he said.

People have been negotiating since the beginning of time. What we will do in this book is to describe the strategies, tactics and approaches that successful business people have used for centuries. We will discover what they are, why they work, and how to protect ourselves when they are used against us. We will learn how to make the best possible deal for both parties without exploiting anyone or being exploited ourselves. With these skills you can be sure to get what you deserve in any negotiation, large or small.

LEARNING TO NEGOTIATE FROM THE CHINESE, THE JAPANESE, THE FRENCH AND THE ARABS

Business people in the United States have a lot to learn from other societies about the ancient art of negotiating. Up till now,

Americans have been lucky. They were able to do well dealing mainly with other Americans. But in order to grow and maintain market share we now have to do business and negotiate with people everywhere, especially those on the Pacific Rim of Asia. These are the nations likely to achieve the highest growth rates of the 21st century.

The challenge we face is that we are far less comfortable or experienced with negotiation than people from these cultures. Less affluent than Americans, they were brought up to bargain for everything they bought or sold. For them, every price and service was subject to intense give and take. The economic well-being of their families and themselves depended on how well they negotiated.

We have much to learn from the Chinese, the Japanese, the Middle-Easterners and the French. What follows are ten powerful approaches that have been honed sharp by centuries of successful use.

FROM THE CHINESE – THREE WELL-TESTED APPROACHES

1. The "Quanxi" Approach

Friendship in the Chinese culture goes far beyond friendship in Western society. To the Chinese, friendship means helping each other to grow, to become independent and to become prosperous. It means doing more than is expected or what convention calls for. It means revealing secrets. In business, it means helping with money, manpower, and technology to solve problems that are unanticipated and unbudgeted.

Friendship and "QUANXI" are closely related. The tradition of QUANXI says that once two parties are friends the dominant or stronger partner implicitly agrees to help the weaker partner in times of need. In return, the dependent party implicitly agrees to assist the other and to stay loyal in hard times. When a Chinese negotiator is refused information because it is a "trade secret," he shows his anger openly: "You are not our friend," he might say. "You are not living up to our agreement in principle, which says that friendship, trust and help are our mutual goals."

The "QUANXI" approach goes beyond the written contract itself. It says that if one side or the other is losing money on a deal, or if new circumstances arise which change the original basis for agreement, either side is free to ask for relief. Furthermore, each side expects that relief will be granted in the name of friendship and trust. The "QUANXI" approach helps the parties to work together to survive periods of economic uncertainty and change, or times when one or the other is having problems. Each is well aware in advance of its responsibilities to the other.

2. "Precision in Words"

There is a parable from Confucius dating back 2500 years which tells us a great deal about the Chinese approach to negotiation.

> A disciple said to Confucius when the reigning prince was negotiating with Confucius to enter his service: "The prince is waiting, sir, to entrust the government of the country to you. Now what do you consider the first thing to be done?" "If I must begin," answered Confucius, "I would begin by defining the names of things."

"Oh! Really," replied the disciple, "but you are too impractical. What has definition of names to do here?"

Confucius replied, "Now, if names of things are not properly defined, words will not correspond to facts. When words do not correspond to facts, it is impossible to perfect anything. When we cannot perfect anything, law and justice cannot attain their ends; and when law and justice do not attain their ends, people will be at a loss to know what to do."

"Therefore, a wise and good man can always specify whatever he names; whatever he can specify, he can carry out. A wise and good man makes it a point to always be exact in the words he uses."

3. The Key to Success – Consistency of Purpose

Chinese as well as those from Taiwan, Hong Kong, and Singapore are unbelievably persistent. They repeat their demands over and over again. Arguments are repeated almost word for word over long periods of time. Once they ask for something, they don't take "no" for an answer.

Issues once apparently settled are raised again. Questions that have already been asked and answered are asked again and again. If there is a difference, however small, between one answer and another previously given, a detailed explanation of the difference is requested and the implications for the negotiation are thoroughly explored. Such persistence and consistency of purpose can wear anyone down, especially Americans, few of whom are used to it. A friend who dealt with the Chinese many times once said to me, "They grind away until they get most of what they want."

Benjamin Disraeli, Prime Minister of Great Britain under Queen Victoria, once said, "The key to success is consistency of purpose." This applies as well in negotiation as it does in all of life's affairs.

FROM THE JAPANESE: THREE ANCIENT WAYS

The Japanese are a wise and patient people. What follows are three powerful but low key techniques which are an outgrowth of traditional Japanese forbearance.

1. The Considered Response and Respectful Silence

One of the best negotiators I ever encountered used an interesting technique I call the "considered response." It worked this way. Whenever I made a demand, his first reaction was to listen carefully and take notes. Then, when I was through presenting my demand, he would say nothing but would proceed to make calculations on a sheet of paper. After what appeared to me a long period of time he would say, "I can't afford to accept your demand." His way of responding indicated to me that he had seriously weighed my arguments, even if he had not agreed with them.

Frankly, I don't know whether he really figured anything out on that sheet of paper. For all I know he might have been doodling. But I do know that his "considered response" gave his answer credibility and respect. It became a stronger "no."

The Japanese handle the "considered response" in quite a different way; they do it with respectful silence. In an article in the Harvard Business Review titled *"How to Negotiate in Japan,"* Van Zandte observes:

Americans often don't know how to cope with silence. When a pause or impasse in the discussions develops, the Japanese remain quiet, not feeling a compulsion to say anything. Many Japanese can refrain from answering when a question is asked them, responding to it by drawing air through their teeth and then sitting back as though pondering what to say.

When a couple of minutes have passed and no comment is forthcoming, Americans become uneasy and feel that they must make some sort of statement. It is at this point that they often voluntarily give in on a disputed point or say something they should not say.

Whether accompanied by a respectful silence or not, the "considered response" is a powerful tool. By disciplining yourself not to shoot snap answers "from the hip," your strength as a negotiator will increase. The rule is this: The next time the other party makes a demand or offer, be it acceptable or not, don't respond to it with a "yes" or "no" right away. Just keep quiet and think about it for a while. Better yet, write down on a paper a few calculations that only you can see. Then answer "yes," or "no," or anything you please. Your considered response will give greater weight to your answer, whatever it is.

2. "Seeking Heavenly Approval"

The Japanese pay more attention to long-term relationships than Western businesspeople do. An important part of their decision to do business with someone is whether they will be able to work harmoniously with them in the future. Even if the price is right, there is little point in dealing with someone who will make trouble later.

The Japanese have formalized the practice of building harmonious long-term relationships into their business culture. When a transaction is about to close, the Japanese use a technique called "Seeking Heavenly Approval." After the facts are in and a written agreement near at hand, a period is set aside for achieving executive consensus as to whether they want to do business with the other party in the long run.

In a well-attended discussion marked by long periods of silence, members of the executive group reach mutual inner understanding and consensus. The Japanese call this moment of harmonious accord "KAN." By having sought and achieved "heavenly approval," they have given themselves a final chance to evaluate whether the agreement will satisfy their needs and give them peace of mind in the future. They are unwilling to deal with those who may cause them aggravation later – no matter how good the price.

3. Time Is Money – Japanese (Not American) Style

Americans tend to think in the short term. They believe that "Time is money." Getting things done quickly is a virtue in our society. In Japan, "time is money" means something else: Giving the negotiation more time means they will gain greater benefits and satisfaction.

The Japanese nurture the bargaining process. They build time for planning and consensus into their schedule, and they resist pressure to finish negotiations quickly. They are incredibly persistent in repeating the needs and logic of their positions; they are patient in discovering and testing the needs and resolve of those they oppose. That's how they make "time into money" Japanese style. The more time they take, the more money they make.

FROM THE FRENCH: TWO VERY GOOD IDEAS

1. Agree in Principle, Then Negotiate the Details

The French do not approach negotiation the same way as the Americans or the English. The French prefer to hammer out an agreement on the basis of broad principles, then settle individual issues by referring back to these guiding concepts.

In contrast, the Americans and English prefer to bargain on an issue by issue basis. When all the issues are settled, the deal is considered complete. For example, if an American were negotiating with a painting contractor to paint a four-room apartment, they would go about it this way. First show the painter exactly what is to be done and request a bid. When all the proposals were in, negotiate with the one who appeared best able to perform the work and whose price was reasonably competitive.

Four issues might typically be involved: the final price, the competence and experience of the painters, the quality of paint to be used, and when the work would start and end. The negotiation would proceed on an issue by issue basis, one at a time. When all issues were settled, the contract would be signed.

The French approach negotiation at a higher level. After they receive all bids on painting the house, they select and begin negotiations with the preferred contractor. They start by searching for agreement on broad principles governing the relationship and its objectives. These agreements will serve as a guide to both parties in negotiating detailed issues later.

As a matter of principle they might agree that the painting job should be of a very high quality. Another agreement in principle might be that the contractor would disrupt the customer's life as little as possible during the work. They could also agree that such a job required competent and highly experienced painters using good quality paint. Finally, they might agree in principle that the final price would be fair and reasonable in relation to the level of quality specified.

Once these agreements in principle were defined and accepted, the parties would get down to detailed issues. For example, let's say the contractor wanted to put two young, relatively inexperienced painters on the job. The customer would respond by referring to the principle that high quality work required highly competent and experienced people. This would lead to a compromise more in keeping with the earlier agreement in principle.

The agreement in principle would also govern the settlement of other detailed issues. The paint to be used by the contractor would have to meet the quality principle. The matter of minimizing customer disruption would be settled by agreeing to start on Monday and complete work in ten working days, each day starting at 8:00 AM and ending at 5:00 PM sharp. No work would be done on weekends. Daily cleanup and final job cleanup terms would be settled under the minimum disruption principle. With respect to the final price, the contractor would be obliged to show and prove that the fair and reasonable price was in keeping with others in the area on a house of this size and complexity. At all times, any differences encountered would be measured against the governing principles agreed to earlier.

Which approach works best? I believe the choice should depend on the nature of the negotiations. The important thing is to recognize that we have a choice of approaches, not just the one most of us are accustomed to. Good planning requires that we ask: "Which approach is appropriate in this specific situation, the French or the American?"

2. "Give Nothing Without Getting Something in Return"

One of our most famous diplomats, Robert A. Lovett, once said, "Do not give concessions to the French without getting something in return. They will not feel gratitude. They will feel contempt for your gullibility." The French do not make unilateral concessions; they do not give something for nothing. Americans, as a rule, do not like to tie strings to their concessions. They consider it bad taste to give with the one hand and take away with the other. From a negotiation standpoint, that is sheer nonsense, and we will show why later in the book.

Open your mind to the French rule of "QUID-PRO-QUO": make no concession without getting something in return.

FROM THE MID-EAST – MAKING NEGOTIATION FUN

Long before oil became a factor in international exchange, trade routes between Europe and the Orient weaved through the desert. The Arabs have been negotiating for thousands of years and continue to do so in their daily dealings in the marketplace and bazaar . Unlike Westerners, who often become uptight when they have to bargain for something, people in the Mid-East have learned to make negotiation an enjoyable experience.

For them bargaining is good fun. The Arabs take special pains to make those they deal with comfortable. They are courteous and solicitous of the other party's personal needs. Tea and soft drinks are provided and served in a gracious manner. Delicious sweets, dates and bakery goods are offered in abundance. You feel like an honored guest at a nice party rather than a participant in a high stakes negotiation.

Nothing is rushed. There is lots of small talk before and during the bargaining. Digressions and breaks are a normal part of the process. Introductions between executives of both sides are carefully made to assure that no one is offended. Gifts are exchanged if the parties know each other from previous meetings.

Frequent interruptions from outsiders are tolerated. Wives and children, friends, secretaries, tea boys, associates, and long lost relatives often come and go during the talks. Much cross-conversation takes place, and it is sometimes difficult to tell where business ends and social conversation begins.

Mid-East negotiators are far less apprehensive about deadlock than Americans are. They are accustomed to deadlock from a lifetime in the bazaar. Part of what they enjoy most in bargaining is walking away from the transaction and coming back again. If the item has been sold to someone else in the meantime, that is not good. But for the Arabs it is the will of Allah. If they cannot close today, it may well be that tomorrow, next month, or never will be good enough.

The game of negotiation is a welcome diversion in the Mid-East, where many Western forms of recreation are not available. For them bargaining is fun. For those in the West, unfortunately, bargaining is too often an intense win or lose contest that is best finished as quickly as possible. I personally believe that people bargain best when they are relaxed. Be like the Arabs, make it more fun.

FROM AROUND THE WORLD – WORDS HAVE A STRANGE WAY OF CHANGING FROM CULTURE TO CULTURE

In 1979, after decades of bitter enmity, Israel and Egypt signed a peace treaty. The treaty was written not in one language but four: Hebrew, Egyptian, English and French. The parties agreed that in the event of a dispute the French version would be binding. Both sides understood that words mean different things in different cultures.

Anyone who has negotiated with people who do not normally speak English knows how difficult it is to communicate across language barriers. Over the years I've kept a small file on how the English language changes meaning when used by people from other cultures.

A good example is a story reported in the Los Angeles Times about a German tourist whose demand to use the toilet on an airplane landed him in jail. The 23-year-old student told a flight attendant in broken English that the "roof would go" when she tried to get him to return to his seat. As the tourist struggled with flight attendants, he told them again and again that the "roof would go." The attendants thought it was a bomb threat and wrestled him to the floor.

After the struggle, the man was permitted to go to the bathroom and then passed out in his seat. The pilot, afraid of a hidden bomb, dropped his fuel load at sea and returned to the airport. When the student woke up, he thought he was in Germany. Instead, he was surprised to learn he was under arrest in Florida.

Facing a maximum sentence of 20 years, he hired a lawyer who reduced the sentence to time already served. It turned out that the phrase "roof would go" means "emptying one's bladder" in German slang, and the court recognized that no threats had really been made.

This story reminds me of a hotel in Tokyo which posted a room sign reading, "You are invited to take advantage of the chambermaid." I saw a sign in a hotel in Egypt which advised, "Patrons need have no anxiety about the water. It has been passed by management." Or the hotel in Moscow whose sign said, "If this is your first visit to the USSR your welcome to it." Or the notice in a Swiss mountain inn which read, "Special today – no ice cream."

English is the language spoken in South Africa. I recently read about a South African woman who was hired as a legal secretary in the United States. The boss asked her, "Can you work on this report?"

She answered, "I'll do it just now."

In twenty minutes the boss returned and asked for the finished report. She didn't understand his impatience. He didn't understand why it was not yet done since it was not a big job.

The problem was that in South Africa the words "just now" mean you will do it as soon as you get a chance to. In the United States it means you will do it right away.

Even those accustomed to speaking English make mistakes. When Vice President Quayle commented during a speech in 1989, "What a waste it is to lose one's mind," he meant to quote the motto of the United Negro College Fund, "A mind is a terrible thing to waste." Or Mario Angelo Procaccino, a 1969 candidate for Mayor of New York City who told a black audience during a speech: "My heart is as black as yours."

More recently, candidate Barack Obama explained in 2008, "Over the last 15 months, we've traveled to every corner of the United States. I've now been in 57 states." And George W. Bush, who once described himself as "misunderestimated," tried in 2000 to relate to those suffering in a difficult economy: "I know how hard it is to put food on your family."

The first Mayor Daley of Chicago often butchered the language. Angry with the press, he once said, "They slandered me, they have castigated me, yes, they have even criticized me." As a negotiator under pressure there are times when you will feel a little like the late Mayor Daley.

Words have a way of changing meaning from culture to culture, and even within a culture words and phrases mean different things to different people. With the best of intentions people misspeak. Nobody's perfect.

When we negotiate with people in Europe, Asia or Africa a good way to reduce the level of future aggravation is to have contracts written in English and at least one other language. Then, have each page proofread and checked by competent translators who are independent of both sides.

CONCLUSION

There is nothing mysterious about being a good negotiator. The more you know about it, and the more you practice, the better you become. Try the low key but powerful ideas in this chapter. They will work for you as they have for others the world over.

TEN NEGOTIATING APPROACHES FROM ABROAD

From the Chinese	The Special Meaning of Friendship and "Quanxi"
	Confucius Says - "Precision in Words"
	The Key to Success - Consistency of Purpose
From the Japanese	The Considered Response
	"Seeking Heavenly Approval"
	"Time is Money" - Japanese Style
From the French	Agree in Principle - Then Negotiate the Details
	Give Nothing Without Getting Something in Return
From the Arabs	Making Negotiation Fun
From Around the World	Words and Phrases have a Strange Way of Changing Meaning From Culture to Culture

2

Winning in Negotiation

FOURTEEN TIME-TESTED RULES FOR GETTING WHAT YOU WANT - THE COMPETITIVE NEGOTIATION

There are two questions I am frequently asked when presenting a seminar or speech. The first is, "What does it mean to be a winner in negotiation?" The other, "Why negotiate when the price is acceptable?" Both are important because the answers can serve as a guide to conducting ourselves in future negotiations. The answers, as we shall see, are not as simple as they seem.

Jack and I have known each other for years. Jack, a Purchasing Manager at General Electric, told me this story about winning and losing in negotiation. His son had an old car with a bashed in fender that needed a considerable amount of body work. The car was an eyesore in a neighborhood of nice homes. Jack knew he had to do something about it, so he got a quote from a local body shop. They wanted $1300. The price seemed reasonable but was more than he wanted to spend on the old car.

One day, purely by chance, two husky men in a truck came to his door offering to fix the bashed in fender for $500. Jack was pleased because he had reconciled himself to paying at least $700 to get the job done. Although the proposed price of $500 was acceptable, Jack decided to bargain for an even better deal. He offered $250. The repairmen reduced the asking price to $450. Jack countered slowly with $300 and then stood fast. The men grumbled but grudgingly agreed to $300. Jack could see they were not pleased as they went to work on the car. He, on the other hand, was so pleased that he couldn't help bragging to his wife about the marvelous deal he had just made.

Eight hours later, sweaty and tired, the men came to the door for their money. Jack went out to look at the job. To his surprise the dent was more or less pounded out, but right in the middle of where the dent had been was a gaping, rough-edged hole about an inch in diameter.

"What's that?" asked Jack. 'A hole," the man answered.

"I know it's a hole," said Jack, "but why?" "I had to drill the hole to pull the dent out," was the answer. "But aren't you going to fix it?" half-pleaded Jack, who had begun to recognize that a renegotiation might be taking place.

"Not for $300," replied the repairman, "but I will do it for $130 more. In fact, I'll touch it up for that." He and his partner were six feet tall and each weighed 225 pounds or more. Jack quickly decided to pay the full $430. The work was done reasonably well. Was Jack a winner in this negotiation? You decide. Many would say that Jack was a winner. After all, he had gotten the work done for far less than the body shop's asking price of $1300, and even less than the $700 he was prepared to pay. Not bad.

But should Jack have bargained to bring the original $500 quote down to $300? Was that fair and reasonable? Would he have been a winner if the repairmen had satisfactorily completed the work for the $450 asked? Some would say he could surely be considered a winner in that case.

But that's not what happened. Jack was induced to re-negotiate the $300 settlement to $430. Less than the $500 originally asked for and a lot less than the $1300 the body shop would have charged. Still, Jack wasn't happy even though the job was acceptable. Years later it continued to rankle him. That's why he told me the story. He still wondered whether he was a winner in that long ago negotiation.

WHAT DOES IT MEAN TO BE A WINNER IN NEGOTIATION?

A winner in negotiation is one who understands what his or her objectives are and takes the time to achieve what is possible through the bargaining process. In addition, a winner strives to leave the other party as satisfied as possible with the outcome. Winners do this by the way they conduct themselves in negotiation and by the way they jointly search for a better deal for both sides.

Please note that I have not said that winners in negotiation achieve all their objectives or get the best of every deal. They may or may not do so. As we all know, it takes two to agree. The other party often cannot or will not grant a "total" victory. Winning in negotiation is definitely not like winning in sports.

By my definition of a winner, Jack did not do as well as he could in this negotiation. On the positive side he did take the time to test the otherwise acceptable $500 opening price. To his credit he was unafraid to start with a low counteroffer of $250 and move up slowly to $300. For his effort Jack achieved a very favorable price. Good, but not good enough.

Jack did not do as well as he could have in other respects. He made no effort to look for the better deal for both parties. For instance, he could have told the men he would recommend them to others in the neighborhood needing body work, or that he would pay them more if they did a very good repair job or if they touched up other parts of the vehicle in addition to the badly damaged fender. He might have offered them an opportunity for steady wash and wax work on his other autos and perhaps those of his neighbors.

With just a little more effort, Jack could have made the men more satisfied with the low $250 offer. For example, he could have said that $250 was all he had or that he couldn't afford to put too much into the old vehicle because he was going to sell it soon. Had they heard this, they might well have been more satisfied with the $300 settlement.

On a personal level, Jack might have increased their satisfaction by offering them a cool beer as they worked in the hot sun. Small amenities often make a big difference in people's attitudes. Jack gave little thought to the matter of satisfaction.

Jack also made another mistake that invited trouble. He did not make the scope of work clear. He hoped that repairing the fender meant the same thing to the repairmen as it did to him. As we know, it did not.

Was Jack a winner in this negotiation? My conclusion is that he was not. Had Jack been more sensitive to the possibility of renegotiating, he might have handled the bargaining in a better way. Had he clarified the work specification and put the agreement in writing, the final outcome might have gone better. Jack did the right thing in testing the original $500 asking price even though it was acceptable to him from the beginning. But he could have done a better job had he given more thought to making an agreement that worked for both parties and to increasing the satisfaction felt by the repairmen.

WHY NEGOTIATE IF THE PRICE IS RIGHT?

Too many Americans have a negative attitude toward negotiating. At best, they think of bargaining as a necessary evil. They say, "If the price is right, why bother to negotiate?"

The answer is: There is no right price except the specific price that the specific buyer and seller agree on for the specific product or service they are negotiating for.

Is there a right price for something as simple as a bushel of wheat? Suppose that you are a bread maker and I am a wheat salesman. You ask about the price of a bushel of wheat. I could quote you $5 a bushel, and I would be correct because that is the price listed in the newspaper. But is that the right price?

Not necessarily. There are many factors that might lead me to quote you more or less than $5: where the wheat is located in relation to your bread factory, how much wheat you want to buy, how much I have to sell, whether you have the money to pay for it, and whether the quality of my wheat is adequate for your bread requirement.

Negotiation is the process that takes all these factors into account. The price I negotiate with you might be a lot more or less than $5 a bushel. If I were desperate for money or stuck with bad wheat, I might sell for $3 if you bought all my wheat and took it off my hands. Negotiation tests the specific forces operating in the market and adjusts the price to reflect the situation and motivations of the specific buyer and seller, not the hypothetical price set by economic theory.

HOW WINNERS WIN: RULES OF NEGOTIATING THAT WILL GET YOU WHAT YOU WANT

How do winners win in negotiation? Are there any rules? Yes. People win when they know what they are doing. That's what this book is about. Good negotiators follow certain patterns. Whether you are a professional buyer or seller, or a consumer trying to make a deal on a home, a car or a home wireless network, the fourteen rules which follow will help you win better agreements.

1.   PICK THE BEST PLACE AND TIME TO NEGOTIATE FOR ANYTHING, INCLUDING A RAISE.

2.   WHAT IS OUR NEXT CHOICE IF THIS NEGOTIATION BREAKS DOWN?

3.   BE STINGY WITH YOUR CONCESSIONS AND LEAVE ROOM TO NEGOTIATE.

4. IF YOU ARE A BUYER DON'T GIVE THE SELLER A QUICK COUNTEROFFER TO THE ASKING PRICE.

5. DON'T SAY "YES" TOO QUICKLY.

6. BUYERS SHOULD ALWAYS TRY TO GET COST BREAKDOWNS. SELLERS SHOULD NOT GIVE THEM.

7. DON'T MAKE THE FIRST MAJOR CONCESSION.

8. WATCH YOUR CONCESSIONS AS DEADLINE APPROACHES – BIG MISTAKES ARE MADE.

9. SHUT UP.

10. BE SKEPTICAL. THINGS ARE NOT WHAT THEY APPEAR TO BE.

11. STOP HOPING FOR THE BEST: HOW WINNERS BECOME LOSERS.

12. WATCH OUT FOR FUNNY MONEY.

13. DOS AND DON'TS IF YOU HAVE TO COMPROMISE.

14. BE A SUPER-WINNER: YOU CAN ALWAYS FIND A BETTER DEAL FOR BOTH PARTIES.

Rule 1- Pick the Best Place and Time to Negotiate

Anyone considering whether to ask the boss for a raise should be aware that there is a right time and place to ask. You have to set the stage for a "yes" answer. Where and when to negotiate are key considerations in your strategy.

I'm a sports fan. Keeping track of team standings in baseball and basketball is a daily ritual which I enjoy. Here are the standings for the National Basketball Association on a March day in a tight conference race:

NATIONAL BASKETBALL ASSOCIATION						
Midwest Div.	W	L	Pct.	GB	Home	Away
San Antonio	43	17	.717	–	26-5	17-12
Houston	40	16	.714	1	23-4	17-12
Utah	42	19	.689	1 1/2	25-6	17-13
Denver	29	29	.500	13	21-8	8-21
Minnesota	16	42	.276	26	10-18	6-24
Dallas	8	51	.136	34 1/2	3-27	5-24

You'll notice that almost every team has done better at home than away. This happens in every sport, with few exceptions.

What does this tell us about negotiating? It says that you are generally better off negotiating on your home turf where, as in basketball, you will be familiar with your surroundings and have the resources you need close at hand. When you are on unfamiliar terrain, even the simple things of life become more complex. Being close to home gives you greater access to information and advice from others. It allows you to communicate efficiently with those in your organization. The home team usually holds the high ground in a negotiation. Usually, but not always, as the following story shows.

Once I knew a man who rented his house to the founder of a major technology firm in Beverly Hills. The rent was $4000 a month. After two years of inflation, the owner decided to raise the rent to $4500. He knew that the stockbroker would be shocked, despite the fact that the raise was, for many reasons, justified. The owner wondered where to negotiate the higher rent.

His five choices were: at the broker's rented house, at the broker's office, in a restaurant, in the owner's home or in a quiet park close by. The owner chose to negotiate the increase in the broker's big office at work. Why? Because at work the broker was accustomed to dealing in large dollar amounts and his office was designed to show how successful he was. The broker agreed to the increase quickly.

In that office setting, his time was most valuable and the increase didn't seem like so much. He was also flattered to be seen by the landlord in such a fine light.

In general, the rule about where to negotiate is this: negotiate at home if all other things are equal. Negotiate away if you can learn more about the other side at their location or if you want to see and inspect certain things there for yourself. Negotiate away from home if you want to isolate the other party from information they might use to their advantage, or if you want to keep them away from your upper level decision-makers.

Of course, there are many occasions when the other party will not allow you the advantage of negotiating at home. The original Israeli-Palestinian talks were conducted in Europe and Washington, the Vietnam talks in Paris and the late cold war negotiations between Presidents Reagan and Gorbachev in Iceland. In each case, neither party would permit the other home court advantage.

When talks must be conducted away from your home office, as when sellers deal with buyers, try to find a neutral place like a restaurant or a hotel conference room. If the seller and buyer are located in different cities, pick a location between them, if the buyer can be persuaded to agree.

One man I know owns a large paper company. He prefers to negotiate at his lodge in Georgia timber country. His private jet flies the buyers to the remote location where they see for themselves how trees are cut and logs processed for market. In his experience, this quiet wooded setting encourages customers to talk more, resulting in negotiations that often end in better agreements for both parties.

The same principles apply to negotiating a raise with your boss. Conduct the discussion where the boss can see the quality of the work you do. Make your output real to him or her. Pick a quiet place where talks will not be disturbed by other people and be sure your cell phones are on silent. Your office is a much better place than theirs. If that's not possible, a conference room is a good compromise. Picking the right place improves your chances for a "yes" answer.

The right time to negotiate is as important as the right place. For instance, tax deadlines or changes in the tax law can make it advantageous for the other party to reach an agreement quickly.

The time of day as well as day of week can also create a negotiating advantage. I once had a job selling machine shop services to a large manufacturer. Most salesmen knew that the best time to negotiate with the buyer was on Friday afternoon at 4:00 because he wanted to clear his desk for the weekend. It was virtually impossible to book an appointment at this preferred time unless you did it weeks in advance. I searched for a better time. Unfortunately, a competitor found it before I did. He locked in his appointments at 3:00 PM on Wednesday, just before the buyer left for the golf course.

When negotiating with your boss for a raise, there are some very bad times to talk. The worst is Monday morning on the day after the boss's vacation. Just as bad is in the middle of some sort of crisis. He or she won't appreciate your timing. Almost as bad is while the boss is enjoying the company picnic or the expensive Christmas party that broke the budget.

The best time to ask for a raise is immediately after you have accomplished something extraordinary for the company, or when you are basking in the glory of a good report sitting on the desk.

We will have more to say about picking the right time to negotiate in Chapter 12, where we discuss time tactics.

Rule 2 – What is Our Best Second Choice if Talks Break Down

Good negotiators will always ask themselves these questions before going to the table. "What will I do if this deal fails? What is my next best alternative?"

I am reminded of the story of the Death Row convict who after many rejected appeals faced the choice of how he wished to be executed. In some states a person can choose to be gassed, hanged or shot by a firing squad. Having lost his first choice – the appeal for a reduced sentence – he settled for his second choice, the gas chamber.

On the night prior to execution it was customary for the warden to ask the desperate man if he had a final request. "Yes," he said, "I want a gas mask." That's what a negotiator has to do, think about his second choice before talks begin.

On a less somber note, let's assume that you and your spouse have carefully shopped for the car you want. Both of you are exhausted, but you have finally decided on a beautiful silver Audi that has just the right accessories.

Before negotiations begin, the two of you should sit down and discuss your opening offer and your target price. Consider what to ask for in return for concessions you may decide to make along the way. Writing these "ask in return" items down in advance will help you and your spouse to remember them later as the give and take of negotiations continues.

Decide together what alternatives will be pursued if talks break down. Agree to do the work to find another car if it becomes necessary. This joint willingness to walk away and start over will strengthen your hand if deadlock appears close. If you have not agreed on an alternative plan of action, you are likely to pay too much for the car.

The same thinking and planning will be helpful in any complex negotiation. It does not matter if the issues in contention involve national defense, diplomacy, labor relations or contract negotiations. The approach is the same: Targets must be set, opening offers decided on and next best alternatives considered. Not to do so weakens your position unnecessarily. To do so adds to your power.

Rule 3 – Be Stingy With Your Concessions and Leave Room to Negotiate

Whether you are selling, buying, or negotiating anything, this rule should be carefully considered: leave room to bargain when you open talks and give in grudgingly as you move toward agreement.

There is a tale from a century ago in the days of the British empire. An Englishman, anxious to be one of the few nonbelievers to visit the Arab holy city of Mecca, slipped into the city by browning his skin and pretending to be imbued with deep religious fervor.

Unfortunately, he made one mistake. He went into the marketplace and bought some bananas. The merchant asked for five coppers, which the man quickly paid. Suddenly there was a crowd around him. Everyone stared. 'An infidel," someone shouted, and the mob threw him into prison after threatening his life. They knew him to be a pretender. He had failed to negotiate for the bananas. No real Arab would have paid the asking price without bargaining.

Americans, as a rule, bargain less than their counterparts in other cultures. Americans are uncomfortable making low offers when they buy. They are reluctant to build much fat into their sales proposals. They don't enjoy the give and take of negotiation; nor do they like the extensive talk and repetition that is so much a part of the bargaining process.

Where you start and how you give in is crucial to how well you will do. For many years I accumulated data on the results of practice negotiations among my seminar attendees. I consistently found that executives who started higher and made concessions in smaller increments did better. Experiments by others confirm this.

What are the practical implications of these research findings? Suppose you are a seller, and your knowledge of the marketplace indicates that something is worth about $10 a unit. It's wise to begin by asking for more than $10. How much more depends on supply and demand factors influencing you and your buyer at the time of the transaction. It also depends on how much difference there is between your product or service and those offered by competitors.

As a buyer, you are well advised to make an opening offer of less than $10. Only that way can you discover how pressured the seller is to sell and how little they will take. The "leave room-give in grudgingly" approach makes good sense. It is surprising that so many people are reluctant to follow this prescription.

Notice that I have not stated any specific starting point for either the seller's demand or the buyer's offer. The starting point depends on how accurate a picture of the market place each party has and what they know of the other's needs. For example, if we were dealing for a rare painting whose market value is obscure, the seller might start very high and the buyer quite low. Each would be wise to give logical reasons for validating their starting point.

On the other hand if we were speaking of a bushel of wheat or a barrel of oil, where market prices are reasonably well known, the seller might ask for a little more than market price. The buyer would offer a little less. Where you start in a negotiation is a matter of business judgment. *Your knowledge of the marketplace and the supply and demand factors specifically influencing the parties in the transaction determine your opening offer or demand.*

As for being stingy, the record is clear. People who are stingy with concessions come out ahead. They hoard concessions by giving in slowly and making the other party work for all they get. When a concession is granted, it is a small one. They signal that they do not have much to give.

Many negotiations are lost when people cave in before they need to. As you negotiate, make sure the other party is never certain whether you will back down further from your position. If you retreat too soon or by too large an amount, the other side will be encouraged to try for more. Negotiators who concede quickly or make large concessions usually do so to move the agreement toward closure. But often this drives the parties further apart by raising the expectations of the opposing side to unrealistic levels.

Everything you do in a bargaining situation affects the expectation level in the other person's mind. Your initial demands set the stage. Your persistence in holding to a position leads the other party to wonder if their goals can be reached. The rate and timing of your concessions determine whether their expectations will rise or fall. Your way of offering concessions will affect their overall satisfaction with the settlement. If concessions are small and grudgingly given, they are likely to be pleased because they will feel that little was left on the table.

Giving in slowly and leaving room makes sense. Concessions, carefully controlled, lead the other party toward closure and provide them with a higher level of satisfaction with the final outcome.

Rule 4 – If You Are a Buyer Don't Give the Seller a Quick Counteroffer to the Asking Price

I'm going to ask a provocative question. In most cases buyer-seller bargaining starts like a game of ping-pong. The seller opens with a proposal offering something for sale at a price. Most buyers respond to the proposal by doing what comes naturally – they promptly make a counteroffer. Should a buyer respond to the seller's initial proposal by making such a counteroffer?

My stand on this may strike you as unusual. I look upon the

buyer's counteroffer as perhaps the most important concession she or he will make. It represents the first concession to the seller.

Some years ago I read a story by Daniel Defoe, the author of Robinson Crusoe. Defoe described a negotiation in which he offered to sell some goods to a prospective buyer. Defoe desperately needed the money and was anxious to sell. The buyer, a shrewd native, was smart enough not to make a counteroffer. Instead he just talked and talked around the subject.

Defoe's reaction to not getting a counteroffer provides us with an interesting insight into human nature. Defoe describes the anxiety he felt while trying to determine whether the native was interested enough to buy. He wondered if he should drop his price or in some other way sweeten the offer. He had time to think about what he would do to raise the money he needed if the buyer walked away. These haunting doubts were relieved much later when he received a low but negotiable counteroffer. Defoe goes on to tell how pleased he was to learn that, low offer or not, the native was at least willing to consider a commitment to buy.

Whether you are a buyer or seller, my advice is that you make the other party work for every counteroffer they get including the first one. They will appreciate your counteroffer more if they have to wait for it. From a psychological standpoint, the difference between getting a counteroffer and not getting one is large. To the person waiting for it, it represents the difference between an opponent who might be willing to deal and one who probably won't.

In that light, buyers who do not respond quickly to a seller's proposed asking price or terms are starting the talks off in the right direction. They are lowering the seller's expectations in a subtle way.

Rule 5 – Don't Say Yes Too Quickly, Even if You Like the Deal

When you are ready to say "yes," learn to say "no" a few more times. Then say "yes." The following story was told to me by Dinah Shore, the late movie actress, while I waited to be introduced as a guest on her television show. Knowing that I was going to talk about negotiation, she said off camera, "I'm the world's worst negotiator." Whenever anyone says that, listen. A good story usually follows.

Some years ago, a Beverly Hills home was for sale at $500,000. The actress liked the house and offered $425,000. The broker immediately said, "We'll take it." Years later, despite the fact that the value of the house was more than $1,000,000 when she told me the story, she was still angry about the $425,000 agreement made earlier. Dinah Shore was convinced that her $425,000 offer was a foolish mistake because it had been immediately accepted. That's why she said, "I'm the world's worst negotiator." But was she really the world's worst negotiator, or was it the broker?

If we wish to see how bad a mistake the broker made, we have only to imagine another scenario. What if the broker had, upon hearing the offer, said "I don't think my client will accept your offer, but I'll be glad to submit it." He could have returned in five minutes and explained that the client, because she was in a divorce action, was willing to take $440,000, still a real bargain. Suppose they then settled at $435,000. Would Dinah Shore have felt that she was a good negotiator or a bad one? Because of the delay in saying "yes," she would have been more satisfied paying $435,000 than the $425,000 she actually paid!

It's ironic isn't it? For Dinah Shore, paying $425,000 represented pain and dissatisfaction. Paying $435,000 would have meant the opposite. There is an underlying principle here: The other party will always appreciate the settlement price more if they believe they have worked for it and gotten closer to the bottom line. If not, their self-esteem will be bruised. They will be angry at you and themselves for a long time.

One final note on why you should learn to say "no" a few times even when you are willing to settle. As many of you know, Dinah Shore was a caring and giving person. If she had not been so nice, her anger about the deal might have caused her to make trouble for the seller in a number of ways.

If she were upset enough, she might have made an excuse to cancel the agreement before escrow or ask that expensive repairs or improvements be made. She might have demanded that the Persian rugs and fireplace accessories be included in the price. People do these things when they get a "yes" answer too quickly. Like most people, rich or not, they hate to feel they were "taken" or that they foolishly left too much on the table.

Rule 6 – Buyers Should Get Cost Breakdowns – Sellers Should Not Give Them

If you are a buyer, always try to get price breakdowns. If you are selling, try never to give them. The good sense behind this rule will soon be obvious.

Suppose you need some plumbing work done in your house. Three contractors bid and the lowest is $2804. You want to get an insight into the plumber's costs, so you ask for an estimate of labor and material. (Usually this is not too difficult to get with a bit of prodding.) The number comes up to $2304 for labor and

$500 for material. You then probe for further cost information and learn that the labor portion consists of two people for two days at the $72 per hour union rate ($2304) and that material consists of copper pipe at $300 and $200 for miscellaneous items ($500). Labor ($2304) plus material ($500) equals the low bid ($2804).

Based on even this minimum amount of information, there is much you can do. You can question whether two people are necessary, whether both are entitled to the $72 per hour union rate, whether two days is too long for the job, and whether they will actually work eight hours a day each day. In the material area you can explore why copper pipe is necessary.

Armed with answers to these questions, it is possible for you to better compare the competitive bids and make a sensible decision. For example, galvanized pipe may be adequate, thereby saving $200. Your probe may reveal that the second person on the job is only an apprentice whose only job is to take things out of the truck. For apprentices the union rate is $30 an hour, not $72. You may decide, based on the information, that getting new bids from non-union plumbers makes sense. Dealing with such plumbers would eliminate the mandatory union rule for a second person and further reduce labor costs.

Before you are through, the fact that a price breakdown was obtained can help bring the $2804 low bid price down to perhaps $2300 or less. Getting good cost breakdowns from competing sellers can, with relatively little work, provide a buyer with leverage to ask for large savings.

United States government procurement regulations have long required sellers to provide a detailed cost breakdown with proposals on negotiated contracts. They would find it much harder to negotiate a fair price and terms without it.

Sophisticated industrial companies have followed the government's lead to good effect. Many now employ professional price analysts in their purchasing departments to help their buyers do what you have just seen done in the simple plumbing example. Buyers who get price breakdowns win better prices. That's why sellers shouldn't provide them unless existing laws or regulations force them to.

Rule 7 – Don't Make the First Concession on a Major Issue

I discovered something in my experiments that may someday save you lots of money. I found that people who made the first concession on an important issue ended by doing poorly. It was as though they were on the defensive from the start.

For quite a while both opposing subjects in my experiments held their ground, neither giving an inch. Then one cracked on a major issue. The one that cracked never recovered. His or her opponent continued throughout the experiment to make fewer concessions and smaller ones.

Do we dare extrapolate from an experiment to real life? I believe that we can, but must be careful. My advice in a business negotiation is to feel free (after holding off awhile) to make the first concession on minor points. Persuasion theory says that this is a good way to reduce resistance barriers. However, when it comes to major issues, I think it best that you not give in first. By making such first concessions, you send an early message to the other party that they ought to raise their expectations. At the least, hold back and find out just how strong their position is.

Rule 8 – Watch Your Concessions as Deadline Approaches

A curious thing happens again and again in the practice negotiations we conduct at our seminars. Attendees are able to control their concession behavior through most of the bargaining. They make relatively modest concessions as the give and take progresses. Then, when I announce that deadline is approaching, one party or the other cracks. They make large concessions which are not reciprocated by the other. The party making smaller concessions as deadline approaches usually does better.

In a formal experiment with 120 professional negotiators, I found that both parties controlled their concession behavior for most of the session. Then things changed. As deadline approached and I began to announce, "three minutes to go," "two to go," "one to go" – a hush fell over the room. The tension mounted. Many participants settled only minutes or seconds before the final bell, although they'd had a full hour to do so.

It turned out that both skilled and unskilled negotiators made their largest concessions as time ran out. Both sides caved in somewhat as they sought to reach settlement, but it was the unskilled who gave most.

A friend of mine who works as a psychiatrist told me he wasn't surprised at these results. He has found that people make very bad decisions under pressure. They behave in an emotional rather than a rational way. His advice to those who come to him as patients is that they are better off postponing a decision in times of stress.

The next time you are in a negotiation, recognize that your tendency will be to give too much as deadline comes close. Discipline yourself to make smaller concessions and spread them out a bit longer. Learn to ask yourself two simple questions as time runs out. First, "why should I give so much in one lump sum right now?" And second, "Why not make these final concessions on the installment plan – a little now, a little later?" These reminders will help you avoid the deadline cave-in crisis. Remember also that most deadlines are themselves subject to negotiation. There is usually time enough to make another concession if you have to.

Rule 9 – Shut Up, Don't Talk So Much: Anything You Say May Be Held Against You

The less the other person knows about you, the better off you are. The more you know about them, the stronger your bargaining power. Of course, some information must be exchanged in the give and take of bargaining. The problem is that what you say and what you show may be used against you if it reveals your weaknesses. How much you choose to reveal is a matter of business judgment. Less is better than more in most cases.

My niece and her husband learned this the hard way. They were buying their first home. It was a nice older place, a fixer-upper. My niece liked the neighborhood and was determined to give the house a thorough inspection before making an offer. While in the bathroom looking under the sink, she heard her husband tell the broker how beautiful the place was and how its location was exactly what they wanted. There she was on her hands and knees worrying about the wrong thing. With every word he said, the final price in the broker's head went up.

But was it really her husband's fault? They were both at fault because they hadn't talked about their strategy beforehand. Each should have warned the other not to say anything that could raise the seller's expectations. Such knowledge only strengthens the seller's power and resolve.

People talk too much. Merchants tell me that they are constantly amazed at how much customers tell them if given half a chance. Some reveal that the $2000 digital camera they are looking at is the only one they've seen that matches their needs, or that a store down the street is selling an older model of the same camera at a higher price. Is it any wonder that these "talkers" fail to win price relief from the merchant?

Salespeople often make a similar mistake when they tell a buyer how anxious they are to win a contract or renew an order because business is slow or inventories high. We know they do so to convince the buyer that they will get a good price and exceptional service if the order is awarded. The trouble is that they may raise the expectations of the buyer so much that a substantial ten or fifteen percent discount may appear to the buyer as a pittance.

Salespeople anxious to make a sale sometimes start negotiating by offering discounts or special services they have provided to other customers. They wrongly assume that the buyer knows that others are receiving these extra benefits at no additional cost. Their assumptions lead them to talk too much and give benefits away before they are even asked to.

As a person with considerable experience in buying and selling, I have found that it is usually not the buyer or salesperson who talks too much. More often it is the engineers, production people, administrative assistants and accountants who reveal more than they should. As a negotiator, you should warn others in your organization that anything they tell the other party's personnel will make it difficult for you to reach a fair agreement.

My advice to those who negotiate and especially to those who are only indirectly involved in the bargaining process: "Don't talk too much. Everything you say may be held against you." You may end up like the missionary in Mark Twain's story who wanted to convert the cannibals. "They listened with great interest to everything he had to say," Twain said. "Then they ate him."

Rule 10 – Be Skeptical. Things are Not What They Appear to Be

Be skeptical – things are not what they appear to be. Like it or not, business negotiating in our society and every culture in the world involves a degree of posturing, partial truths, and conflicting interests. That's the way it is.

There is an old Hungarian saying, "Every saint folds his arms toward himself." Each party will present its viewpoint in a way favorable to its position. They will include what helps their side. They will leave out what doesn't. Salespeople put on their best face to sell their goods or services. That's their job. Buyers will forever tell salespeople why their competitor's product is just as good or better at a lower price. That's their job.

I have learned from hard experience to be skeptical. Sellers and buyers who appear to be firm often make concessions over time. I've heard buyers say, "This is all the money I've got," only to have them find more funds when it was worth their while to do so. I've heard sellers say, "We'll lose money if we sell any cheaper," only to accept a lower price for this reason or that. When I hear someone say, "We never do that," or "We never negotiate," I know that "never" is a pretty broad statement and rarely means what it says.

Be skeptical. The information provided by the other party may not be complete. Their expert may not be an expert at all. What you are not told may be more important than what you are told. The product or service you receive after an agreement is reached may not be what you bargained and fought so hard for. If this harsh view of business negotiation offends you, it is not meant to, but I believe it to be realistic.

Let's face it, the other party will present the information that best suits their position. Your job is to be politely skeptical. Search for the big picture. Search for what may have been left out. Test everything you are told and all that you see. Things are rarely what they appear to be.

Rule 11 – Stop Hoping for the Best: How Winners Become Losers

People who consistently do poorly in negotiation suffer from a common human failing. They make one or more of these four "hope for the best" mistakes:

> ONE: Going into negotiation without a plan.
>
> TWO: Agreeing on something that isn't clear.
>
> THREE: Signing a contract without reading it.
>
> FOUR: Not following up to see that they got what they bargained for.

With respect to the last point I'm reminded of a baseball negotiation in the 1950s – when ball-players received far lower salaries than they do today. The story reported by the Times went like this.

Billy Loes, a Brooklyn Dodger pitcher, was offered $14,000

by Buzzie Bavasi, the team general manager. Loes held out for $15,000. Bavasi finally said, "OK, sign the contract."

"But it's blank," said Loes.

"I know, I'll fill it in later," said Bavasi.

At the end of the season, Bavasi told Loes, "Hey, wise guy, I bet you think you made $15,000. Well, I paid you only $14,000 because I knew you wouldn't add up the checks." Of course Bavasi was a good guy and gave Loes a check for the $1000.

The trouble with "hoping for the best" in negotiation, as in life, is that it's a dangerous way to live. It trades today's peace of mind for tomorrow's aggravation. Billy Loes hoped for the best when he signed the blank contract and didn't check his weekly pay stub. He was lucky because Bavasi was a nice guy. You may not be so lucky.

What amazes me is how often people go into important personal transactions without thinking through what they want or what their plan is. Real estate brokers and car dealers confirm that most customers do a poor job of negotiating for these high ticket items. Only occasionally does someone come along with a strategy for getting what they want. Most just flounder around and hope all will go well. For them, the "best" never happens. They get less for their money – less car, less service, fewer extras and less satisfaction.

Professional buyers and salespeople also suffer from "hope for the best" syndrome. They go into negotiations, sometimes multimillion or billion dollar deals, without adequate preparation. They hope for the best by agreeing to terms that are not clear enough, only to find themselves on the short end of the deal later. Luckily for some of these professionals, things sometimes work out better than they deserve because the other party is equally unprepared. They too fall victim to hoping for the best and thereby relinquish the advantage they could have had.

"Hoping for the best" is the lazy man's way to success. It won't work. The person who puts his or her fate in the hands of luck is sure to lose over the long run. The person who plans will be better prepared for the unexpected. In our free enterprise system, "hoping for the best" is one of the major factors that convert winners into losers.

Rule 12 – Watch Out for Funny Money

Those who own the gambling casinos in Las Vegas know that customers place a $100 bet using a plastic chip faster than they would if they had to place a $100 bill on the gambling table. It is easier to sell a $60,000 car if you tell the buyer it's only $699 a month. Funny money is money that doesn't seem real but is.

Good negotiators think about real money. The column on the left is funny money. The other column is what smart negotiators think about. As you compare them it becomes clear how different they are.

FUNNY MONEY	REAL MONEY
1. The buyer says, "You are asking 20 cents a pound. We'll give you the order right now at 19 cents. It's only a penny."	The seller should be thinking. With 2 million pounds involved, that comes to a $20,000 concession. Too much. I'm going to hold at 19.8 or 19.7 cents.
2. The electronic component salesperson says, "We'll sell your company those ultrafast microchips at $1100 per 100. They will make your processors far faster"	You should be thinking, "But I need 20,000 chips. That comes to $220,000. I'll make a deal for $180,000 if I take the lot."
3. The bank is charging 11.25% on the $30,000 personal loan for five years.	In real money that's $9,061 in interest and it's not deductible. If I can bring the rate to 9% I save $2,000.
4. The interior decorator works on a cost plus 35% basis. The decoration will cost $20,000-$25,000 which means her fee will be $7,000 to almost $9,000.	Which way should I negotiate? I can offer a fixed fee of $5,000 for the whole job or try to bring the 35% down. I think I can do better dealing in a flat dollar amount.
5. The overseas phone support contractor says, "We can't give you the 10% fee you ask; 0.8% is all."	The subcontractor should be thinking. "On this $3 million dollar job a 2% drop in fee is worth $60,000 in real money. That's too much. A drop of 0.4% is okay.
6. The transportation seller says, "We charge you only $5 to fill out an export document. You know that it would cost you three times that if you did it yourself.	The transportation buyer should be thinking, "With 4,000 foreign shipments a year, that person is asking us to give $20,000. That pays for a full-time clerk for a year.

7. The banker says, "We can't reduce the interest rate from 9.2 to 9% on the mortgage for your new manufacturing plant."

The controller should be thinking, "Over a thirty-year period that .2 percent is worth $300,000. Wow! $300,000 is worth negotiating for."

8. The union negotiator says, "We need an extra two minutes on the break to allow people to go to the bathroom."

Management should be thinking, "Two minutes a day for 2,000 employees for one year is worth $500,000. Wow!"

9. The big executive says, "Let's split the difference on this $50 million deal. We are only $2 million apart.

The big executive should be thinking. "Our whole company earned only $5 million last year. Maybe we ought to try a $200,000 concession instead."

People are wise to train themselves to think of real money whenever they transact business. Only then can they decide whether they want the talks to revolve around such abstractions as percentage rates, cost per pound, price per unit, employee-hours, overhead rates, or labor rates per hour. If the other side wants to negotiate in terms of funny money, that's their problem not yours. People who deal in funny money without converting it to real money usually make larger concessions than they should.

Rule 13 – The Art of Concession-making and Compromise – A Summary of Practical Dos and Don'ts

In most negotiations, both sides move from their original positions. Each compromises by making some concessions to reach an agreement. The following dos and don'ts of concession-making will help you do better in future negotiations.

1.   Never fear to negotiate. Resist your embarrassment or fear of trying.

2.   Leave some room to compromise.

3.   Get something in return whenever you make a concession.

4.   If they say "Let's split the difference," you can say, "I can't afford to. I need 75% of the difference."

5.   Learn to give concessions that give nothing away. Good listening, courteous consideration and strong backup for what you say are examples of such concessions.

6.   If you can't get a dinner, get a sandwich. Don't be too shy to nibble.

7.   If you can't get a concession, get a promise. A promise is a concession with a discount rate. It's better than nothing and, in some cases, quite valuable.

8.   Tit-for-tat concessions are not necessary. If they give 100 you can give 80 or 60. If they give 20 you can give 10 or nothing in exchange.

9.   Don't negotiate for "funny money" unless you have thought it through in terms of real money. Think of every concession this way, "Have I figured out what I am about to give away in real money. Is it too big a concession?"

10. Keep track of your concessions and theirs. They may be

giving more concessions than you are, but yours may be worth more. One concession can be worth a lot more than four.

11. Don't be ashamed to back away from a concession you've already made. It is the final settlement that closes the negotiation, not the agreements in between.

12. If you want to dampen the expectations of the other party and have them appreciate what they get, give them lots of no's, make small concessions over a long period of time and concede in smaller and smaller amounts as you move toward agreement. Make them work for what they get.

Bobby Knight, the outstanding basketball coach at Indiana University, once considered leaving basketball for a television career as a sports commentator. In an interview he said, "I would have gone to CBS if they hadn't screwed it up. I said just give me the best offer you have. I don't negotiate. They came back with a figure and I said no. They came back and offered me two and a half times the original figure. The more they offered the more upset I got. They could have offered me a million dollars a year and I wouldn't have taken it."

A lot of people, like Bobby Knight, don't negotiate. They pay a high price for that privilege. In a complex society like ours, give and take is increasingly called for. It is far better for a person to learn about and engage in the art of negotiating. Bobby Knight was negotiating whether he knew it or not. He used a tactic we describe in Chapter 11, "Give Me Your Best Offer." CBS responded in a way that Knight should have expected. When people say to me, "I don't negotiate," I think to myself, "There's

no dishonor in not negotiating but there's no honor in it either."
I believe that in business, as in life, you don't get what you deserve
you get what you negotiate. Why not do it as well as you can?
These rules of concession-making are sure to help.

Rule 14 – Be a Super-Winner. You Can Always Find a Better Deal for Both Parties

By now you can see that the rules for becoming a winner in
negotiation are really quite simple. Anyone can do it with a little
bit of practice. Yet there is an even higher level one can reach –
the Super-Winner level. The best negotiators are Super-Winners.
What they do every time they negotiate is find a better deal for
both parties – a deal that neither side imagined possible when
they first met. It isn't as hard as it sounds. We can all do it.

The road to becoming a Super-Winner begins when you recognize
that negotiation is not a contest. Unfortunately, most people see
negotiation as a battle. They believe that if there is a 10-inch
diameter pie cut in ten pieces the winner is the one who gets six
or more pieces. They see it as a process in which one person gains
at the expense of the other – a zero-sum game. This naturally
makes them tense and often leads to deadlock.

A Super-Winner in negotiation knows that elements of
competition are built into every bargaining situation. However,
the Super-Winner also recognizes that both parties win more
when they search together for innovative ways to create value that
they can then share between them.

CONCLUSION

Whether you are a consumer who only negotiates once in a while or a professional who does so daily, the rules we have covered will improve your performance. They will also lead you to be more comfortable in any bargaining situation from now on.

HOW WINNERS WIN IN NEGOTIATION

Rule 1   Pick the Best Place and Time to Negotiate for Anything, Including a Raise.

Rule 2   What is Our Next Choice if This Negotiation Breaks Down?

Rule 3   Be Stingy With Your Concessions and Leave Room To Negotiate.

Rule 4   If You Are a Buyer Don't Give the Seller a Quick Counteroffer to Their Asking Price.

Rule 5   Don't Say Yes Too Quickly.

Rule 6   Buyers Should Always Try to Get Cost Breakdowns. Sellers Should Not Give them.

Rule 7   Don't Make the First Major Concession.

Rule 8   Watch Your Concessions as Deadline Approaches – Big Mistakes are Made.

Rule 9   Shut Up.

Rule 10   Be Skeptical. Things are Not What They Appear to Be.

Rule 11   Stop Hoping for the Best: How Winners Become Losers.

Rule 12   Watch Out for Funny Money.

Rule 13   Dos and Don'ts if You Have to Compromise.

Rule 14   Be a Super-Winner: You Can Always Find a Better Deal for Both Parties.

3

The Super-Winners in Business Are Always Win-Win Negotiators

WHAT IT IS AND HOW TO DO IT -
THE VALUE BUILDING NEGOTIATION

This is the most important chapter in the book. If you want to be a SUPER-WINNER in negotiation, win-win is your key to success. The magic is that it is so easy to do and the payoff so great.

This chapter will show you how to make win-win agreements every time you negotiate. We will illustrate how to do so in a step-by-step way using two common negotiating situations: when, as a consumer, you buy or sell a home and when, as a professional salesperson or purchasing executive, you negotiate for products, materials, or services.

To understand win-win negotiation, imagine a 10-inch diameter pie cut into ten equal pieces. You and I are negotiating over how many of these ten pieces each of us will get. If you get six, I'll only get four. If I get eight, you'll only get two. This type of competitive negotiation is not win-win but a contest for shares of the pie.

Most people look at negotiation in the wrong way. They see it as a contest, a game in which the gains of one come only at the expense of the other. They feel that the goal of most bargainers is to get six or more pieces of the 10-piece pie and leave the other four or less. No wonder they are nervous about negotiating; they don't want to be the one who gets only three or four.

The power and magic of negotiation is that it is far more than a contest. It has the potential to be a win-win process by which we work together to produce a 12-inch pie which is bigger and tastier than before. We then cut the larger pie into twelve pieces and share it more easily than the original ten smaller, less tasty pieces. Think of your family. Wouldn't it be easier to share twelve pieces of a bigger pie than ten pieces of a smaller pie that wasn't so good?

Super-winners recognize that win-win is the way to negotiate. What they try to do in every negotiation is increase the size and quality of whatever they are negotiating about. They search for a better deal for both parties. Only after searching and finding the bigger and better deal for both do they worry about how to share it.

The basic principle of win-win negotiating is that there is ALWAYS a bigger and better deal for both parties if they are willing to search for it. Both buyer and seller increase their PROFIT and SATISFACTION without hurting each other. The win-win principle says that the negotiating pie can ALWAYS be made larger and better before sharing it with the opposing side. **ALWAYS.**

With this in mind we will now show how win-win negotiating can be applied to the real world of buying and selling. Two examples will be developed in a step-by-step manner. One involves buying a home for $300,000, the other a large contract for guest internet service for a hotel chain like Holiday Inn. First, we will show how to make a better deal for both the buyer and the seller of the home, then we will show how to handle the high-dollar drinking glass negotiation in a win-win way. You will see that the principles and techniques in both situations are virtually identical.

HOW TO NEGOTIATE FOR A HOUSE USING THE WIN-WIN STRATEGY: SMART NEGOTIATING

You are buying a house. The seller has had it on the market for a year. She now wants $300,000, a reasonable price. You open by offering $250,000 and explain why your offer is reasonable. After some discussion, the seller reduces her price to $280,000. Then, after a period of standing fast, you gradually raise your offer to $265,000.

Now, after both of you have said the same things to one another many times, there doesn't seem much more to say. The seller is locked in at $280,000 and you remain at $265,000. You are heading toward deadlock. Both of you are tense. Yet the seller wants to sell, and you want to buy.

You make a strategic decision. You will not continue to talk about price until you and the seller search jointly for ways to make the transaction better for both. Together you explore eight areas where win-win opportunities are likely to be found in any bargaining situation.

1. TAXES
2. PAYMENT TERMS
3. WHAT IS INCLUDED OR NOT (SPECIFICATION)
4. TRANSPORTATION
5. DELIVERY OF PERFORMANCE DATE OR MOVE-IN DATE
6. QUANTITY
7. WHO DOES WHAT FOR WHOM
8. RISK AND CONTRACT TYPE

1. TAXES

One of the best payoff areas lies in tax savings. Sellers who are going to make a profit on a house will surely be interested in reducing their tax liability.

One possible tax suggestion is to have the buyer pay 29 percent down and take the mortgage directly from the seller. The seller could then spread the capital gains tax over many years rather than pay a large lump sum now. This could be a substantial gain for the seller at no loss and possibly at a gain to the buyer.

It is easy to see that the tension of bargaining is likely to be less than before. Both parties can now search for other ways to build the 10-inch pie into a 12-inch pie – that is, to create joint value together.

2. PAYMENT TERMS

Most homes are bought with about 20 percent down and a 30-year mortgage. A better deal for the buyer may be a longer or shorter mortgage. A couple may prefer to start with low payments and move to larger payments later on. Or, knowing they will inherit money soon, they may favor a big two-year second mortgage. The seller, for reasons of his or her own, may prefer these non-conventional alternatives. Payment terms always provide win-win opportunities.

3. WHAT IS INCLUDED (SPECIFICATION)

Items included or not included with the house can lead to both-win opportunities. For some people, it may be best to include the drapes, stove, and refrigerator. Other home buyers might want to purchase the existing furniture because it fits perfectly into a corner of the new house. Conversely, the sellers may want to get rid of some very nice pieces at bargain prices because they are moving to a small condominium and no longer need them.

A buyer moving to Los Angeles from the east would probably need a second car. The seller of the home moving to New York City might well be delighted to sell the car so easily. What is included or not included in any deal is open to win-win possibilities.

4. TRANSPORTATION COSTS

At first glance, it is hard to see how transportation costs affect a house purchase, but it does. Both parties are moving, one in and the other out. It is possible for buyer and seller to make a three-way arrangement with the moving company by which the trucks bringing the buyer's furniture to the house can haul away the seller's. It may also be possible for the buyer to start moving things into the new house while the seller is still there, thereby saving trucking charges.

Occasionally, creative buyers and sellers share the cost of renting a "U-Haul" truck and help each other move.

5. DELIVERY OR CLOSING DATE

You, the home buyer, are moving to Los Angeles and want your children in school by September 15. Your present lease expires on that day and you want to move out by then. It may be possible for both parties to arrange the closing date of escrow for September 15 in order to meet your needs. This would represent a substantial benefit to you at little or no cost to the seller.

6. QUANTITY

There is no way a person would buy two homes to live in at once. Or is there? A year ago a friend of mine bought a resale condominium in Florida and asked the seller if he owned any other property. It turned out that the seller had a vacation cottage on a lake in North Carolina. My friend bought both properties at a discount. In your negotiation for the house, it might be wise to explore whether he or she owns any other property which might be included in the deal. I've known people in Florida who were given a very good discount for buying two condominiums in the same development. Later they sold the extra one at a nice profit.

Another man I know always buys two adjoining lots, although he plans to build on one only. Later, when the area develops, he sells the other lot at a large profit.

7. WHO DOES WHAT FOR WHOM

If I were a carpenter and you were a tailor, I might build some custom book shelves for you and you might sew some custom suits for me. In any transaction, each person has different talents to contribute to the exchange.

In a similar vein, it might be best for the seller of the house to put in a swimming pool before escrow closes. In that way the new buyer can spread the added pool costs over a 30-year mortgage at a lower rate of interest – a large saving and convenience for the buyer.

8. RISK AND TYPE OF CONTRACT

There are ways to obtain the use of a house without buying it. These alternatives include leasing, a lease with option to buy, a contract sale, or a trade. Third parties such as relatives, banks or trustees may participate in a beneficial way if it serves the purpose of one or both parties. For example, the seller's bank may be willing to lend money to the buyer at a lower rate if his or her parents co-sign the note. The point is that there are various types of contracts that can reflect the risk-taking propensity and needs of those involved.

• • • • •

Each of the win-win opportunities above were designed to help the buyer or seller of the house gain something at little or no expense to the other. They were developed to help the parties bridge the price gap by building what I call "intersecting spheres of mutual interdependence."

The fact that the parties are now interconnected by tax savings, a vacation cottage, a tailor made suit and the extra car will surely help them bridge the existing $15,000 price gap. They are now bound by "intersecting spheres of mutual interdependence." That is how win-win negotiating brings people together.

HOW SELLERS AND BUYERS IN BUSINESS CAN MAKE A BETTER DEAL FOR BOTH PARTIES EVERY TIME: NEGOTIATING LIKE AN ENTREPRENEUR

Suppose now that you are a buyer for Holiday Inn and you are ready to place a purchase order to upgrade internet service for hotel guests. You've gotten ten bids and the best will charge $1.00 per room per day for internet service. You call the lowest bidder into your office to look for ways to reduce the price and, at the same time, increase the seller's profit margin. Is it possible to do so? You will soon see that it is.

Once more let's look at the eight avenues for both-win opportunities:

1. TAXES
2. PAYMENT TERMS
3. WHAT IS INCLUDED OR NOT (SPECIFICATION)
4. TRANSPORTATION
5. DELIVERY OR CLOSING DATE
6. QUANTITY
7. WHO DOES WHAT FOR WHOM
8. RISK AND CONTRACT TYPE

1. TAXES

A safe assumption is that the other person's tax situation differs from your own. For example, as the seller I may not care when Holiday Inn takes actual possession of the hardware components as long as I get paid. But the Holiday Inn treasurer may care a great deal because he or she now has to pay an inventory tax which could easily have been avoided by delaying shipment one day.

Sales taxes vary from state to state. Perhaps the order should not be placed from New York with its high sales tax rate, but from someplace where sales taxes are lower. Federal tax rates may go up or down if merchandise is owned on December 31 rather than January 1. That's why it's so important to coordinate buyer/seller tax needs and to check out possible advantages with accountants. Doing this is especially critical in foreign transactions where more than one country is likely to be involved in tax collection matters.

2. PAYMENT TERMS

Once, when I worked at Hughes, I dealt with a vendor who didn't want to be paid. He refused to invoice us for two years after doing the job, despite the fact that we badgered him to bill us. (If you've ever worked for a large company, you know how disconcerting it is to the accounting department to have an unpaid purchase file hanging around that long.) Only when he retired was an invoice sent. He held out because he wanted to pay taxes at a lower rate when his earnings were less.

If Holiday Inn had lots of cash and the seller was low on funds, the best payment terms might be progress payments, or some payment in advance, or cash on delivery. Between the quick payment that some people need and the slow payment my old vendor preferred, there are many win-win variations.

3. WHAT IS INCLUDED (SPECIFICATION)

Holiday Inn specified name brand modems for their guest

internet service. The seller bid $1.00 per room per day based on that specification.

Was this the best arrangement for both? The answer is, "not necessarily."

Suppose the seller informed the buyer that their own brand of modems could provide service for 80 cents because they manufactured these themselves for numerous customers. Might not the buyer change her mind and save $200,000 on the order? At the same time, the seller could earn a larger profit than before by selling modems they produced themselves and in bulk. For the hotel guest, the change to a different brand of modem would make little difference.

The best way to look at a specification is to assume that a better deal for both parties may be possible if some changes are made to blend the seller's specific production capabilities to the buyer's specific use. If the specification change is large, it may be necessary to reopen the bidding process, but specifications are negotiable in many situations.

4. TRANSPORTATION COSTS

Most people who buy and sell know very little about transportation and its high cost. Yet, with just a few minutes work and the help of a transportation specialist, substantial benefits can be gained. Transportation is the hidden funny money of buying and selling because no one pays attention to it, except those who sell transportation services. Rates vary enormously between truck, rail, air, United Parcel, and Postal deliveries. Differences between one and three day delivery prices are quite large. For example, this book can be shipped by media mail for less than $3 or by overnight express service for over $100.

Transportation costs can be reduced at no expense to either party. Sometimes buyers are better off handling freight themselves because their empty trucks pass the seller's factory. In other situations, the seller may ship in such large quantities they are favored with low bulk rates.

The more you look into transportation, the more win-win opportunities you discover.

5. DELIVERY DATE

The Holiday Inn buyer wanted the upgraded modems and service installed in four equal phases over the course of the year. The seller agreed to do so. But might they not do well to consider an alternative schedule for delivery and installation?

For example, suppose the seller normally laid off employees in July and August when business is slow. Perhaps they would be willing to reduce the cost if they could install service during these months. Both sides could benefit if Holiday Inn could handle the staffing and payment problems. The reality of business is this: A buyer's delivery requirements never represent the seller's optimum production economics. Tie the two together and you've got a win-win combination.

6. QUANTITY

When a buyer says he or she wants to upgrade service at a thousand hotels, the seller has to bid on a thousand hotels. But it is well for both to recognize that a thousand doesn't necessarily represent the best amount for either. For instance, the Holiday

Inn might prefer a three-year contract upgrade service annually so that it doesn't have to reopen bids every year, and the service provider might benefit from the security of a long-term contract by negotiating a lower interest rate on a loan from its bank. One of the best win-win strategies I know is to close a price gap by changing quantity.

7. WHO DOES WHAT FOR WHOM

When Holiday Inn purchases installation of upgraded guest internet service, they are indirectly purchasing not only the end service, but also an entire production line. They are indirectly buying into both supply chain and service development ranging from production of wireless internet hardware and development of companion software to the internet service provider's system design and integration as well as the training of installation teams.

The point is, if you want to find a better deal for both parties, look carefully at the seller's procedures, whether on the production or service development side. You are sure to find operations that can be omitted, excess packaging that can be dispensed with, more efficient ways of transporting products in bulk, and ways of developing option-rich software to cut down on the cost of tailoring systems to each buyer. In my experience, the surest path to finding a better way to do anything is to study the detailed production, paperwork, and electronic tracking processes.

8. RISK AND TYPE OF CONTRACT

All business involves risk. The other day, I had a plumber repair some pipes in the attic. He wanted a time and material contract to protect his profit if something unforeseen came up. I preferred a firm price. We compromised risk by agreeing on a time and material basis limited by a not-to-exceed dollar amount. This served to guarantee satisfaction on my part. The plumber came in about 10 percent under the not-to-exceed amount and we were both pleased.

I would be the first to agree that a firm price contract is probably best for a large production order like modems and service, but other alternatives could be considered. A cost plus or time and material contract would likely be foolish. However, a tight incentive arrangement might serve both parties by balancing the seller's risk with the potential for earning a greater profit.

That's exactly what was done in the contract for repairs made to the earthquake damage to the 1-10 freeway in Los Angeles. The contractors were given an incentive of $100,000 a day if they beat the contract completion date. If they missed, they lost $100,000 a day.

The freeway was repaired sixty days early. The contractor earned an extra $6 million. The people of Los Angeles were delighted to get the busiest freeway in the world operating so quickly. It was a good deal for both parties.

HOW TO APPLY THE WIN-WIN APPROACH WHEN SOMEONE ASKS YOU FOR A RAISE OR WHEN YOU ASK FOR A RAISE

A friend of mine is a department manager at a large company. His secretary requested a 10 percent raise. She was worth it. The problem was that 10 percent represented a large raise compared to the 5 percent other employees had received. Was there a creative both-win way out of this problem?

As they explored the possibilities several ideas emerged.

The company starts work at 8:00 AM and closes at 5:00. The manager learned that his secretary encountered heavy traffic every evening on the way home. They agreed to have her work from 7:30 AM to 4:30. This saved her at least 20 to 25 minutes driving time. Certainly a benefit to her at little or no expense to the company.

They then studied her job in detail. Before long they jointly developed a new description which gave her more responsibility and, at the same time, more interesting work. Both parties benefitted from the changed scope of work. The raise itself was then discussed. A compromise was reached by agreeing on a 6 percent raise for three months and an additional 2 percent later if the new responsibilities were adequately performed.

What was accomplished in this management situation was to move the talks from a confrontation and a contest to a win-win arrangement. Negotiation on the higher win-win level did the job. Together they created values and satisfactions that were not there before, values that both sides welcomed. The company gained by enlarging the scope of work in exchange for a raise that was less than the 10 percent requested. The manager also gained something that was even more valuable, an employee who knew she could work with her boss in a creative both-win way.

CONCLUSION – THE POWER OF WIN-WIN NEGOTIATION

The win-win strategy of negotiating is without a doubt the most important concept in this book. In each of the three examples in this chapter we illustrated how the parties created enlarged "spheres of mutual interdependence and interests" which helped them discover benefits far beyond what each thought likely or possible when talks began. Like successful entrepreneurs everywhere, they found hidden opportunities in what each could do for the other.

That is the essence of win-win negotiating. It deals with more than price or terms, though each is important in its own right. Win-win raises the stakes – it raises the level and content of the relationship between the bargainers. It generates new values and connections that were not visible before they jointly searched for them.

In this chapter, we explored only eight areas in which win-win benefits were generated. There are, in real life, many more than eight value generating payoff areas. For example, in the Holiday Inn internet service upgrade negotiation, we might have considered such matters as paperwork flow, alternative hardware and software suppliers, distribution, installation processes and a myriad other possibilities to make the final agreement even better for buyer and seller.

Another benefit of win-win negotiating is that it reduces the tension inherent in bargaining. I have found there are few phrases which more quickly capture the attention of the other party than,

"Let's find a better deal for both of us." What follows, like magic, is that we find creative both-win opportunities every time. A 10-inch pie becomes a bigger and better 12-inch pie which is much easier to share than the smaller, less tasty one. Our relationship with the other side becomes stronger, less likely to fall apart. We both become SUPER-WINNERS. That's the magic of win-win negotiating.

There is little question in my mind that the road to exceptional success in negotiation is the win-win road. In subsequent chapters of this book we will see how the win-win approach enhances your bargaining power, helps break deadlocks and allows you to gain and maintain the initiative under pressure.

AREAS TO LOOK FOR
WIN-WIN SOLUTIONS

Area 1	Taxes
Area 2	Payment Terms
Area 3	What Is Included or Not (Specification)
Area 4	Transportation
Area 5	Delivery of Performance or Move-In Date
Area 6	Quantity
Area 7	Who Does What for Whom
Area 8	Risk and Contract Type
and	Many More Value-Creating Synergies

4

Bargaining Power: Making the Most of The Power You Have

Power is the most important factor in determining outcome. Experienced people are aware of this and experiments confirm it. Power is the ability of one person to control the resources and benefits of another. To the extent that one person can control something another needs, that person has power over the other. This chapter shows you how to build your base of power and how to limit the leverage of the other side.

Power is rarely what it appears to be. *People have more power than they think because they are more aware of their own limitations than those of the other side.* They recognize the losses they would suffer if agreement cannot be reached. What they cannot do is look into the mind of the other party and accurately assess how worried they are about losing the deal if deadlock occurs.

Additionally, both parties always have some constraints upon their action, even when they are in a strong position. These limits may be legal or moral, economic or physical, geographic or organizational, imagined or real. These constraints limit the negotiators' capacity to use all the power they have.

For example, assume that you have not made a mortgage payment for six months. The bank has threatened to foreclose and take possession of the house. They have every right to do so. Your negotiating position is not good. What limits the bank in taking over your home?

The bank may have too many foreclosed homes in your area. It may cost them too much to maintain the property in saleable order. They are bankers not property managers. Vandals may damage the empty property. The bank auditors may determine that the bank has too many bad loans and raise their reserve requirements. The bank may be optimistic and believe the economy will turn upward. This may allow you to get a better job and make payments, or sell the house at a better price yourself. If you are a popular, community-spirited person, the bank may be embarrassed to foreclose.

Despite its superior financial and legal power, the bank is limited in its willingness or ability to use all the strength it has. Similar constraints exist in most negotiations.

Power is part of the exchange system. People deal with one another because they wish to increase their satisfaction by exchanging resources and benefits. They give something to get something they want. To best leverage our power, we should know what the other party wants and what we can do to gratify or deny those wants. Ben Franklin said it another way: "Would you persuade, speak of interest." In the next section we will speak of the interests that motivate a negotiator.

THE ICEBERG THEORY OF NEGOTIATION POWER MOTIVATORS

There is a theory of negotiation called "The Iceberg Theory." It is obvious people want money, goods, and services, but this theory contends that many things which a person also needs remain unseen and unspoken, hidden like the underside of an iceberg. Money, goods and services are the tip of the iceberg. If you want power, you must understand and know how to gain access to and use the parts below the surface as well as the parts that show. It will be harder to reach a workable settlement if you fail to be aware of and satisfy the other parties' unspoken needs.

Four hundred years ago, Sir Francis Bacon had this to say about power, persuasion and wants: "If you would work any man, you must either know his nature and fashions, and so lead him; or his ends and so persuade him; or his weaknesses and so awe him; or those that have interest in him, and so govern him." If you and I and Sir Francis were each asked to make a separate list today of what people want, it is likely that our lists would be much alike. Human beings have not changed much in four centuries and neither has power and its relationship to negotiation.

What follows are some of the unspoken issues affecting both parties in every negotiation:

- They want to make their lives easier.
- They want others to think them competent.
- They want peace of mind.
- They want to be listened to.
- They want some freedom of choice.

- They want to keep their jobs or position.
- They want to be treated with dignity.
- They want to be dealt with honorably.
- They want recognition in some tangible way.
- They want to be liked.
- They want to avoid future troubles and aggravations.
- They want to minimize personal or business risk and uncertainty.
- They want reliable and satisfying relationships.
- They want to keep what they already have.
- They want to satisfy their own needs as well as the needs of others who depend on them.

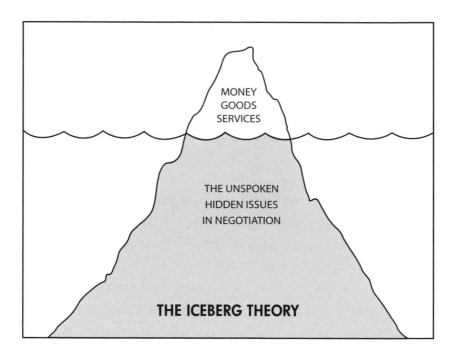

These are the hidden issues in every agenda. You have never seen a purchase order for a pound of "make my life easier," or three dozen "no future troubles," or a yard of "I want to keep my job."

Yet whether you buy or sell, that's what the other party wants. They won't say "yes" until some of these wants are filled.

The key to gaining power is to recognize that if we are to persuade anyone we must "pay them well," not necessarily in terms of dollars, goods and services, but in satisfaction. As Shakespeare suggests in The Merchant of Venice, "He is well paid who is well satisfied."

BUILDING YOUR POWER BASE

The cowboy gunslingers of the old west used to say, "A kind word and a gun will get you much further than a kind word alone." That's one way to look at power, but in these more civilized days we can leave the gun behind.

One thing to recognize about power in business affairs is that it may be more imagined than real. An ancient Chinese warlord once said, "The first rule of power is that you have a closed door. The enemy must never know what, if anything, lies behind the door." Power is in the head as well as the fist.

In the rest of this chapter we will consider seven time-tested approaches to building a base of power in any negotiation. We will also discuss two tough negotiations: first, the seller who must make a deal with a buyer who has many suppliers to choose from and second, the buyer who must close a deal with a sole-source seller, one who has no competition. These are the most difficult situations buyers and sellers face because the balance of power clearly favors the opposing party.

BUILDING BARGAINING POWER – APPROACH #1
THE POWER OF TIME

Time is a crucial element in bargaining power. If I have time to reach an agreement and you don't, I have a measure of power over you. The difficulty with time is that we tend to underestimate our strength because we are aware of the time pressures on ourselves, not those on the other side.

Below are seven ideas to help build time power:

1. Leave time to shop around. Don't wait for Christmas Eve to buy or sell. When forced to act quickly you won't do well.

2. Be on time for the meeting. It's a small thing, but it will help you get started in a relaxed way.

3. Give yourself time to think. Caucus often. Short sessions with breaks in between are better than long sessions.

4. Avoid marathon talks unless you are well satisfied with where you stand and want to carry the agreement over the goal line.

5. Pick the best time to negotiate. If you are bargaining for bananas at the market, approach them at 5:00 PM on Saturday afternoon before they close for the night or weekend. There is usually a best time for everything.

6. Leave time for things to go wrong. Murphy's Law applies to negotiation as well as life – things will go wrong if they can. Have a contingency plan when talks are delayed or things bog down. Start on the assumption that your time

will be wasted in unforeseen ways. Instead of getting nervous or caving in at deadline, build a fallback position. Have second options available or have extra cash around to maneuver with. You'll need flexibility to maintain your bargaining position. The time to worry about "buying time" is long before you need it.

7. Leave enough time to plan. Use that time to plan rather than hope for the best.

8. Leave enough time to negotiate with your second choice if your first choice talks break down.

In addition, there are three useful questions involving deadlines which I suggest you ask yourself before and during any negotiation. They will help you relieve the pressure of deadline more effectively.

Question 1: What self-imposed or organization-imposed deadlines am I under that make it harder for me to negotiate? Self-imposed deadlines are often more difficult to cope with than those coming from the other party.

Question 2: Are the deadlines I've imposed on myself or my organization real? Can I negotiate an extension with my own people? Many deadlines are amenable to change.

Question 3: What deadlines are putting pressure on the other party and his or her organization?

You are not the only one under time pressure. They may be under greater pressure than you.

BUILDING BARGAINING POWER – APPROACH #2
MAKING WORK WORK FOR YOU

The "Hard Work Theory" says two things: first, the harder you work in negotiation, the better you are likely to do and second, the harder you make the other party work, the higher will be their satisfaction with the agreement.

Lazy people make poor negotiators. A recent book by an expert on how to buy a car observes that most buyers are too lazy to shop the market. For that reason they become easy prey for the hard-working seller. The expert's strongest recommendation in negotiating for a car is that the buyer be prepared to walk away from the dealer and start shopping all over again. Car dealers have a nasty habit of backing away from offers they have made. They do so to test the buyer's resolve. The buyer who makes up her or his mind that "there's always another car" if this deal collapses is best able to show resolve and obtain a better price.

There are three other principles involving work which can serve as guides to action in building work power. The first is called "The Least Effort Principle." It says that people prefer to make their lives easier. There's nothing new or brilliant about this idea, but it's quite useful in a negotiating context.

According to this principle, people would rather say "yes" to a passable deal than complicate their lives by bargaining longer for a better one. It says that buyers don't want to look for new sources if they can find reasons to stay with the old source. It says that sellers don't want to find new customers to replace old customers, even if the business isn't too profitable. The "Least Effort Principle" says that neither party wants to endure the stress of further negotiation or the work it takes to start over again with someone else. But it also says that the party that is willing to go beyond "least effort" gains power.

The next work power principle is called "The Wasted Work Principle." It says that people don't like to waste their energy. Once they have worked on something, they want the effort to payoff. The more work they have done, the more they want the deal to close. Real estate brokers know that the buyer who has spent lots of time shopping for a home, talking about it and negotiating for it is a very hot prospect. So also is the software developer in a billion-dollar negotiation who has invested a great deal of time, effort, emotional equity and money in the sales proposal. He or she will be desperate to close.

The final "power of work" principle is what I call the "Easy Come – Easy Go" Principle. This was discussed briefly in Chapter 2 where I suggested that saying "yes" too quickly is not wise. People do not appreciate what they get too easily. In fact, it's worse than that. I believe that people who get things without working for them tend to put down what they get and often resent the giver. There is a scene in Strindberg's play "Miss Julie" in which the servant wins the sexual favors of the beautiful countess but complains the next morning that the victory was so easy it didn't mean much to him.

Groucho Marx put it another way. He said, 'Any country club that would accept Groucho Marx isn't good enough for Groucho Marx." In negotiation it pays to be somewhat "hard to get." It will raise the other party's satisfaction with the final outcome.

BUILDING BARGAINING POWER – APPROACH #3
THE POWER OF PERSISTENCE

Webster defines persistence as the "refusal to give up when faced with opposition." Negotiators who are tenacious move the balance of power in their direction.

Normally, sales managers urge their salespeople to be persistent in selling their products. They correctly say, "Don't take no for an answer. Keep selling." Research shows that successful salespeople stay close to the buyer. They are better able to persist in the face of "no."

I have seen the same advice work well for buyers. The buyer who keeps after the seller whose price is too high has a good chance of winning a reduction. Persistence pays off for the buyer who is willing to take on a firm price, just as it works for the seller in defending it.

Good negotiators are persistent. The Russians, Arabs and Chinese don't hesitate to test their opponent's resolve by repeating their arguments over and over again. An American negotiating with the Vietnamese reported that for two years they came to the talks every morning and ceremoniously said the same thing with little or no change. It almost drove the Americans crazy.

Persistence has the power to break down walls of resistance. I knew a young man who wanted to buy a home owned by a widowed old woman. The man had a good job but little money for a down payment. He called on the old woman for a year telling her again and again that he loved the home, would take good care of it and could make the payments. Before the year ended they were good friends.

Persistence won out. She sold him the house for market price with a small down payment. The price was determined by an independent appraiser that she chose. At the last moment, after realizing that she didn't have to pay a broker, the woman sweetened the deal by taking $500 off the price.

Persistence is a good approach to negotiation. It allows the relationship to mature. It flatters the person being pursued and gives him or her time to accept your ideas. It works as well in social and love affairs as it does in business.

BUILDING BARGAINING POWER – APPROACH #4 THE POWER OF KNOWLEDGE AND INFORMATION

In his book Managing for Results, Peter Drucker argues persuasively that knowledge is the only thing that any business has for sale. Knowledge, as he sees it, is the power source that converts money, machines, materials, land and human energy into marketable products.

Knowledge and information is power in negotiation.

The surprising thing is that much of what you need to know in bargaining is not too hard to get if you determine in advance what you want to know and where to look for it. What follows are nine relatively simple questions which a seller should try to answer before negotiations begin or while talks are in progress:

1. How is the product I sell used and by whom?

2. Where does the money come from? Who really pays the bill? If it's the buyer's customer, would they be sensitive to a higher price for what you sell?

3. Who is the real decision-maker in the buyer's organization?

4. What are the time pressures on the buyer and his or her organization?

5. How is the buyer appraised? Many buyers are not judged on how good a price they get but on whether their agreements create problems. Others are measured by whether they get their purchase orders placed on time.

6. What are some of the hidden personal motivators under the buyer's iceberg?

7. How did the buyer (or the buyer's organization) negotiate last time? They may use the same approach this time.

8. What is their track record? Will they make trouble later by adding extras or changes?

9. What are the needs of the buyer's organization? Remember that these needs increase pressure on the buyer.

As a buyer, here are ten things you should try to discover about the seller. They will give you leverage in the give and take of bargaining:

1. Why is this order important to the salesperson and the salesperson's organization?

2. How did they negotiate last time? Do they come prepared, stand firm for a while, then cave in? What's the pattern?

3. What are the time pressures on the seller? Are there

quotas, quarterly bonuses or commissions to consider?

4. What three competitors is the seller most afraid of? Why?

5. How is the product or service made? How can we get good cost breakdowns?

6. What are the standard markups, discounts or services available to the buyer? How negotiable are they historically?

7. How is this salesperson measured by his or her organization?

8. Who is the seller's real decision maker?

9. What is the market and distribution structure for this product or service? Can I buy it cheaper on the used market?

10. What are some of the hidden personal motivators driving this salesperson to close?

Information has been called the mother's milk of negotiation. The more you know the better you will do. Yet it is well to remember that knowledge is only potential power if it is organized into a plan of action to achieve goals.

BUILDING BARGAINING POWER – APPROACH #5
THE POWER OF RISK TAKING

All negotiation involves work, discovery and taking risks. The person willing to suffer uncertainty has a better chance to tip the balance of power in their favor than those less bold. Courage is always part of the deal. One must have the courage to try, to probe, to ask questions, to wait, to deadlock or to commit oneself to an agreement. Every course of action carries with it a degree of financial or emotional risk.

Most people prefer security over uncertainty. This tendency spills over into negotiation and leads them into fearing to negotiate or giving in before they should. To counteract this tendency, it's well to understand the kinds of risks that people try to avoid:

THE RISK OF DEADLOCK – People are afraid of deadlock. They prefer the deal in hand to the one in the bush. They know that by walking away there is a chance to do better. On the other hand, they might lose what they've already gained or, worse yet, have to start all over again with someone else. Given such a choice, most people prefer to settle once they have spent time negotiating for a significant period of time.

THE RISK OF "ROCKING THE BOAT" – People who work for large corporations will agree that it isn't wise to rock the organizational boat. Negotiators have been known to lose their reputations and their jobs for making agreements that second guessers in their own organization thought inadequate. I know many a buyer who is afraid to negotiate a low price for fear that the seller may later respond by shaving on quality or delivery. When this happens, management tends to forget the low price and question the business judgment of the buyer who won it.

Never forget that the other party has a lot to lose on a personal level. Their jobs, their reputations, their business judgment, their relationships with others, their commissions, their bonuses and their next raise are on the line. From a personal standpoint, they may be better off with a poor but easily explained settlement than a better one which has a chance of falling apart later.

THE FEAR OF LOSING WHAT ONE ALREADY HAS – People would rather forego gains than lose what they already have. For example, most of us are conservative in investing money. We would rather take a low, but secure, interest rate from the bank than put our funds into speculative stocks. A key human motivation is to control and conserve that which we have striven hard to get.

In business, it works this way. A seller has a steady customer who pays on time. The trouble is that the profit margin on these sales is less than it should be. In a subsequent negotiation with the customer, the seller tries to raise the price, but encounters stiff resistance. One thing the buyer can count on is that the seller is balancing the risk of losing a small but safe margin against the gain of a higher price. The fear of losing what they have will weigh heavily on their decision.

THE RISK OF LOSING AN OPPORTUNITY – Unless a negotiation involves big dollars, there is a tendency on the part of the buyer to assume the sale is not important to the seller, especially if the seller is a large company and the profit margin small. Yet I have seen many situations where sellers were willing to take unprofitable orders. Why?

Below are some hidden opportunities that motivate a seller even when there are no profits in the short run:

- Breaking into a new market or account
- Developing a product
- Learning how to do the job
- Building a relationship with the decision-makers
- Selling another product
- Covering fixed costs

- Proving a seller's competency to do the job
- Using the customer as a reference
- Reaching break-even
- Getting the opportunity to raise prices later on

In keeping with this matter of opportunities I am reminded of the story of Kennedy, a jeweler who was teaching his son the ins and outs of the jewelry business. "This is my best money maker," he said, pointing to a case of wristwatches. "They cost me $200 and I sell them for $200."

"If they cost you $200 and you sell them for $200, how can they be your best money makers?" asked the son.

'Ah, but that's not the point," the old man replied. "The profit comes from repairing them. They always come back to me."

There is leverage in recognizing that loss of potential opportunity plays a role in bargaining, even when the present stakes appear small. Salespeople are particularly sensitive to this possible loss of future opportunity. They often complain that by pricing so high, sales management "never misses an opportunity to miss an opportunity."

BUILDING BARGAINING POWER – APPROACH #6
THE POWER OF PRECEDENCE, LEGITIMACY AND HABIT

Habit and custom exert power. Some years ago, a television show demonstrated how strong an influence habit is in controlling behavior. The camera crew put a traffic light in the middle of the sidewalk on 5th Avenue, one of the busiest streets in New York. As usual, the sidewalk was choked with people going in both directions. First they put the light on green. Everyone kept walking. Then they switched it to red. You and I know that a red light in the middle of a sidewalk makes no sense. But to the television viewers' amusement, throngs of busy New Yorkers stopped and waited for the light to change. Only when it turned green did they continue walking. Such is the power of custom and habit.

The past also exerts pressure on present and future behavior. Past dealings and precedents affect future dealings. What merchants charge today for their goods or services affects what they can comfortably charge tomorrow. What they charge one person partly determines what he/she feels comfortable charging another. If the seller gave you a discount last year, you are likely to expect one this year. Other customers will also expect one if they learn of it. In labor negotiations, precedent is all important. When teachers in Los Angeles get a 5 percent raise, teachers in San Francisco want one too. Precedent, custom, and habit can add substance to your base of power.

Another good way to gain leverage is to find policies and procedures that add credibility and legitimacy to your position. The British Prime Minister Gladstone said, "Good laws make it easier to do right." The power of standard terms, policies, procedures, rules and regulations is profound. There isn't a person I know who hasn't at one time or another succumbed to the phrase, "We can't change the procedure," or "It's against company policy."

If you want the other party to look favorably at your position, find a good rule or regulation to support it. When Moses came down the mountain with the Ten Commandments, they weren't just ideas in his head. They were engraved in stone. Who was going to negotiate a change when every word was chiseled in granite and blessed at the highest level of authority?

Since we cannot publish price lists in stone, printed lists will have to serve instead. Published price lists, printed discount sheets, advertisements in a trade magazine or a fancy color catalog carry weight to the bargaining table. They are far stronger than telephone conversations, chalk on a blackboard, or words in a presentation.

Legitimacy, precedents and habit add strength to a negotiator's position. They allow arguments to take the high ground. Legitimacy, precedents and habit imply that the weight of organization and history is behind the negotiator. Like Moses with the Ten Commandments, a negotiator backed by precedent or habit becomes a more persuasive bargainer.

BUILDING BARGAINING POWER – APPROACH #7
THE WIN-WIN STRATEGY: THE POWER OF INTERSECTING INTEREST AND INTERDEPENDENCE

Win-win is a powerful way to build leverage in any bargaining situation, be it a one shot deal involving the purchase of a consumer product or a long-term business transaction worth millions. The rule is simple – the more opposing parties develop intersecting spheres of mutual interest and interdependence, the more bargaining power they are likely to exert.

The diagram below describes in graphic terms the difference between competitive, "If you get more – I get less", zero-sum negotiating and the win-win approach, "Lets find a better deal for both parties." As the diagram shows, the intersecting spheres of mutual interest and interdependence between the buyer and seller is far greater in a win-win situation. This difference has profound effects in determining the outcome. The larger the intersection, be it of a personal or business nature, the higher the level of satisfaction both will share.

INTERSECTING SPHERES OF MUTUAL INTEREST AND INTERDEPENDENCE

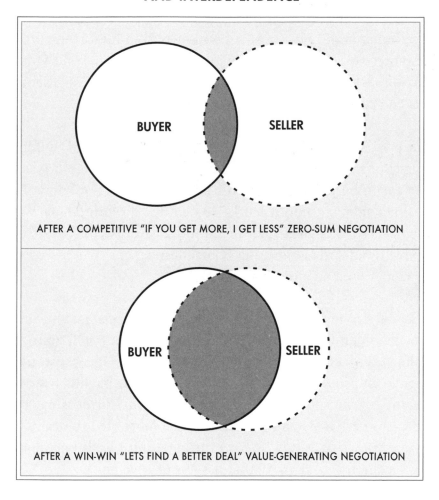

AFTER A COMPETITIVE "IF YOU GET MORE, I GET LESS" ZERO-SUM NEGOTIATION

AFTER A WIN-WIN "LETS FIND A BETTER DEAL" VALUE-GENERATING NEGOTIATION

The enlarged sphere of mutual interests leads to positive results at the table. Not only does it reduce the stress of bargaining but it serves to bind the opposing sides closer together after agreement is reached. Both tend to pay attention to the other's viewpoint because they are interconnected in a web of enhanced contributions and benefits. Neither is inclined to start anew with someone else.

Smart salespeople are aware of this source of bargaining power. They set the stage for an intersecting personal and business relationship long before negotiation takes place. Every visit to the buyer's organization is more than a business visit. It is accompanied by some favored goodies, a few jokes, small personal and family talk, some kidding around and a sprinkling of buyer-friendly facts and rumors.

As expressed earlier, Arab negotiators make the most of building interactions on a personal level. They are gracious hosts who make the bargaining process as much fun as possible. They know that the other side will find it harder to be difficult with people who have favored them with consideration and respect. Friendship, goodwill and interconnecting contributions and benefits count for a lot at the bargaining table.

When buyers and sellers build areas of joint personal and business interest and interdependency, it is unlikely they will want to exploit each other. Why should they? Having spent the time to build improvements in the specification, in payment terms, warranties, transportation, distribution, joint advertising and end-customer satisfaction, neither will be motivated to deal with anyone else. That is how win-win negotiation builds bargaining leverage, even for the party that has less relative power.

BUILDING BARGAINING POWER – THE POWER AND LIMITS OF COMPETITION FROM THE BUYER'S AND SELLER'S VIEWPOINT

Americans as a whole believe in competition. They are convinced that it results in better products at lower prices. The interesting thing is that I've rarely met a seller who was fond of competition in their own business. The reason is obvious: the more competition they faced, the harder it was to win the order, and the lower the price they had to accept. Despite all the lip service paid to competition, smart sellers do all they can to limit its effects on their sales, while buyers do all they can to make the most of it.

In this section we will explore two aspects of competition and its limits in negotiation. First, we will see why sellers have more power than they think, even when a buyer is lucky enough to have many suppliers who want the business. Then we will look at the power a buyer has when dealing with a seller who is in a sole source position obviously a very difficult negotiation from the buyer's standpoint.

The salesperson who understands the limits of a buyer's ability to make use of all the competition that exists will negotiate with greater confidence. So too will the buyer who recognizes that even sole-source suppliers, the only ones who can do the job, have limits in exploiting their strength. From a negotiating standpoint, it is my contention that buyers facing a single-source and sellers facing heavy competition both have more power than they think. If they have power in these difficult situations, then so will you when the balance of power against you is less extreme.

THE POWER OF SELLERS, EVEN WHEN THEY FACE INTENSE COMPETITION: FACTORS WHICH LIMIT A BUYER'S POWER

Competition is intense in most industries. Salespeople meet with rejection every day. They lose orders to others who bid less or offer more than they do. For those who sell in the face of intense competition the question is, "What limits a buyer's power to use the seller's competitors?" The seller who understands the buyer's limits will find they are in a better position to make more profitable agreements.

As a procurement executive with considerable experience in large companies, I can tell you first hand of a buyer's limits in using competition, even when suppliers are fighting for the business. Below are some constraints that lessened our ability to make a better deal.

1. Some sellers fell by the wayside because my engineer or manufacturing head didn't like them.

2. Some fell because I didn't like them for failing to make a critical delivery in the past, making me and the company look bad.

3. Some were too small to deal with. Too much risk was involved. Maybe they couldn't do the job.

4. Some were producing Cadillacs when all I needed was a Honda.

5. Some offered marvelous features which raised the price for those who needed them. I didn't need them.

6. Some had bad reputations.

7. Some did a painstaking job of telling us why their product fit our specific needs. Others didn't bother tailoring their proposal to us. Those who didn't eliminated themselves.

8. Some were too far away to deal with.

9. Some didn't bid on my requirement, even after I invited them to do so. Some bid late.

10. I didn't know of some suppliers. They had never called or advertised.

11. I didn't get around to some because there wasn't enough time built into the purchasing process. By the time I learned that someone in my company required the service, there was no time to shop.

12. Some offered better terms and credit. That made lots of difference to our controller. This was especially true when our credit wasn't good or cash was scarce.

13. Some were so busy they couldn't meet our delivery requirements.

14. Some suppliers were eliminated because we had little experience with them. Suppliers with whom we had a satisfactory long-term relationship had the edge. Who likes to change? Track records are important.

15. Some did not offer good warranties or quality control.

16. Some were in financial trouble. We had to be sure they would not go bankrupt in the middle of our work.

17. Some were so smart that they helped our engineers write the specification around their product or service so nobody else could compete. That eliminated a lot of possible choices and reduced my power.

18. Some did not offer the mix of products and values I needed. It meant that I would have to deal with more than one firm to fill my full requirements. This meant additional risk and work for me, which I preferred to avoid.

19. Somebody, usually our engineer, told the preferred seller that they were preferred "because." That made it hard for me to negotiate. The seller already knew they had an advantage and acted accordingly.

20. Some were priced so high it made no sense doing business with them.

It is said that the buyer is "king." As you can see, there were many times I didn't feel that way. Yet the sellers usually thought I was. They made concessions I never dreamed possible. Often, all I had to do was act like there was lots of competition. I told many sellers that all that mattered was price since all of them were offering essentially the same package of goods and services. It was never quite the case, but most chose to accept it anyway.

An understanding of the buyer's limits in using all the competition that exists is important. For those who sell, it means that the salesperson who is more aware of the buyer's limits will be in a stronger position than those they compete with. Because of this, they may not have to agree to a larger discount or feel coerced into offering costly added services at no charge.

For the buyer, the task is different. In order to make the most of existing competition, the buyer and their organization must look at the overall procurement system to eliminate those constraints that forfeit power to the seller. If the seller understands the limits of the buyer's power, they will be in a position to circumvent those limits and to negotiate the best deals possible.

THE POWER OF BUYERS, EVEN WHEN THEY DEAL WITH SOLE-SOURCE SUPPLIERS: FACTORS WHICH LIMIT THE SUPPLIER'S POWER

All of us know how hard it is to negotiate against a seller who has no competition. The purpose of this section is to show that even such a strong seller has real limits in exploiting their superior bargaining position. What follows are ways a buyer can generate competition where little or no competition appears to exist. If you know how to bargain with a seller who has no competition, dealing with one who has will be a lot easier.

One thing a buyer can do is to decide to do the work themselves. They can favor a "make" decision rather than a "buy" decision. I have seen many organizations make just such a decision after being exploited by a single-source seller for years. Not only did the seller lose the business, but they found themselves confronted by a new and formidable competitor.

A buyer can also create competition between the seller's long-term interests and their short-term profit goals. The buyer can reduce the size of their order or spread it out over a longer time period. They can break the requirement into parts-some parts to be eliminated, some given to other suppliers, and still others done themselves. This has the effect of creating internal competition within the seller's organization. Those who sell, those who price, those who need cash and those who perform the work in the seller's organization have different needs and goals. These needs and goals may be in conflict.

I have seen alert buyers create competition against sole source suppliers by dealing with others in the distribution system. Some moved toward the used market. Others have found that dealers at lower distribution levels, burdened with heavy inventories, can be induced to sell at lower prices than original manufacturers.

One company I worked for financed a second source to compete against the exploitative sole-source. They found that by splitting the order between two sources, costs dropped by 25 percent. The second source investment paid off in a short time and continues to do so to this day.

Some buying organizations have learned to deal with their sole-source suppliers in a productive "win-win" way. They are forming partnerships with them. The basis for such a partnership between customer and supplier lies in the synergy created by both parties in finding better ways to market and perform the work to be done. Experience in Japan and many companies in the United States and Europe indicates that quality is improved and costs go down in well organized buyer-seller partnerships. More will be said about creative both-win partnerships in Chapter 6.

Buyers do business with single-source suppliers not because they want to but because they fill a critical need. Resisting such suppliers will always be difficult. It always involves risk-risk of losing the source of supply, risk of making them angry and having to pay a higher price for doing so, and the risk of wasting time and effort without results.

Yet, despite these risks, taking on a sole-source supplier is possible and worthwhile. The buyer who chooses to be passive, or who gives in too easily in the face of the sole source's superior power, is likely to be exploited even more at the next negotiation.

TEN SIMPLE THINGS YOU CAN DO TO BUILD BARGAINING POWER IN ANY NEGOTIATION

Bargaining power, as we have seen in this chapter, is a key factor in determining outcome. The ten suggestions which follow will help you build bargaining power in any negotiation. You will find them discussed at greater length at various points in the book. They are presented here to show that the balance of power between parties is not exclusively a matter of major factors like supply and demand or control of vast resources. Small things, well done, can contribute to nudging the balance of power in your direction.

1. Set the stage for a "yes" answer. Bring good things to eat and drink. Find personal areas of mutual interest to talk about like sports, films or family affairs. Make things comfortable. Break bread together.

2. Take notes about what is said and agreed to. Your notes have the power of legitimacy if the other side wants to renege on a prior concession. It's amazing how often people forget what was said yesterday.

3. To be successful, learn to dress two or three levels higher than you are. On the other hand, if you want to show that you don't have much money for negotiating purposes, then dress that way. You can always dress like a country gentleman on the weekend.

4. Don't go into the negotiation alone. Bring a friend who can help you listen, answer questions and observe the reactions of the other side. Too much goes on too fast to catch it all by yourself.

5. Bring published rules and regulations. Price lists, articles, policies, standards, proof statements, references and data also help to support your viewpoint. The more the better.

6. If you are going into a negotiation alone-take the time the night before to do a dry run rehearsal of the talks. That alone is more than most people do.

7. The key to successful negotiating-search for as many second choice sources as you can before talks begin. The more choices you have, the more you will project a sense of power to the other side.

8. When the negotiation is over write the memorandum of agreement yourself. It will add strength to your position.

9. Shut up. Don't tell the other party anything that will raise their expectations or show them how badly you need them. If someone attends the negotiation with you, spend a few minutes coaching them to do the same.

10. Be ready to walk away from a negotiation and walk back again as many times as it takes. Negotiators who are

prepared and willing to do this have the best chance of discovering what the other party's bottom line really is.

CONCLUSION

You have more power than you think. In this chapter we have examined the sources of power available and provided an insight into the hidden needs that drive people toward agreement. With these tools, you can tip the balance of power more in your favor. Power is, to a great extent, what we make it and how we take it.

BUILDING NEGOTIATING POWER

Seven Power Building Approaches

Approach #1　Power Through Putting Time on Your Side

Approach #2　Power Through Making Work Work for You

Approach #3　Power Through Persistence

Approach #4　Power Through Gaining Knowledge and Information

Approach #5　Power Through Taking Risks

Approach #6　Power Through Precedence, Legitimacy and Habit

Approach #7　Power Through a Win-Win Strategy

And:

The Power of **Sellers**, Even When They Face Intense Competition

The Power of **Buyers**, Even When They Deal With Sole-Source Suppliers

Ten Simple Things You Can Do to Build Bargaining Power in Any Negotiation

5

New Insights: What Makes a Good Negotiator and a Successful Team

One major factor which determines settlement outcome is people power. In this chapter we will learn what makes a good negotiator and how to put together a winning team. A good place to start is with new insights from research on how people behave in one-on-one bargaining situations. Then we will see how they interact when part of a team. There are important differences in how people behave when they negotiate alone and how they bargain in teams – differences that result in favorable agreements or disastrous ones.

NEW INSIGHTS ABOUT PEOPLE IN NEGOTIATION – WHAT THE RESEARCH TELLS US

Several experiments are relevant to those who negotiate for themselves and those who own or manage any organization. Research has focused on seven questions related to people in bargaining situations:

1. HOW DOES THE SIZE OF A TEAM AFFECT A NEGOTIATION? IS ONE PERSON BETTER THAN MORE THAN ONE?

2. WHAT IS THE EFFECT OF THOSE IN ATTENDANCE AT THE BARGAINING SESSION ON THE PERSON WHO NEGOTIATES?

3. WHAT HAPPENS WHEN PEOPLE ARE OUTNUMBERED IN NEGOTIATION?

4. WHAT HAPPENS WHEN THERE ARE OPEN DISAGREEMENTS IN THE TEAM?

5. HOW DO THE OPENING REMARKS IN A NEGOTIATION AFFECT RESULTS?

6. HOW DOES A NEGOTIATOR'S ACCOUNTABILITY FOR RESULTS AFFECT HOW WELL HE OR SHE PERFORMS?

Question #1 – The Size of Team – Is One Person Alone Better Than More Than One?

The first of these questions is especially important. The size of a team has a profound influence on results. It affects how well the members plan together and how long they take to settle. In my experiments, I deliberately matched teams one on one, two on two, and three against three. I found that three-person teams took longer to plan and did a better job of it than smaller ones.

When a person negotiated alone, he or she spent hardly any time getting ready. My conclusion is that if you want better planning, have three people (or at least two) work on it together.

I also learned that three-person teams took longest to close. When people were matched one on one, they settled quickly. This result is understandable because people in teams have to satisfy each others' needs and have to reconcile their differences before they can say "yes." The larger groups recessed often to talk things over. One-person bargainers did not recess at all. If you believe as I do that a longer negotiation is usually a better one, then go into the session with people at your side.

Question # 2 – What is the Effect of Those in Attendance at the Bargaining Session on the Person Who Negotiates?

What is the effect on the person negotiating when others, besides the opposing team, are in attendance at the talks? First, it is well to recognize that there are three audiences whose respect the negotiator is anxious to win: the people they represent back home, those on their own team and, in a strange way, the opposing party.

Research indicates that people seek approval from an audience. In that respect they are like actors on a stage. One experiment found that even the presence of a complete stranger at the conference was enough to change a person's bargaining style from passive to aggressive. Another found that people tried harder when their boss attended the talks.

Researchers have also found that negotiators are anxious to appear strong and decisive before an audience. They strive to win the respect not only of their own people but of those on the other side. This desire to win respect makes saving face all the more important. Once you cause someone to lose face in front of others, added resistance follows. A person who has lost face will try to regain self-respect by joining others against you, or will deliberately create deadlock. Research indicates that people who lose face often choose to forego gains, or even suffer personal loss, if in so doing they can prevent the other party from gaining anything.

Many people have a very strong need to be liked by the person they are negotiating against. This has dangerous implications. People with a strong need to be liked are especially vulnerable in negotiation. When such a person is separated from the opponent by the formality of a conference table, all may be well. But if the talks move to the informality of one person to another in a restaurant, the need-to-be-loved person may talk too much or make large concessions in their desire to please.

Question #3 – What Happens When People are Outnumbered in Negotiation?

The third question concerns how people feel when they are outnumbered. To test this, I matched negotiators two against one and then asked the outnumbered person what went on in their head. In hundreds of trials, almost all of those outnumbered reported that they felt intimidated. A few, for their own reasons, explained that they enjoyed the experience. In another two-against-one experiment, it was found that salespeople made greater claims for their services or products when facing a single buyer than when facing two.

A sensible rule is to keep both sides approximately matched in numbers and status. Of course this has to be considered from an economic standpoint. Whether or not to negotiate with a large team also depends on the importance of the transaction, the expected duration of the talks and the cost of transporting and maintaining the team on location. My preference leans toward having at least one person at my side when I negotiate. The team, albeit small, helps me do a better job than I would alone.

Question #4 – What Happens When There are Open Disagreements in the Team?

The fourth finding confirms common sense. Whenever open disagreement between team members surfaced during my bargaining trials, that team did poorly. The atmosphere surrounding the team much resembled the atmosphere in a restaurant after a small grease fire. The opponent sensed an opportunity and pushed home a favorable settlement. An effective team leader demands a show of unity at the table but encourages disagreement in the privacy of the planning and caucus room.

I have been in large negotiations where our team leader lost control. Not only were we embarrassed by the internal dissension but probably paid a high price as well. As I write this, I'm smiling because it happened some time ago. I remember how surprised everyone at the table was when our team leader flung his half-eaten donut at the engineer on our side who had just openly contradicted him. It was as though our team had formed a circular firing squad with their guns aimed at each other.

Question #5 – How Do the Opening Remarks Made in a Negotiation Affect Results?

The fifth finding will be of interest to those preparing for an especially difficult negotiation. One researcher tried this: he had two high level executives, one from each side, launch the talks with a short introduction. They jointly announced to both sides at the table: "We expect you to come to an agreement because our companies put a high value on doing business together. We know you can do it." With those words they left the room. The experimenter found that this simple statement by higher level executives facilitated settlement. It paved the way for mutual cooperation and trust. Perhaps that's why the Japanese open important business negotiations by having senior executives from both sides say a few words encouraging agreement.

Question #6 – How Does a Negotiator's Accountability for Results Affect How Well They Do?

The sixth research question concerns the effect of accountability on bargaining performance. Research has found that if you want tougher negotiators, you must make them accountable for results. Department store buyers are tough because they are accountable for selling the merchandise they buy. So is the software salesperson who has promised the boss that they will close a sale at $4 per unit. The buyer who tries to push below $4 is in for a battle. Disciplined target setting and clear accountability help achieve good results.

NEW INSIGHTS ON WHAT MAKES A GOOD NEGOTIATOR

Top executives in sales and purchasing ask, "What is the most important trait we should look for in selecting a good negotiator?" If I were to restrict my answer to a single trait, it would be the ability of negotiators to deal with people in their own organization. Good negotiators should be good networkers. Only in that way can they understand the needs of those around them and balance their expectations and priorities. A diplomat's success in dealing with other world leaders in trade negotiations will, in the last analysis, be dependent on his or her ability to deal with the President, the Cabinet, the Congress, the press, the people, and the CEO's of the major corporations involved.

Here are some other traits that good negotiators share:

ONE: An ability to work with the other party in searching for creative win-win ideas to bring the parties together.

TWO: A logical mind. The ability to present his or her position in terms of principles that can be easily communicated. Abraham Lincoln once said of another politician, "He can compress the most words into the smallest ideas of any man I've ever met." That man, I'm sure, was not a good negotiator.

THREE: A dedication to painstaking preparation and detail.

FOUR: A willingness to tolerate disagreement and confrontation.

FIVE: The ability to live with ambiguity for long periods of time. Things are rarely black or white in negotiation.

SIX: Good judgment. As the old farmer who was known for his wisdom said when asked why he was so wise, "I've got good judgment. Good judgment comes from experience; and a lot of experience comes from bad judgment."

SEVEN: Patience and willingness to let the situation evolve.

EIGHT: Persistence and a refusal to give up in the face of opposition.

NINE: Hard work and stamina. Lazy people make poor negotiators.

TEN: The ability and willingness to become involved with the other party on a personal level.

ELEVEN: The ability to listen carefully and focus full attention on other people's ideas.

TWELVE: A broad time perspective. Most negotiations affect the past, the present, the near future and the far future. The negotiator with a broad time perspective can integrate these time scales and thereby make more intelligent agreements.

THIRTEEN: Self-confidence in understanding the issues to be discussed. Knowledgeable about the product, the service, or the matter being negotiated.

FOURTEEN: A sense of humor is not essential but it helps.

FIFTEEN: Tact and discretion.

SIXTEEN: The flexibility to give and take. A negotiator can't be like the Australian Bushman who got a new boomerang and spent the rest of his life trying to throw the old one away.

SEVENTEEN: The courage to cope with reasonable risk. All negotiation involves an element of risk.

EIGHTEEN: An understanding of the negotiating process and the emotional, psychological and tactical factors that make things happen.

The common sense and flexibility to make decisions under pressure is also important. I'm reminded of the story of the old mountain man who came down from the hills pulling his donkey loaded with fur pelts. He tied the donkey up and went into the town saloon. A drunken cowboy, seeing the old mountain man, decided to have some fun. He pulled his gun and said to the old man, "I want to see you do a jig, as he fired several shots at the old man's feet. The mountain man didn't hesitate. Without a word he started doing a jig. The drunken cowboy jumped with glee and fired more shots. The old man danced faster. Then, as the drunken cowboy reloaded, the old man grabbed his own gun from the floor where he had dropped it. He held it next to the cowboy's head and said grimly, "Have you ever kissed a donkey's behind?"

The young cowboy, sobering quickly, looked at the old man, at his gun, at the donkey and said decisively, "No sir, but I've always wanted to."

A look at international diplomacy provides us with further insight into what makes a good negotiator. When the history of the twentieth century is written, only a few will be regarded as the skilled negotiators of this era. Henry Kissinger and Chou En-Lai of Communist China are sure to be mentioned. Chou shared with Kissinger the ability to survive under turbulent political conditions. In a society where a single mistake in judgment could mean death, Chou survived jail, purges, and the Long March. Later Chou's exceptional judgment helped him survive the Cultural Revolution in which thousands of Mao's closest followers were liquidated or sent to Mongolia. Chou was indeed a man who could function effectively under difficult conditions. For forty years, Chou was China's top negotiator. A Western diplomat who knew Chou well described him this way:

"Chou was a tough and persuasive negotiator, with an immense capacity for absorbing detail, and immense patience

in bargaining. With him, it was always a matter of give and take. He was frank and outspoken and he expected the same. Disagreement did not upset him. He expected a good deal of disagreement, but was disappointed if it could not be supported in intelligent terms. His eyes were bright, penetrating, and looked right at you. You felt that you had all his attention, that he would remember you — and what you said. It was a rare gift."

The question of selecting the right negotiator interested Sir Francis Bacon hundreds of years ago. He advised those in authority to:

"Use such persons as affect the business wherein they are employed; for that quickeneth much: and such as are fit for the matter; as bold men for expostulation, fair-spoken men for persuasion, and crafty men for inquiry and observation. Use also such as have been lucky, and prevailed before in things wherein you have employed them: for that breeds confidence, and they will strive to maintain their prescription."

Bacon's prescription continues to be as valid today as it was in the seventeenth century.

PUTTING TOGETHER A SUCCESSFUL TEAM: WHAT TO LOOK FOR

The day of the one-man negotiating team is over in business and personal affairs. If you want to do well, negotiate with someone at your side.

Not long ago, the government would assign a person to go from plant to plant closing multimillion dollar deals. Government negotiators were like traveling preachers. It was an absurd practice because most contracts were too complex for a single person to handle well. There are still a few industrial companies who continue to depend on an "all-wise itinerant negotiator." They would, in my view, be better off with two or three persons on the team if the size of the contracts or the importance of the issues warranted the extra cost.

The advantages of team negotiations are overwhelming. Teams bring a broad base of knowledge to the table. They are more creative than individuals. Properly organized, they are less apt to overlook important details. They plan better and, as a group, think better.

Research indicates that teams tend to take greater risks in setting higher targets than individuals. However, when risks entail large losses that are potentially life or organization threatening, they become conservative. Groups of people on the same team perceive power differently from those who bargain alone. Individuals tend to dwell on their own side's limitations, whereas groups reinforce each other's strength by challenging their team assumptions and constraints.

Teams serve another important function after the contract is signed. Having many people from various departments participate in the bargaining helps sell the final agreement internally. It provides each department with an understandable basis for allocating budgets and committing themselves to performance. Griping and "Monday morning" criticism about the agreement are reduced.

Team bargaining does have drawbacks. Good leaders are not easy to find. It's hard to lead a cavalry charge if you don't look good on a horse. Leaders have to look and act the part. They have to be tactful and flexible.

One difficult responsibility of the team leader is to control the content and flow of discussions. Discussions sometimes drag on interminably on points hardly worth talking about. I'll never forget a session where eight people at the table wasted three hours because an engineer asked how the bubble in the gyro was extracted. It was interesting, but not useful. The team leader should have cut the discussion short. Most of us have been on teams where the leader allowed team members to speak at the wrong time and reveal too much information. These dangers notwithstanding, go into the talks with someone knowledgeable at your side if the stakes warrant it. This will enhance your bargaining power.

PRACTICAL TIPS FOR BETTER TEAM RESULTS

Winning and super-winning in negotiation are not hard if the right people work together and are well led. These 16 suggestions are designed to help management and the team leader do a better job. They apply as well to consumer negotiations as they do in business.

1. Each team member should contribute an area of expertise. Don't settle for half a specialist just because he or she is the only one available.

2. Each member should be given a specific job to do. Don't let them answer questions which are not their concern or in their area of expertise.

3. Have a few easy to understand signals that tell your people to "shut up."

4. Prior to negotiation, assign each specialist an area of responsibility for gathering information about the other

side's positions, vulnerabilities and inclinations for or against the position you plan to take on an issue.

5. Make one person responsible for information gathering and security. See that all relevant information passes through this central point and is communicated as needed to others on the team.

6. Make sure that every person knows where and when the negotiation is to take place.

7. See that your team is free from other pressing work for as long as the talks go on. Team members who are harassed by other responsibilities will not do well.

8. One of the worst things that can happen in a negotiation is when you are depending on a knowledgeable engineer or specialist to defend a particular position and you learn at the last minute that this team member is on vacation. The fault lies with the leader in a case like this. It can be avoided.

9. Occasionally, a team member simply doesn't like negotiating and resents wasting time on it. Get him or her off the team. Also don't negotiate with anyone at your side who thinks negotiating is a belittling business. The signals he or she sends will adversely affect your bargaining style and raise the other parties' expectations. Remember, there are lots of people who look down at negotiating. Many dislike the process. Others are afraid of it. Keep them off the team.

10. The power of a team is enhanced by planning together several times before the session. Don't leave planning for the night before.

11. Never let your team be significantly outnumbered. Recognize that if the other party has ten members on their team, you better have at least three or more. If they field three people, you should field at least two.

12. Assign each team member as an observer of his or her counterpart on the other side. Make them responsible for determining how their counterparts fit into the knowledge and decision-making structure of the other party.

13. Let one person on your team be the official note taker, observer, and listener. Have that person take copious notes while others do the talking. Share the official observer's findings with the team during recess periods. Good notes are a source of bargaining power.

14. Caucus frequently. Give yourselves time to think. Formulate new plans as you learn more.

15. Prevent open conflict between team members at the table. Encourage disagreement in the back room. The other party will pick up even the most subtle of team conflicts.

16. Conference and hotel rooms, as well as telephones, are sometimes "bugged." If the stakes are high, assume this possibility exists and protect yourself.

CONCLUSION

Never go into a negotiation without giving serious thought to who should do the negotiating, who should be on the team, who should lead it, and who can best support the leader. The organization that doesn't give thought to this source of bargaining power is making a costly mistake. In experiments with professional negotiators, it was no accident that skilled negotiators outperformed those less skilled. They do so in real life also.

TIPS FOR PUTTING TOGETHER A WINNING TEAM

Approach #1   Choose the Best Team Leader Possible.

Approach #2   Give Members Time for Planning Sessions Before Negotiations Begin.

Approach #3   Use Opening Remarks to Set the Tone of Negotiations.

Approach #4   Include Enough Members to Deal with the Complexity of the Issues and the Size of the Other Team.

Approach #5   Be Cautious about Adding Team Members with an Excessive Need to Be Liked, or Who Dislike the Negotiating Process.

Approach #6   Assign One Team Member to Control Information and Security.

Approach #7   Assign a Team Member to Observe and Take Notes.

Approach #8   Make Sure Each Team Member Has an Area of Expertise.

Approach #9   Assign Each Team Member to Observe His or Her Counterpart on the Opposite Team.

Approach #10   Make Sure All Team Members Are Available.

Approach #11   Caucus Frequently.

Approach #12   Keep Team Disagreements in the Back Room.

Approach #13   Develop Signals to Tell Team Members to "Shut up."

Approach #14   Make Negotiators Accountable for the Deals They Make for Both Parties.

6

The Strategy of Long-Lasting Relationships and Partnerships

MAXIMIZING WIN-WIN SATISFACTIONS FOR BOTH PARTIES

This is the story of a long-term relationship and what happened to it. It concerns my gardener Joe. The situation, though small in scale, reflects the dangers inherent in any relationship which continues over a period of time.

Four years ago, my previous gardener retired. This, we thought, was fortunate because he hadn't been doing his work. He was growing old and had slowed down over the years. I proceeded to look for a new gardener. During the next month, I interviewed five men, showed them about the premises and explained in detail what was to be done. When you hire a gardener you have to select someone who is not only competent but honest since he will often be on the premises when you are away. After considerable effort, I selected Joe. It was a relief to get it over with.

The trouble began when Joe's quality began to slip about six months after we hired him. He spent too much time on what wasn't needed and too little on what was. One thing he did well was to take care of my wife's roses. From her point of view, Joe was satisfactory, but not from mine. It seemed wise to talk things over.

We talked not once, but many times. Three years later, I was still trying to correct the situation but to no avail.

Why, after so long a time, did I still retain him?

There are many reasons and inertia was one of them. Of course, his work was still marginal, but we were used to it by then. He had reduced our expectations. Less is what we aspired to, and less is what we got. Every month as I wrote him a check, I promised myself to search for another gardener. But it was such a chore I put it off until next month.

Another reason was organizational. I preferred to lay him off, but my organization wouldn't hear of it. Because of his success with the roses, he had won my wife's allegiance and friendship. Whenever I wanted to say "go" she told me "no." So the downhill relationship with Joe went on like this for years. It seemed like it would go on forever unless one of three things happened: if he quit, if I sold my house or if we tried to do something we hadn't tried before to make it work.

WHO GAINS MOST FROM LONG-TERM RELATIONSHIPS

Does the buyer or seller benefit most from a long-term relationship? This is an important question when one considers that most transactions in business are part of a continuing interaction rather than one-time affairs.

Long-term relationships can be beneficial to both parties, but they can also be dangerous. On the plus side, such relationships can provide reliability, friendship, and peace of mind. From the seller's standpoint, it takes far less effort to maintain an old account than to win a new one. Conversely, many a buyer has been glad that a seller valued past business sufficiently to supply scarce materials during periods of shortage.

On the negative side, there are problems which long-term relationships create for both buyers and sellers. From a negotiating standpoint, it becomes increasingly difficult to keep the proper distance. Each side may know more than it should about the other's bargaining style and power position. Personal convenience factors tend to dominate the long-term relationship instead of rational arm's-length business judgment. Both parties have a tendency to grow complacent as they take each other for granted.

Who benefits most from such a relationship? It's hard to tell because it depends on the intentions of the parties and how well one or the other checks to see that the performance or services promised are being rendered as agreed to. In my experience, one side or the other begins to benefit more in the long term. That's the danger.

There is no way of telling in advance whether the buyer or seller will benefit most from the relationship. Which it is depends on many factors. In the next two sections we will first see how sellers can gain from such a relationship. Then we will consider how buyers can gain the advantage and what sellers can do to keep things in balance.

HOW SELLERS CAN BENEFIT FROM LONG-TERM RELATIONSHIPS AND WHAT BUYERS CAN DO ABOUT IT

An alert seller can gain most from a long-term relationship if the buyer is not assertive and painstaking in exercising his or her rights. There are many factors favoring the seller which buyers should be sensitive to.

The seller generally has greater access to the buyer's organization than the buyer to the seller's. A salesperson is expected to visit the buyer's decision-makers and end-users. After an agreement is signed, he or she has easy access to the buyer's engineers and production people. The seller can cement friendships with the buyer's accounting and shipping personnel on an ongoing basis. Important secret information can be learned from these contacts concerning the buyer's budgets, manufacturing processes and costs. An alert salesperson can also learn how dependent the buyer's marketing strategy is on the seller's product or service in satisfying the buyer's end customer.

This point was once made clear to me by a woman who sold fragrances to soap and lotion companies. Competition is fierce in the fragrance business. Soap company buyers try to reduce fragrance costs by playing one supplier against the other. One day during a quiet lunch with a lower level marketing analyst for the soap company, she learned that soap manufacturers never dare to change a fragrance once a soap is accepted by the market. This insight helped her win new sales by bidding low on original requirements and increasing the price later.

The case of Joe, my gardener, is indicative of the perils of long-term relationships to a buyer. Joe gradually learned to cater to one part of my organization (my wife) in favor of the other (me). He learned that he could increase prices over time even as he reduced services. He understood that customers like me don't like to change gardeners unless they absolutely have to. The two hours per week he agreed to spend on our garden gradually was reduced to one hour and forty-five minutes and eventually to one and a half hours. Who could keep track? My wife and I were working while he gardened. In the beginning he didn't charge for small extra planting services. Later he did. That's the way it works when customers are not alert or assertive about their rights and unwilling to change vendors.

My advice to those who sell is to break into a new account, even if you have to suffer initial loss. The buyer will be reluctant to let you go if you do a reasonably good job and maintain warm rapport. Salespeople who go one step beyond by befriending the end-users of their product or service, such as the engineering or manufacturing people, will build an almost impregnable barrier against losing the account.

The idea of "buying-in" to gain a customer seems risky, but it usually isn't. In my experience, buyers take good care of vendors who have been with them for a long time. They are willing to pay higher prices to suppliers who give them no trouble.

One more factor that works for the seller is that the specifications for most products or services change over time. These revisions always benefit the current supplier more than their competitors. Changes serve to increase the seller's profit margin. A marketing executive I know used to say, "Changes are profits in escrow." He understood that a losing job can quickly become a profitable one as the specification or scope of work changes.

What can buyers do to offset the seller's advantages? The seven strategies which follow can help turn things around in favor of an alert buyer:

ONE: Don't be lazy. Search for competition. Keep the sellers on their toes.

TWO: Don't be passive about settling for a gradual reduction of services or performance. Be alert and assertive. Face the problem early or you will soon get less for your money.

THREE: Rotate buyers. There is nothing like a new buyer to stimulate a seller's lagging interest in an old account.

FOUR: Dual-source your requirements whenever possible, even if you have to pay a premium to start with. Competition works wonders.

FIVE: Try to learn as much about the seller's business as they know about yours. Find out what their costs are, how they make the product, and how badly they need your business.

SIX: Negotiate cost not price. Buyers do better when the basis of discussion is cost. Get breakdowns and negotiate each element of cost.

SEVEN: Work closely with the seller to find better arrangements for both parties. Creative changes for mutual benefit are sure to follow if you look for them. More will be said about this powerful win-win strategy later in this chapter when we deal with the subject of partnerships.

Long-term relationships are a fact of business life. The main danger for the buyer is complacency. The buyer who learns to treat each negotiation with an old supplier as a new test of the market will keep the seller from exploiting the relationship. In the long run, this will make for a healthier, more durable association that benefits both buyer and seller.

HOW BUYERS CAN BENEFIT FROM LONG-TERM RELATIONSHIPS AND WHAT SELLERS CAN DO ABOUT IT

Some years ago I customized an Effective Negotiating® program for bankers. Having grown up in a world where those who lent money called the tune and those who borrowed danced to it, I was in for a surprise.

Bankers are sellers of money and borrowers are buyers. In customizing the seminar, I wondered who benefitted most in a long-term relationship, banker or borrower?

Before a loan is made, bankers are usually in the driver's seat. To protect their loan they insist that the borrower provide current business forecasts, income statements, asset and liability balances, and cash flow forecasts. The borrower is required to maintain minimum checking balances and to report any change in money borrowed from others or in the ownership of the business. Most of us would agree that these financial controls are quite reasonable.

To protect themselves further, banks also insist that whenever equipment or assets are bought, sold or leased during the loan period, a new report must be submitted. Personal guarantees by the owner and his or her spouse are often demanded and secured. On the surface it looks like the banker, as the seller of money, is in a very good long-term position. Let's see how it really works.

The trouble for bankers is that borrowers soon begin to nibble at the tight agreement. Once the borrower's track record of paying installments on time is reasonably established, they begin to erode the bank's terms and conditions one by one. The bankers, anxious to avoid conflict with a good customer, tend to overlook the nibbles or fail to recognize that nibbling is taking place.

Before long, the stringent loan security requirements are eroded. When the loan is later renewed, it is the borrower who is in a good position to negotiate a less demanding agreement and a lower interest rate. Most bankers I have spoken to are convinced that the borrower benefits most in the long term if they make the monthly payments with some degree of regularity and are reasonably responsible.

In the world of buying and selling, buyers who are aggressive in demanding extra services usually get them from sellers who are afraid to lose older customers. Such buyers end up paying bills slowly, winning higher levels of quality than they originally agreed to accept, and getting more free training than the contract called for. Aggressive buyers facing passive sellers gain most from a long association.

Paradoxically, in order to save the long-term relationship, passive sellers create the conditions that will in the end destroy it. The buyer's gradual erosion of contract terms with the seller's quiet acquiescence makes the relationship unstable, a Humpty Dumpty arrangement. If seller tries to correct the situation later by taking away the buyer's privileges or by raising the price, it will create buyer resentment. The seller is likely to lose the next order as the angry buyer looks elsewhere for a new supplier.

A LONG-TERM RELATIONSHIP THAT BECAME A MARRIAGE – THE CASE OF JOE, THE WIN-WIN GARDENER IN A CUSTOMER-SUPPLIER PARTNERSHIP

You're probably wondering how my relationship with Joe worked out. Well, I didn't sell the house and he didn't quit. We are still together, but our whole relationship has changed.

To accomplish this I tried a new strategy. I decided to work more closely with Joe to find creative ways to make a better deal for both of us. We became CUSTOMER-SUPPLIER PARTNERS and stopped dealing with one another in continuous low-level conflict. It wasn't that Joe was not working hard or that his employees were lazy. That wasn't the problem. They were good workers but inefficient.

Joe and I tackled the problem by looking for better ways to do things. We got rid of plants that grew too fast or required too much care. We replaced them with colorful shrubs that were easier to control. Because we were working together on a win-win basis we got along better. In exchange for replacing plants to reduce work, Joe reciprocated by charging me wholesale rather than retail prices.

He also reduced my labor costs by hiring less expensive itinerant labor to remove the old growth.

Our new partnership benefitted him in other ways. Joe had little capital so he used older, less efficient equipment. I advanced him a modest loan, and by combining it with his meager savings he was able to purchase a faster lawn mower, new power shears for clipping bushes and a more efficient, less noisy leaf blower. My advance was repaid in a year by reducing my monthly gardening fee. To further reduce his work I invested in trash barrels with big wheels that allowed him to remove cuttings easily.

Joe is now doing a better job than ever. The garden looks good even though he spends only an hour and a half a week on it. Joe has become a more efficient businessman not only on my job but with other customers. We are loyal to each other and always in search of new win-win ideas. After all these years, we are now partners.

Customer-supplier partnerships, like the one I have with Joe, are on the rise in the United States and worldwide. Of course they are often more complicated than the one I described, but the benefits to both parties are much the same conceptually.

CUSTOMER-SUPPLIER PARTNERSHIPS AND NEGOTIATION: WHAT YOU BETTER THINK ABOUT IF YOU WANT A GOOD PARTNERSHIP

A recent book on partnerships predicts that their increasing popularity will mark the end of negotiation between customers and suppliers. The author feels that negotiation will no longer be needed. Nothing could be further from the truth. Partnerships will require more negotiation than ever.

What follows is an interview on partnering that appeared under my byline in Purchasing, the largest publication for procurement managers in the United States. I have been their Contributing Editor on Negotiation for several decades. The interview discusses the increased complexity of negotiation in the age of customer-supplier partnerships.

Partnering is a Marriage – Not a Long Date

Interview: Dr. Karrass discusses partnerships, their problems, and how they will change buyer-seller dealings in the future.

"In the age of partnering and win-win problem solving, can there be any need for negotiating?"

Good question, says Dr. Chester L. Karrass, the nation's renowned authority on negotiating. As Karrass sees it, win-win and partnering make business negotiations more numerous and more complicated.

While pointing out that partnering is a significant development on the industrial scene, Karrass suggests that it has to be looked at "as a marriage, not a long date." In the process of setting up the marriage, he notes, partners need to negotiate some very tricky issues that are unique to partnering.

"In traditional buying," says Karrass, "I buy so much of this item, for this amount of money, and here's how and when I want it. I don't give a damn about how you run your business." Partnering greatly complicates the relationship. In a partnership, how each company conducts its business is of great importance. Indeed, partnering opens up a long list of items that need to be explored and negotiated. Among them:

• What are acceptable labor, profit, overhead costs?

• What are the rights of the buyer and seller in relation to other customers? For instance, what right does the supplier have to sell that new design to a competitor? What right does the buyer have to use the design in another product with another supplier?

• When the buyer downsizes, who takes the gaff?

• What accounting system is used, and do partners have the right to audit each others' accounts?

• What kind of change control system is used?

Karrass also notes that there are "a bunch of issues involved in breaking the marriage. Once there is a marriage there has to be a divorce procedure. Suppose both parties put money into developing a design. What happens at termination? How are costs settled? Who owns the project? Is there a non-competition clause to protect secrets and techniques? How about sharing trademarks, copyrights, patents, tooling, drawings, techniques, data?"

NOT AN EASY TRANSPLANT – Although Karrass deeply believes "the buyer-seller partnering relationship is here to stay," he doesn't expect it to work as well in the U.S. as in Japan. "There are many cultural, organizational, and emotional reasons – in addition to the way the Japanese people relate to each other as individuals – that makes partnering more workable in Japan than it's ever going to be in the U.S."

He also suggests that many people say they partner, but few actually do it. "Many people I meet say they are partnering, but when I get close to it, I find I'm looking not so much at partnering as long-term relationships."

WIN-WIN IS NOT EQUAL SHARING – Karrass also feels that many – in and out of procurement – miss the main point about win-win negotiating. In his view, win-win is the most powerful tool in the negotiator's toolbox, but it's not all that new to the negotiation process. He notes, for instance, the role of negotia-

tion in value analysis and value engineering.

Karrass strongly challenges those who suggest that the need to win concessions is being supplanted by the idea of win-win. As Karrass sees it, win-win is a "mode of negotiation," and in today's setting is only part of the negotiating process. Win-win, he says, is concerned with "creating value where none was recognized or searched for before."

On the other hand, he notes that win-win, "doesn't tell you how to share" the winnings. The biggest mistake that can be made, he suggests, is to go into any kind of a relationship with the idea of sharing everything equally. He sees two main benefits resulting from the "win-win mode": (1) it always allows both parties to find a better deal and (2) it's a good way to avoid or break deadlock.

Inherent in the success of a win-win negotiation, however, is the fact that every win-win negotiation needs to be followed by a competitive negotiation. Karrass compares the win-win negotiation to one in which the two negotiating parties sit down to divide up ten marbles, and they end up creating three more. Together they have created more marbles to divide up, but that doesn't mean both parties will share equally.

A SECOND NEGOTIATION – After win-win negotiation there has to be another negotiation to determine "What are we each entitled to take out of this bigger pot?" says Karrass. "How difficult it is in the context of a partnership! Say you're the seller and you invest some of your money and you reduce the cost of making a component from $50 each to $40. Who gets the benefit? We're partners – buyer and seller. We decide how much for each partner by negotiating, and there can be serious, honest disagreements over the answer. This can only be resolved by competitive negotiation."

As Karrass looks at it, there will always be issues on which the buyer and the seller seriously disagree. There will always be changes, and benefits, and contributions that involve unknown or uncertain sharing requirements. "The right formula will always be unknown and uncertain. There will always be an imbalance of power between the two parties in the sharing of benefits and contributions."

CANDOR VS. NAIVETE – Those who are most outspoken against negotiation, says Karrass, usually base their dislike for negotiation on these two assumptions: (1) each side should tell the other everything, and (2) both sides in a transaction will instinctively be fair and reasonable. "I think such assumptions are absolutely naive. There are a lot of people who will not tell you everything you want to know. In most important business transactions there will be issues that will require very difficult negotiations. Partnering is not the end of negotiations, it's the beginning."

"People who say put everything on the table – even in a partnership – are naive as hell," says Karrass. "There are two important traits of any good negotiator – tact and discretion, and he or she must think like this: What should I say? How much should I say? When should I say it? And in partnering – which I compare to a good marriage – there are things I say, things I say partially, things I say later, and things that are never said because they would only cause tension."

NEW ROLES – With the change in the type of negotiation used will come a change in purchasing's role, says Karrass. "The purchasing pro will be more of a contract manager, a manager of relationships – rather than just a buyer – among quality control people, manufacturing people, design people." Karrass also sees a change ahead for the role of the salesperson. He or she also will become more of a contract manager. The initial sell in getting into the buyer's plant will remain about the same, but once the partnership is established the salesperson will have a contract manager role."

OPEN INFORMATION BETWEEN BUYERS AND SELLERS IN THE AGE OF PARTNERSHIPS

I would like to add one more thought that was not covered in the interview. It concerns the question of how open information channels between buyers and sellers should be in partnerships.

In the United States and Europe there are deep seated structural barriers separating the organizations of sellers and buyers. For partnerships to work best, openness between the parties is necessary. However, there is a difference between openness and penetrability. Openness allows you to look at the other party's processes, methods and even its books and accounts. Penetrability is different. It poses the question of whether you can become an important part of their business process, their long-term strategy, and of their decision making structure.

It is not unlike what the United States faces in dealing with Japan and its large trade surpluses. We want the Japanese to be both open and penetrable. The question is, "Is this likely or possible?" The following, which appeared years ago in the New Republic, is apropos to our discussion.

To understand this issue (openness vs. penetrability), recall the Tarzan movies of your childhood. The jungle may be closed to you because the natives, led by the chief, are shooting poisoned arrows at you. But if they are not, and the jungle is open (and inviting because of the gold that it promises), the progress of the safari through the jungle is constrained by the tall grass and the thick vegetation. Then again, the path through the jungle is hazardous because of the dangers posed by traps, laid by natives to hunt animals but inadvertently dangerous to the safari as well. In short, openness and penetrability are different things.

The difference between openness and penetrability can be seen in the accounting statements of failed financial institutions like Lehman Brothers. The government regulators and the public had access to their quarterly reports, but they could not penetrate the reality of what was going on. Many of these failed financial institutions actually looked good on paper just days before they failed. Only after they failed did the harsh truth reveal itself.

At this stage in the American development of partnering, there is still a big gap between openness and penetrability, especially as it applies to buyers and sellers of goods and services. Hopefully the jungle will become more penetrable, but it is likely to take much more time in the United States and Europe than in Japan.

Supplier-customer partnerships continue to grow world-wide for good reason. They are effective in reducing cost even as they raise quality. However, this only happens when both the supplier's and the buyer's highest level executives participate in nurturing the new arrangement. The partnership must be organized into joint company mandating committees whose job is to search for better ways to do things. Partnerships are still strange relationships in the business world. Buyer and seller organizations have been conditioned to be adversaries in our culture. People have to be retrained to share sensitive information about cost, profit, and strategy. Both sides will need help in working together and negotiating how contributions and benefits will be shared.

As a consultant I have found that partnering is not an easy relationship to maintain. Those involved do not know how much to share or how trusting they should be. Only after considerable time do joint company committees learn to work together. It is then that a true win-win, long-term relationship of the highest order emerges.

HOW THE GROWTH OF PARTNERSHIPS WILL CHANGE HOW SELLERS WILL SELL IN THE FUTURE

With the growth of partnerships, sellers will be under pressure to sell in a new way. Only a short time ago, sellers competed differently than they do today. For most products and services there were local, regional and national firms in competition for the business available from anyone firm in the area. For example, if a company like General Motors, Weyerhaeuser or Phillip Morris had divisions in different parts of the United States, each division had its own purchasing department and each, for the most part, focused independently on its own major procurement needs.

Local and regional sellers were in a good position to win the division's business. If they lost the order this year, they would try to position themselves through price or service to win the order when bids opened again next year. Losing a million-dollar order was serious for them but not catastrophic in relation to their total business. Today things are different for local and regional sellers; the stakes are far higher.

Hardly a day goes by without reading about a large corporate merger or the layoff of thousands of employees. Few companies are immune to these changes. One day it's Intel, the next Sony and a day later a small firm like Dixie Wire Nashville that moves to Mexico because it cannot compete with other wire supply firms unless it reduces labor costs.

Three major trends have changed the economic picture for American manufacturing firms. The first is the ever-growing tendency of companies to merge with others into larger corporations.

The second trend is the globalization of competition. This is an age when almost every product and many services can be exported: the Apple iPhone is produced in China and many major call centers are now in India. The advent of faster and more interactive networks across telephone and internet platforms has woven every point on the globe into a single marketplace.

The third trend is the Deming phenomenon. W. Edwards Deming, a management expert whose theories were put into practice by the Japanese in their rise to economic power, believed companies would be wise to reduce the number of suppliers providing their purchasing needs.

Deming reasoned that if an auto manufacturer presently placed its business with four suppliers of tires, it would be better off from a quality and price standpoint to place its entire requirement with only one. He believed that the product purchased would be continuously improved as seller and customer worked together in a win-win partnership arrangement.

These seller-customer partnerships reached prominence in Japan in the last five decades. Now they are on the rise in the United States. This trend toward partnerships continues to accelerate and is profoundly affecting American business.

The time of "high-stakes shoot-outs" has arrived. In their search to be competitive in the world market, giant corporations strive to cut costs on every product and service. For example, instead of each corporate division purchasing its own packaging products, the corporation with thirty divisions now prefers to buy packaging from one or two suppliers rather than thirty.

Each of these thirty suppliers once bid on million dollar orders from their local division customers. Now, world-class packaging companies bid on $100 million contracts. They bid to satisfy the needs of all a corporation's divisions in the United States or the world in a single contract. Procurement contracts are not for one year as most used to be. Now they bind the parties for three to five years.

Negotiations in the world of partnering are different. They are concerned not only with price and service but also with the ability of the seller to do research, finance factories for special needs, design a wide variety of packaging, while reducing costs, improving quality, and enhancing appearance over the contract period.

The result is predictable. Only five to ten firms are large enough to participate in this high-stakes, winner-take-all game. Local and regional firms cannot break in. To survive they must downsize to service small market niches or sell out to large corporations.

The "high-stakes shoot-out" is probably the most difficult selling problem now facing local and regional suppliers still in the marketplace. The cost of making a winning proposal has risen dramatically. The ability to meet the customer's stringent partnership and volume needs has narrowed the field. Once an order is lost it will be lost for five years, perhaps forever.

Partnerships are changing the way sellers must sell. They are also changing the individual job description of the salesperson and the corporate buyer to whom they sell. Both will suddenly find themselves far more involved in the world of contract management and in the administration of continuous contract changes. Both will need to learn new and difficult skills.

Yet, with all its difficulties, partnering is worth the effort. When it is well done the payoff to seller and buyer is enormous.

7

Setting Reachable Targets: "Ready - Fire - Aim"

Once there was a business professor who was interested in marksmanship. He learned of a fantastic sharpshooter in the backwoods of Kentucky and decided to visit him to discover why he was successful. Upon arriving in the village, the professor was astounded to learn that the crack marksman was known as the village idiot. "What can I possibly learn about marksmanship from a person like this," he wondered. Having traveled so far, he decided to stay an other day to watch the village's annual shooting contest.

Five contestants preceded the sharpshooter. As custom dictated, each marksman set up his own target. The contestants were all very good. At last the sharpshooter's turn came. It was incredible. As the professor and villagers looked on, the sharpshooter took six shots in rapid succession. Everyone rushed to the target. There, for all to see, were six holes in the bull's eye. It was uncanny. When the professor asked if the performance was typical, the villagers proudly replied that they had seen him do it time and again.

The professor, determined to learn the secret, befriended the marksman. This wasn't easy because the sharp-shooter didn't have much to say. After considerable wining and dining, he divulged the full story. "It was easy," he said with a twinkle in his eye. The trick, the professor learned, was not in the shooting, but in mounting the targets. What he did to achieve success was to mount his own targets – targets which already had six holes in the center. The bullets were blanks.

The professor returned to the classroom a bit wiser. Were not many so-called negotiating targets a bit like that? Did not negotiators also shoot fast, obtain results, and then adjust the explanation to the results. In a sense, they took six shots and fitted them into the bull's eye by moving the target where they wanted it to be.

Negotiation is one area of business where the village idiot's approach to target setting is expensive. All to often, negotiators are more concerned with explaining results than in the results themselves. Something has gone wrong in the great scheme of things: like the village idiot, the bull's eye has become the point at which we settle rather than the target we shoot for. Unfortunately, READY - FIRE - AIM is the way we approach negotiation targets.

WILL THE REAL TARGET PLEASE STAND UP?

Some years ago, there used to be a show on television called "To Tell The Truth." It was about the appearances of reality and reality itself. The guests all claimed to be a certain person, but only one was telling the truth. The problem facing the show's panel was to find out who the real person was by asking penetrating questions. When all the questions had been asked, the panel members voted on who was truthful. The master of ceremonies then said, "Will the real Mr. Jones please stand up." More than half the time the panel was wrong.

In negotiation we have a similar problem that I call, "Will the real target please stand up." Imagine you are a salesperson. Your company has submitted a proposal for selling coaxial cable in bulk at 5 feet for $1.00. Before the negotiation, your boss tells you, "Try to get the $1.00 asking price, but if you can't get that, 98 cents is good. Under no circumstances go below 95 cents." Which is the target: $1.00, $.98, or $.95? I believe that most of us would say that 98 cents is the target rather than 95 cents. But in the world of buying and selling, is 98 cents the real target?

One company in the mid-west tried a marketing experiment. They told salespeople in Chicago that the asking price was $1.00. They also told them to try to get 98 cents if they couldn't get the $1.00. Under no circumstances were they allowed to close at less than 95 cents. In Cleveland they did only one thing differently. They told the Cleveland salespeople not to close at less than 96 cents.

What was interesting is that most sales in Chicago closed at 95 cents. In Cleveland most sales closed at 96 cents. It became obvious that how targets were set had a lot to do with results.

On a personal level, let's assume that you and a friend are interested in purchasing a mahogany table and chairs for your dining room. While not yet an antique, the set is over 80 years old and in fine condition. The dealer is asking $1600, a little high considering the competition.

The two of you decide that your friend will do the negotiating. Both of you agree to try for $1300 but not to pay more than $1550. Will the real target stand up? Is the real target $1300 or $1550? What will you probably pay?

What I dislike about the target setting approach I have just described is that in the hands of a skilled antique dealer, you are likely to pay close to $1550, the price both of you have already decided is acceptable.

My suggestion to buyers is that they stop talking about the most they are willing to pay. Concentrate instead on your opening offer and your target: the price you intend to achieve or do better than. My advice to the sales manager we met earlier is similar. Stop talking about 95 cents, the least you are willing to take, or you'll end up settling for just that.

If I were the sales manager, I would tell my salesperson: "Sell the quality of cable and the services our company provides. Be patient and go for the $1.00 price. If you are put under pressure by the buyer do not settle at a price be low 98 cents until you speak to me."

The salesperson is likely to try hard to close at the 98 cent price rather than get into another discussion with the manager. However, if a 98 cent closure fails, the manager could say to the salesperson: "I authorize you to close at 97 cents if you ask for and get a larger order, 96 cents if you ask for and get a two-year contract rather than a one-year contract, or 95 cents if they give you a larger order, a longer contract and agree to pay in 30 days instead of the 45 days they want."

By requesting the salespeople to ask for something in return for concessions, they may resist dropping to 95 cents quickly. The buyer may also accede to some of the seller's demands. Even if none of the demands are won, the buyer is likely to be more satisfied with the 95 cent outcome, having worked harder to win it.

How we set targets in negotiation determines how we will settle. A well thought out target forces the negotiator to test the other party's power, to challenge their assumptions, and to resist giving in too easily.

We will now learn how expectations and targets go up and down in a person's mind during the give and take of bargaining. Everything – yes, everything – you say or do in a negotiation affects the picture in the other party's head.

HOW THE PRICE GOES UP AND DOWN IN THE OTHER PERSON'S HEAD

People set targets in negotiation as they do in life. They change them as success or failure is experienced. A negotiation is an information system. Targets, tentative or not, are set by buyer and seller. Feedback then follows. Every demand, concession, threat, delay, fact, deadline, authority limit and question has an effect on people's expectations. The price goes up or down in their heads with every new statement, every new fact and every gesture or body language sign.

Research in how expectations change is of special interest to those who negotiate. This is what the studies indicate:

1. Most people raise their expectations after a success and lower them after a failure. Every concession can have the effect of raising the other side's expectations. Concessions may be perceived by the other party as a success. Every "no" can have the opposite effect.

2. A great success leads to a great rise in aspirations. A mammoth failure results in a severe drop. Never make too big a concession or give one too easily. By raising aspirations you may drive the parties further apart rather than closer together.

3. A mild success leads to a small rise in expectations. Small concessions, reluctantly and slowly given, are not likely to raise expectations very high.

4. Moderate failure leads to a small fall in aspirations or none at all. People appear to have downside resistance to small failures. Just saying "no" once or twice may not be enough to reduce the other party's expectations.

5. It takes a series of extended small failures to drive expectations down. Your low opening offer may not be enough. It may take five or ten no's to depress the expectations of the other party. That's why persistence and repeating yourself pays off.

6. People who set targets in a group tend to set higher tar gets and aspire to more.

Every tactic affects the "price" in your opponent's mind. He or she waits anxiously on your words and actions for a signal as to whether things are going well or not. This rise and fall of expectations affects the final outcome.

Sam Walton, of Wal-Mart fame, had an especially keen interest in the question of expectations and performance. During our negotiating seminar at Wal-Mart, the subject of aiming higher came up. Mr. Walton smiled and nodded his head affirmatively.

He explained to me that he believed that the rapid growth of Wal-Mart was largely a product of a phrase he originated and repeated continuously to his executives. That phrase was, "High expectations are the key to everything." Then he added, "I'm not at all surprised you found it so in negotiation."

FROM RUSSIA – "NO, NO, A THOUSAND TIMES NO"

Although the Soviet Union hasn't existed since late in the twentieth century, modern Russian history and its style of negotiating dates back at least to Peter the Great in the 1600s. Russia has long been an international economic power. They will be strong again. There is much we can learn from them.

The Russians know how to say "no." They do it in a number of interesting ways. Sometimes they say no by repeating their arguments like a broken record with little, if any, change. At other times they walk out in great anger. Sometimes they do so by saying nothing while letting the other party keep talking. After a while, the Russian silence convinces their opponent that they had better make some concessions to move talks along.

What the Russians count on is that few of us are persistent in testing a firm "no." Most people think that if someone says "no" many times, they probably mean it. History has shown that many Russian "no's" may well mean "yes," and many, many can mean "maybe." Saying "no" many times over a long period has a way of wearing people down and reducing their expectations. The Russians also know that even if they make a slight concession after lots of "no's", the other side will feel they have won a major victory – their satisfaction level will rise even as their expectations fall.

HOW WELL DO YOU SET TARGETS? TARGET SETTING FOR PROFESSIONAL BUYERS AND SELLERS

I'm going to propose a challenge – How well do you set negotiating targets for your company? Take the Target Setting Quiz on the next page and score yourself by adding the numbers circled. Please don't read on until the quiz and scoring are completed.

TARGET SETTING QUIZ

(Circle the number you believe best fits your approach.)

1. Does your target setting approach result in a better prepared negotiator and team?

NOT AT ALL   1   2   3   4   5   6   7   8   9   10   YES FOR SURE

2. Does your target setting approach force a thorough discussion among your own people? Are differing needs, priorities, risks, and viewpoints surfaced?

NOT AT ALL   1   2   3   4   5   6   7   8   9   10   YES FOR SURE

3. Does your approach to target setting elicit a strong commitment from the negotiator to perform to target?

NOT AT ALL   1   2   3   4   5   6   7   8   9   10   YES FOR SURE

4. Does your target setting approach force greater participation of management in the planning of strategy and setting goals?

NOT AT ALL   1   2   3   4   5   6   7   8   9   10   YES FOR SURE

5. Does your approach to target setting tend to lead toward harder-to-reach or easier-to-reach targets?

EASY TARGETS 1 2 3 4 5 6 7 8 9 10 HARD TARGETS

EASY TARGETS

6. Does your approach to target setting force the negotiator and the team to question the limits of the other party's power?

NOT AT ALL 1 2 3 4 5 6 7 8 9 · 10 YES FOR SURE

7. Does your target setting approach force you to surface and test your assumptions?

NOT AT ALL 1 2 3 4 5 6 7 8 9 10 YES FOR SURE

8. Do you have written procedures outlining an approach to negotiation planning and target setting?

NONE 1 2 3 4 5 6 7 8 9 10 VERY WELL
THOUGHT OUT

YOUR TARGET SETTING SCORE

If you scored less than 27, you and your organization are not approaching target setting in the best way. If the score was 56 or higher, you are likely to do well in negotiation.

The purpose of the quiz was not merely to get a score but to stimulate thought about the way you set targets in your personal negotiations and those for your company. If your method of setting targets contributes to better planning, a lively internal debate and a clear understanding of priorities, then you and your company are on the path to success.

CONCLUSION – UP YOUR ASPIRATION LEVEL

Those who aim higher in negotiation do better than those who do not. Experiments by others and myself verify this. This tendency appears to be true in life as it is in bargaining. Expectations are self-fulfilling. People who aspire to less get less.

The danger with aiming high is that it involves risk. Those who aim high tend to deadlock more often than those with modest or lower goals. Another problem with setting high targets is that one must work harder, prepare more carefully, and be more persistent to achieve them. It's easy to say, 'Aim higher and you'll do better." But there is a price paid for the greater success enjoyed. For the negotiator willing to pay that price and incur the risk of deadlock, 'Aim higher" is good advice.

SETTING and REACHING
BETTER NEGOTIATING TARGETS

Tip Number 1 Up Your Aspiration Level.

Tip Number 2 Be Clear about Targets; Don't Specify Fallback Positions That Lower the Aspirations of Your Own Negotiators.

Tip Number 3 Make Sure Your Team Understands the Real Target.

Tip Number 4 An Effective Target Setting System Always Encourages Useful Team Debate.

Tip Number 5 Recognize That Everything You Say or Do Before or During a Negotiation Affects the Other Party's Expectations, Targets and Satisfaction Level.

8 | The Strategy of Taking on a Firm Price

FOR THOSE WHO BUY ANYTHING AS CONSUMERS OR IN BUSINESS

In business as in life we are bombarded by firm prices. Everywhere we shop as consumers or industrial buyers, those who sell confront us with a price tag that tells us in bold letters, "THIS IS THE PRICE." Most of us accept the price without challenge. We've gotten used to doing so.

In this chapter we will see that "firm prices" are less firm than they appear to be. Many will crack if tested. Before we consider the many ways to challenge such prices, I would like you to take the 'Are You Too Timid to Negotiate?" quiz on the next page. Please do not read on until you have completed the quiz and computed your score.

ARE YOU TOO TIMID TO NEGOTIATE?

1. How uncomfortable do you feel when facing direct conflict?

(a) Very uncomfortable.
(b) Quite uncomfortable.
(c) Don't like it but face it.
(d) Enjoy the challenge somewhat.
(e) Welcome the opportunity.

2. What kind of deal do you go for?

(a) A good deal for both parties.
(b) A better deal for you.
(c) A better deal for them.
(d) A very good deal for you and better than no deal for them.
(e) Every person for themselves.

3. How do you feel about ambiguous situations – situations which have many pros and cons?

(a) Very uncomfortable. I like things one way or another.
(b) Fairly uncomfortable.
(c) Don't like it but can live with it.
(d) Undisturbed. Find it easy to live with.
(e) Like it that way. Things are hardly ever one way or another.

4. How would you feel about negotiating a 10% raise with your boss if the average raise in the department is 5%?

(a) Don't like it at all. Would avoid it.
(b) Don't like it but would try it reluctantly.
(c) Would do it with apprehension.
(d) Make a good case and not afraid to try it.
(e) Enjoy the experience and look forward to it.

5. How confident are you in your business judgment in matters of negotiation?

(a) Experience shows it's very good.
(b) Good.
(c) As good as most other people or business executives.
(d) Not too good. I seem to get taken more than I should.
(e) I hate to say it but I guess I'm not quite with it when it comes to business matters.

6. How do you feel about getting involved on a personal basis with the other party in a negotiation?

(a) I avoid it.
(b) I'm quite uncomfortable.
(c) Not bad – not good.
(d) I'm attracted to getting close to them.
(e) I go out of my way to get close. I like it that way.

7. When you have the power in negotiation do you use it?

(a) I use it to get what I want.
(b) I use it moderately without any guilt feelings.
(c) I use it in behalf of fairness as I see fairness.
(d) I don't like to use it.
(e) I generally take it easy on the other person.

8. How do you feel about making a very low offer when you buy?

(a) Terrible, don't do it.
(b) Not too good but I do it.
(c) I do it occasionally.
(d) I try it often and don't mind doing it.
(e) I make it a regular practice and feel quite comfortable.

9. How do you usually give in?

(a) Very slowly if at all.
(b) Moderately slowly.
(c) About at the same pace as they do.
(d) I try to move it along a little faster by giving more than they do.
(e) I tend to give hefty chunks and get to the point. I want to get it over with quickly.

10. How do you feel dealing with people of higher status than you are in a bargaining situation?

(a) Very comfortable.
(b) Quite comfortable but a bit apprehensive.
(c) Mixed feelings.
(d) Somewhat uncomfortable.
(e) Very uncomfortable.

11. How would you feel if you had to say, "I don't understand that" four times after four explanations?

(a) Terrible – wouldn't do it.
(b) Quite embarrassed.
(c) Would feel awkward.
(d) Would do it without feeling too badly.
(e) Wouldn't hesitate.

12. You are the buyer of some construction services. The design is changed because your spouse or friend wants something different. The contractor now asks more for the change than you believed fair and reasonable. You need the contractor badly because they are well into the job. How do you feel about negotiating down the added price with the locked-in contractor?

(a) Jump in with both feet.
(b) Ready to work it out but not anxious to.

(c) Don't like it but will try sometimes.
(d) Dislike it very much.
(e) Hate the confrontation.

13. Are you persistent?

(a) I can stick with my position for long periods.
(b) I want to get it over quickly and usually do.
(c) I feel a bit stupid saying the same thing over and over again.
(d) I hang in longer than most people whom I oppose.
(e) I almost always come up with reasons why it is not worth the aggravation to hang in there.

14. What is your usual reaction to taking on what looks like a merchant's "firm" price?

(a) Love it. Tackle it with fervor.
(b) Like it and do it quite often.
(c) Neither like nor dislike it but do it most times.
(d) Rather dislike but do it rarely.
(e) Hate it and hardly ever do it. Feel embarrassed.

15. How do you feel about walking back into a store after the deal between you and the merchant breaks down because you are too far apart?

(a) I won't do it. I hate it.
(b) I hate it. I rarely walk back.
(c) I don't like it. I do it sometimes but not often.
(d) I don't mind walking back too much and do it often.
(e) I don't mind at all.

16. How successful is your bargaining track record on buying products like houses, property, cars, appliances, etc., in terms of getting a better deal than the seller originally asked for?

(a) I usually do very well.
(b) I have many more hits than misses.
(c) My record is mediocre. About as good or bad as most people.
(d) Mostly I am not successful, but occasionally I win a small concession or two.
(e) I rarely do any good at all. It's hardly worth trying anymore.

HOW TO SCORE YOURSELF

To find your Timidity Quotient, add your positive and negative scores separately according to the answer key at the end of this chapter. Subtract them from each other. This will give you a point score from a low of minus 298 to a high of plus 309. (For example, if you selected answer (c) to question 1, your score would be 0. Selection of answer (d) to question 2 scores -10 and so on.)

Now that you have completed the quiz and arrived at a Timidity Score you can evaluate the results. If your score was between 227 and 309, you have a positive attitude that will help you feel comfortable in bargaining. If your Timidity Quotient was between 1 and 226, you have a good attitude toward negotiating, even in difficult situations. You are not hindered by being too timid to bargain. If you scored between -1 and -142, you may not be aggressive enough. Those who scored below -143 are probably too timid for their own good.

The important thing about this quiz is not your score but your willingness to try the ideas we will soon suggest. With each success, your Timidity Quotient will improve. You will find yourself taking on firm prices you never did before and winning concessions you never thought possible.

HOW TO TACKLE A FIRM PRICE WHETHER YOU BUY AS A CONSUMER OR PROFESSIONAL

Americans as a whole are hypnotized by firm prices, more so than those who live in other societies. We are inundated by what appear to be firm prices. They blare at us in newspaper advertisements, over television, in four color price lists and in the stores themselves. Is it any wonder that we have grown accustomed to paying the asking price without testing it?

Not so in other cultures. There, when they see an $800 price ticket on a piece of furniture, they say, "That's the most the seller wants. I wonder what the least they will take is." Americans see the $800 price tag differently. They say, "That's what the seller wants. Do I want to buy it or not?" The result of this difference in approach is that most Americans, if they want the product or service, pay the price asked.

From now on, whenever you encounter a firm price, say to yourself, "That's the most the seller or merchant wants. I wonder what the least they will take is?" Test the price – there is usually some flexibility in the seller's offering or terms. There are good reasons for this.

Day in and day out salespeople lose sales because people cannot or will not meet their demands. Each loss forces sellers to reevaluate a firm position. This interaction with potential customers leads the seller to consider creative alternatives to close a sale rather than lose it. The consumer or professional buyer who tests the firm price can rest assured that they are not the first to do so, nor will they be the first to succeed in winning concessions.

To help take on a firm price, we can learn as much from little things as from big ones. The principles of testing the price on products or services are alike whether it be for a case of Scotch, a new condominium, a new laptop or the interest rate you pay on your mortgage. We shall illustrate these techniques by testing a department store price on a refrigerator.

Sears, Macy's and other department stores are tougher than most merchants or industrial sellers because they have had a century of experience in holding the price line. If you can take on a department store, you will be able to test the price on any product or service, whether large or small. The principles are the same.

Imagine that you are in a department store. The refrigerator which you like has $1400 boldly printed on a large sign on top of it. In addition, the sign says that colors other than white are available at $30 extra, that delivery is free for 20 miles and that the deluxe ice maker is optional for $200 more. Can the price be reduced? The answer is "yes." But you must ask for the reduction or you will never get it. NEVER.

What follows are 33 approaches that can win concessions in any negotiation involving a seller's or merchant's firm price. Have the courage to try these ideas. They will work for you because they are win-win ideas.

1. **Quantity.** They bought a stove and a refrigerator and got a discount on both. If they owned an apartment house, they might have bought two or three refrigerators instead

of one and obtained an even larger discount.

2. **Mixing.** They bought something on which the price could not be changed together with another item that could be reduced such as a warranty extension.

3. **Payment.** They paid the full price in three monthly installments without interest. This, of course, is the equivalent of a discount. Or they paid cash for which they received a 3 percent discount in lieu of using a credit card. One person at our seminar learned that she could get a one-day 20 percent discount if she opened a store charge account Since she was buying $500 of merchandise, she opened the account.

4. **Billing Date.** They arranged to be billed a few days later and thereby picked up a month's free money on their charge account.

5. **Seconds.** They found a new refrigerator with a slight dent on the side.

6. **Special Item.** They bought a new refrigerator which had been used as a floor demonstrator.

7. **Back Time.** They bought the one that was on sale last week and paid last week's price. All they had to do was ask when it was on sale.

8. **Forward Time.** They bought the one on sale next week. The salesperson told them about the forthcoming sale when they asked when it would go on sale.

9. **Obsolete.** They bought last year's model.

10. **Advanced.** They bought next year's model at today's price.

11. **Distribution.** They bought the same refrigerator from the catalog, the wholesale department, the return outlet or from the industrial catalog instead of the one in the store and received a lower price.

12. **Commission**. They convinced the salesperson to give up some of the commission on the sale.

13. **Trade-In.** They traded in their old model against a new one.

14. **Free Labor or Transportation.** They got the refrigerator delivered and connected in place. Also, the department store agreed to remove the old one and properly dispose of it as required by law.

15. **Delivery.** They got a discount for picking it up themselves or got it delivered earlier or later to meet their own schedule.

16. **Holding Option.** They got the salesperson to hold the refrigerator until they had the money.   This option can sometimes be arranged with a small deposit.

17. **Nibbling.** Extra ice cube trays and crispers were thrown in as well as installation charges on the ice maker. They also got the salesperson to deliver forty miles away at no extra charge.

18. **Warranty.** The warranty was extended to one year instead of 90 days at a nominal cost. A free damaged food insurance warranty was also included.

19. **Service Contract.** A service contract for two years at a reduced rate was obtained. Also a guarantee of service in six hours or the service call would be free of charge.

20. **Specification Close-Out.** The salesman found a somewhat different model which was reduced because it had not sold well.

21. **Time Pressure.** After trying all week with no success to get the price below $1400, they returned just before 4:45 PM on Saturday on the last day of the month. The salesperson made the deal before the store closed at 5:00PM and won the February "Store Salesperson" prize. The final price was $1200 with the ice maker thrown in for only $50 more.

22. **Go to Jakarta.** They found an item that was amazingly similar to what they wanted in Jakarta or Bangladesh.

23. **Spare Parts.** They arranged to buy future spare parts such as a compressor at today's price schedule.

24. **Special Options.** Though they didn't buy the ice maker today, they got an option to purchase it within a year at today's price or at a wholesale price with installation thrown in.

25. **Satisfaction Guaranteed.** They obtained a guarantee that if they weren't pleased, their money would be refunded.

26. **Price Protection.** They prevailed on the salesperson to include a clause stating that if the product went on sale within a month, they would be given the benefit of the lower price.

27. **Price Guarantee.** They obtained a guarantee that if a competitor sold the same model at a lower price the department store would meet the lower competitor price and provide an extra 10 percent bonus on the price difference.

28. **Exchange Privilege.** They reserved the right to exchange the product for full credit (or some reduced credit) for a period of time.

29. **Concession.** They asked for another 5 percent discount and copper color at no charge. They didn't get the discount but did get the copper color free. The salesperson was anxious to get the bargaining over with and go home.

30. **Another Store.** The merchandise they wanted at the lower price was sold out in the Macy's store in Westwood, so they asked the salesperson to see if any of the other Macy's stores in California still had it in stock. One store did.

31. **Friend.** They bought the item through a friend who was a contractor or interior decorator and thereby took advantage of the contractor or decorator discount.

32. **Go To The Manufacturer.** They found out who the manufacturer was and bought the item directly from them.

33. **Discounts of All Kinds Are Available.** They bought it through a cousin who worked at the store. Or they availed themselves of discounts for seniors, auto club, price clubs, union, association, government, credit cards, or any other organization they belonged to.

For those who cannot find a good reason to challenge the price, my advice is that you just ask for a reduction offering no reason at all. You will be surprised at how often "just asking" wins a reduction. Not asking gets you less than you may deserve.

TWO MORE POWERFUL TOOLS FOR BREAKING THE FIRM PRICE BARRIER

There are two other well-tested techniques for challenging the firm price barrier which deserve special attention. The first is "taking on higher authority." Most of us are intimidated by people in authority. Yet in the opinion of experienced negotiators, you can make a better deal with those higher in a company than at lower levels. Grit your teeth and take on higher authority.

The other approach to testing a firm price is basic to all negotiation. Learn to walk away from the table, then come back. Then, if necessary, walk away and come back again. It takes courage to do so, especially for Americans. They've had so little experience at it. Americans tend to perceive reopening a deadlocked negotiation as a loss of ego or face. Europeans, Africans, and Asians view walking away as routine. They attach less personal significance to it. The sooner you practice walking out on small negotiations, the easier it will be when the stakes are high.

My advice is that you learn to test an apparently firm price even when the stakes are low. Some day you will buy a boat or vacation home in Florida. The practice you get on small deals will save you tens of thousands on the larger ones. As for those of you in business, the savings on a million dollar computer system may be as high as two or three hundred thousand dollars. Not a bad return for the time and effort spent taking on the million dollar firm price.

CONCLUSION

The magic of taking on a firm price is that it works. Concessions will be won. Fight your fear of trying. If you are too timid to try, you will never find out if the price was really firm or not.

TIMIDITY QUOTIENT SCORING SHEET

Question	(a)	(b)	(c)	(d)	(e)
1	-18	-10	0	+10	+18
2	+18	+6	-10	-10	-18
3	-19	-10	0	+16	+20
4	-19	-4	+8	+20	+19
5	+20	+12	+4	-12	-20
6	-19	-14	0	+16	+19
7	+20	+14	+4	-10	-14
8	-20	+10	+6	+16	+20
9	+20	+14	-8	-16	-20
10	+18	+12	0	-14	-18
11	-19	-16	-4	+10	+18
12	+18	+12	+6	-6	-16
13	+19	-6	-10	+12	-19
14	+20	+16	+8	0	-20
15	-20	-5	+5	+20	+18
16	+19	+14	+4	-10	-19

9

The Strategy of Defending Your Selling Price

There is a Russian proverb which applies to sellers who are under pressure to reduce their price: "It's not the horse that pulls the cart. It's the grain." It is not the buyer who pulls the price decision cart, it is the seller's mix of products and services which feeds the buyer's deeper needs and leads them toward decision.

In this chapter we will discuss thirteen approaches by which sellers can best defend their price and still close the sale. These thirteen defenses apply whether you are holding to a firm price or to a price that has very little give.

1. IF PRICE WAS THE ONLY REASON PEOPLE BOUGHT ANYTHING THE WHOLE ECONOMIC WORLD WOULD BE DIFFERENT.

2. DON'T LET YOUR JOB WORK AGAINST YOU.

3. WOO, WOO, WOO, WHILE YOU SELL SATISFAC-TION.

4. THE TOTAL COST APPROACH TO HOLDING THE PRICE LINE.

5. DON'T BE IN A HURRY TO COME TO THE POINT.

6. GIVE YOUR SELLING PRICE THE POWER OF GOOD BACKUP.

7. BUYERS DO NOT EXPECT TO WIN ALL THEY ASK FOR.

8. STOP DISCOUNTING YOUR BENEFITS – CON-VERT THEM INTO CUSTOMER DOLLARS.

9. SAY "NO" FOR A LONGER TIME THAN YOU USU-ALLY DO.

10. GIVE BUYERS TIME TO VENT THEIR FRUSTRA-TIONS.

11. MAKE CONCESSIONS THAT GIVE NOTHING AWAY.

12. DON'T BE AFRAID TO THROW SOME ATTEN-TION GETTING INFORMATION LITTER ON THE BUYER'S LAWN.

13. USE THE WIN-WIN STRATEGY TO MAINTAIN YOUR PRICE POSITION.

The First Sales Defense – If Price Was the Only Reason People Bought Anything the Whole Economic World Would Be Different

If price was the only reason why people bought anything the whole economic world would be different. Despite this, most buyers tell salespeople that price is the only thing that counts in making their decision. They tell the seller, even when they themselves don't believe it, "Your competition offers essentially the same package that you do. If you want the order, reduce your price." However, as we know from experience, price is not the only factor in determining what and where we buy.

If price was the only reason that buyers bought a product or service, there would soon be only one price for that product or service. Quality wouldn't matter, user friendliness wouldn't matter, delivery wouldn't matter, design wouldn't matter, supplier financial stability wouldn't matter, follow-up service wouldn't matter and payment terms wouldn't matter.

If price was the only reason that buyers bought anything, there would soon be one supplier. The supplier who could produce at the lowest cost would drive others out of business. Then, as a monopoly, they would control the price to keep others out.

If price was the only reason that buyers bought anything, we wouldn't need salespeople. Computers could do the job. Push 1 to get the price. Push 2 to place the order. Push 3 to enter the delivery date. Every customer would be the same in terms of needs and interests.

That's not the way the real world works. Most buyers know this.

Why then do they keep saying, "Price is the only thing that counts with me"? Because salespeople so often believe them when they shouldn't. Successful salespeople know that price is rarely, if ever, the only factor in making a purchasing decision.

The Second Sales Defense – Don't Let Your Job Work Against You

The trouble faced by most salespeople is that they let their jobs work against them. Not long ago we developed a negotiating program for a prominent rod and reel company. Management was convinced that their people were making larger concessions than necessary to discount retailers and sports stores.

In the process of customizing our seminar we went into the field with their salespeople. It soon became evident how their jobs were working against them. Despite the fact that the company had made fine fishing gear for eighty years, it seemed that few of those selling valued their products highly.

Faced with buyers quick to tell them that their prices were too high and their equipment no better than the competition, the salespeople quickly lowered their expectations. Concessions soon followed. Was that any surprise? Hardly.

Never in their many sales calls had a buyer told them how low their prices were or how highly the fishing public valued their fishing gear. Buyers with common sense rarely say things to a seller that will raise their expectations.

To better understand what was going on, the company decided to hire an outside polling company. Three focus groups were surveyed. While there were many questions asked, the essential one was, "Which of the major manufacturers do you believe makes the best rods and reels for the price?" The focus groups surveyed were: company sales people, sports store buyers, and the general fishing public.

The survey revealed that their fishing gear was rated first by both the general public and the professional buyers for the discount and sports stores. Surprisingly, the only people who rated the competition higher were the company's own salespeople. They rated their own rods and reels lowest of the major competitors.

Was it any surprise that these salespeople made concessions easily? They had learned from the many buyers they faced daily that their products weren't so good and their prices too high. After being on the job for a while, they began to believe that the best and perhaps the only way to close a sale was to lower the price. It was this tendency that management sought to neutralize in the bargaining process.

The first defense in holding price is to recognize that most salespeople get brainwashed by their jobs. They allow the accumulation of buyer rejections and negative comments to erode their confidence in the positive values of their own products and services.

The next time you hear a buyer "throwing garbage on your lawn" by downgrading your offering, recognize that they are just doing their jobs. They will never tell you how good your product is or how favorable your price. Never. Your job is to tell them again and again why your price, product and service will deliver what they need.

Professional buyers, in my experience, are quite rational in making purchasing decisions. Don't let their verbal fireworks get you down. They are probably saying the same thing to your competitors. They do so because it's effective.

The Third Sales Defense – Woo, Woo, Woo, While You Sell Satisfaction

The seller with the best chance to close a sale without making significant concessions is the one who woos the customer. Buyers prefer to give the order to people who show they want and appreciate the business. They are, however, wary of those who appear desperate. Buyers, in that respect, are like bankers who are afraid to lend money to borrowers who show they are in terrible need.

For the salesperson, woo, woo, woo and sell, sell, sell is good advice. Don't be afraid to be a broken record. Tell the buyer again and again how much you want to please them. Tell them how much your company deserves the order. Tell them again why your proposal offers benefits which the competition does not or cannot provide. Quantify the benefits for them.

Don't be in a hurry to reduce your price. Take the time to woo them and to sell them. Sell your product or service and your added values. When you run out of new things to say, say what you already said once more. Tell the buyer again and again why his or her decision to deal with you will be a wise one. Sell to their interests not yours. As William James once said, "Interest alone gives accent and emphasis, light and shade, background and foreground – intelligent perspective."

Persistent wooing pays off, providing it is done without conveying a sense of desperation. The man or woman who woos the person he or she hopes to marry has a better chance of succeeding than one who doesn't. The "woo-ee" can hardly help but be pleased. Wooing works the same way in selling as in social affairs.

The Fourth Sales Defense – the Total Cost Approach

One of the best strategies for defending a firm price is what I call the "Total Cost Approach." If price appears to be the sticking point, do what Albert Einstein suggested when he said, "No problem can be solved at its own level." Direct the level of discussion to total cost instead of price.

Every product or service offered by those who sell is part of a broader economic context. What I mean by this will become clear in the following examples. The first involves a simple product. The second a service.

Assume for a moment that I am buying tires for my car. It's obvious that my total cost of purchasing the tires includes more than the price of the tire.

It includes the time and effort of going to several tire stores, of learning about tires, of selecting the right one among many. It includes wheel balancing and mounting and waiting around to get it done. It also includes the need to rotate the tires every 6,000 miles and the work and money it takes to get it done. And then there is the matter of eventual tire punctures and, finally, replacement at 40,000 miles. The original price is only part of the total cost of a tire. The same is true of most goods and services we buy as consumers or industrial buyers.

If I were a salesman selling tires at $120 each and you objected to my price, one good way I could respond to your pressure is by switching the discussion to total cost. I would show that my tire includes free rotation and balancing every 6,000 miles – an added value added worth let's say $5 per rotation for five visits ($25). I would point out that my tire store is a short walking distance from your home. This will enable you to save time and energy while taking advantage of the free rotation policy.

In addition, I would demonstrate that regular rotation will allow you to travel 88,000 miles on the tire instead of 80,000, saving you at least $20 per tire. It would also be easy to show that our free puncture repair policy is worth at least $2 per tire over its life. Now, using the total cost approach, our $120 tire would really cost only $73 ($120 less $25 less $20 less $2 = $73). No other store could compete with such a low total cost for a Grade A, totally safe performance tire.

That's the way the total cost approach is used to defend a firm price. Notice that we have not merely verbalized the benefits of our tire package. We have put quantified provable dollar values on our offer to make the benefits as real as possible to the buyer.

The total cost approach is a powerful tool for any seller under price pressure. It would be helpful to illustrate its use in another way. My company conducts seminars in luxury hotels. To do so we have to reserve a large conference room for several days, rent a large LCD projector with screen and speakers. Also necessary are whiteboards, flipcharts, lavolier microphones and hotel rooms for those who present the programs.

In addition, we make arrangements with hotel catering to provide a fine lunch and refreshments for morning and afternoon breaks. The hotel bill for two days often exceeds $15,000 in many cities.

The hotel which won the contract in New York and Chicago was not the one with the lowest price. What they did was smart. They analyzed our total annual requirement. They studied, in detail, what we had to do to put on a seminar. Before they were through they understood our needs and costs perhaps as well as we did.

What won the order for them was a total cost package. They suggested that we purchase our own projectors, whiteboards and microphones. The hotel allowed us to store this equipment in a controlled area on their premises. The savings in rental costs alone came to $100,000 a year in just five major cities. There are more cities to come.

The hotel also made their billing and planning software available to us. This allowed us to audit invoices quickly and easily. These total cost adjustments not only assured that hotel billing would be accurate but reduced accounting expenses as well. By integrating our planning process, we were able to streamline our preparations by predicting and communicating lunch requirements and special accommodations promptly and accurately at additional savings.

The hotel succeeded in capturing our business not because it thought in terms of offering a low price but because they thought in terms of reducing our total cost. This approach allowed them to maintain their profit margins. To this day we are both well satisfied.

The Fifth Sales Defense – Don't Be in a Hurry

Let's assume that you have made a proposal to the buyer and they call you to discuss it. You believe the firm price will be challenged at the meeting. You are anxious about it but have developed strong arguments supporting the price. Should you bring up the difficult issue of price or should you leave it to the buyer to do it first?

I believe that it is rarely wise for a negotiator to come to the point quickly in any negotiation – especially if the point of discussion involves a difficult issue. In my experience, negotiators who do not come to the point on sticky issues do better than those who do.

Start the negotiation by talking about the World Series, the weather or golf. There are good reasons for starting with casual conversation rather than coming straight to the point.

(a) You may discover how anxious the buyer is to get the work started or how badly she wants to place the order and get on to something else.

(b) Your assumption that the buyer views price as a critical issue may be wrong. She may see delivery or quality as the "sticky" issue.

(c) You may, by talking amiably about other things, take some of the edge or focus off the buyer's objections.

(d) You may give the impression that while you want the business you aren't too anxious.

Don't come to the point too quickly is good advice for anyone who negotiates. There are advantages to letting the other party do it first.

The Sixth Sales Defense – Give Your Selling Price the Power of Good Backup

When taking a position in defense of price, be prepared to back it up. If your price is as good or better than others, show them that it is. If your price is consistent with what you charged last time, prove it. If your price is in line with the consumer's price index, bring the evidence. If your price is in line with prices shown in trade publications, bring the publication with you and let the buyer see it.

Whenever you provide the other person with facts or figures that add legitimacy and precedence to your price position, you make it more likely that you will get a "yes" answer.

When a price is supported by good backup, it is easier to defend. For example, if your price is the same to all customers, allow the buyer to see your invoice and accounting records. If this is not prudent or possible, provide the buyer with a "most favored customer" certification as a clause in the contract. This is the position taken by many companies whose price is the same to all.

Good backup has another use which is valuable but often overlooked. When a seller finds it necessary to make a price concession, it's wise to do it on a reasoned basis, even if the amount conceded is small. Don't just drop your price. Defend your concession with all the power of backup and legitimacy you can muster. A well defended concession will reduce the buyer's demand for further concessions and increase their satisfaction. An unsupported price concession may leave the buyer hungry for more concessions.

The Seventh Sales Defense – Recognize That Buyers Do Not Expect to Win All They Ask For

Ann Douglas, in her extensive research in bargaining, discovered that negotiators often ask for things they never expect to get.

Why do they bother?

In her research interviews with many negotiators she found that they did so for a variety of reasons. Some did it to test the other party's resolve. Others to develop trading points for winning concessions on unrelated issues. Still others did it just to satisfy the expectations of other executives in their own organization who insisted that this or that point be demanded for reasons of their own.

Negotiators rarely deal entirely for themselves. In most cases, they are part of an organization. Such an organization may be personal, as when a spouse or friend is involved, or corporate, as when the buyer's boss or the engineering department have a stake in the outcome.

It is important for the salesperson to understand that the buyer may be asking for concessions in payment terms that their controller would like to win but that may be unimportant to the buyer. Once the buyer is requested by the controller to ask for better payment terms, they will be obliged to demand it. The buyer will probably be forgiven by the controller for not winning the concession, but would not be forgiven for failing to ask. In complex negotiations, many buyer demands are made to satisfy legal, accounting, operations, or engineering interests that mayor may not be crucial.

Some demands fall into the "straw-issue" category. Straw issues are introduced by buyers to create trading room. They are put forth as demands only to be exchanged for other things the buyer values more highly. Early in the negotiation, it is not easy to differentiate between straw issues and those the buyer really wants. Later, most straw issues disappear, especially as closure comes near.

For these reasons it makes sense for sellers to defend their price with tenacity. The buyer may have less resolve in winning concessions than it first appears. The only way to find out is to patiently test their resolve. Buyers know they cannot win on all issues.

The Eighth Sales Defense – Stop Discounting Your Benefits – Convert Them into Customer Dollar Values

There is little question that sellers who understand and have confidence in the benefits of their product or service do better in negotiation. This is especially true when the seller is able to present these strengths in terms of the customer's needs and objectify them by putting dollar values on the benefits the customer will receive. The trouble is that too many salespeople do not do so.

Sellers who have to remain firm in the face of strong price pressure will find their effectiveness improved if they take the following three actions:

1. Customize Your Benefits. Learn to communicate the benefits of the product or service you sell in terms of the buyer's customized needs and viewpoint. The seller who describes the benefits of his offering in terms of a generalized customer will find it harder to close the sale.

2. Objectify Your Benefits. Do all you can to put a dollar value (calculated in terms of the buyer's specific needs) on every benefit and added value you offer. Objectifying your benefits will put you ahead of your competition because most salespeople don't do it or don't do it well. Why? Because it's not easy to do.

3. Dry Run the Sales Presentation – The Manager's Role. Customization is the wave of the future. It isn't enough for us to say that the salesperson should understand the specific customer's specific needs and customize the product benefits in the buyer's terms. Manager intervention in the sales presentation is essential.

The sales manager who takes the time to evaluate the sales presentation before talks begin will get better results in holding the price line. Customizing product or service benefits and objectifying their value is hard work. If your salespeople are taught to do it right and if they know you will be present at the dry run, they will do a better job when they meet the buyer.

The seller who is willing to take these actions is certain to be more successful in defending a firm price than one who does not.

The Ninth Defense – Say "No" For a Longer Time than You Usually do

As we have said earlier most cultures are more comfortable saying "no" than Americans. From now on, when defending a firm price learn to say "no" for a longer time than you are presently accustomed to.

A polite "no" supported by logic, evidence and persistence goes a long way in reducing a buyer's expectations. Any concession, however small, which the seller makes after saying "no" for a long while contributes to a higher level of buyer satisfaction.

Surprisingly, some buyers even welcome a well defended seller's "no" because it saves them the time and trouble of further negotiations. Still others value the seller's firm "no" because it makes the final price easier to defend to their own organization. There are good ways to say "no" that do not slam the door on further talks. The Japanese are especially adept at saying "no" in tactful ways. Instead of saying "no" directly, they are accustomed to say things like, "That will be very difficult" or "No, maybe" or "That will require further consideration" or "Yes, but." Some Japanese show resistance by breathing deeply with a slow sigh and "whoof" sound. One way or another they stick to their position for a long time. We can learn much about defending our price from them.

The Tenth Sales Defense – Give Buyers Time to Vent Their Frustrations

If you are going to stick to a firm price or hold reasonably close to your last offer, be sure to give the buyer time to vent his or her frustration. Recognize that whenever you restrain a person's freedom of choice – and that's what a firm price or firm position does – it creates resentment.

Let the buyers complain as long as they wish. At the least, it will allow them to get it off their chest and relieve the pressure somewhat. At best, it may help display to others in their organization how hard they tried to win a better price. If you provide the buyer ample time to express anger, sooner or later they will run out of things to say. If you interrupt to defend your position too soon, the buyer will become harder to deal with.

The Eleventh Sales Defense – Make Concessions That Give Nothing Away

How can a salesperson make concessions that give nothing away – concessions that provide the buyer increased satisfaction but without giving away goods, money or services? Successful sellers know it is wise to make such concessions, especially when defending a price which has little or no room for compromise.

Sellers have the power to increase a customer's satisfaction in a number of ways. One way is by providing credible backup. They can assure the buyer that the product or service will meet their needs by providing a list of satisfied customers. They can listen responsively to the customer's viewpoint. They can show their commitment to customer satisfaction by having them meet with their company president. Each of these concessions costs little but provides the other party considerable satisfaction.

I remember two salesmen who used to call on me when I was a purchasing agent. Both had a simple technique for making the price negotiation more pleasant. One always brought delicious muffins. I looked forward to seeing him, no matter how difficult the problem to be discussed. The other salesman gained my respect and attention by bringing along useful trade, price, and product information that helped me do my job.

Did these amenities help them to better hold their price? To some extent I believe it did. Both raised my satisfaction level by making concessions that gave little or nothing away at the table.

The Twelfth Sales Defense – Be Discreet, but Don't Be Afraid to Throw Some Attention-Getting Information Litter on the Buyer's Lawn

The industrial buyer confronted by a firm price is likely to be frustrated. Many will vent their displeasure by threatening to take their business elsewhere. They are also apt to tell the seller that the price is too high and their product and service no better and perhaps worse than the competition. The buyer's purpose in throwing such "garbage on the seller's lawn" is to reduce the seller's aspirations and to make them anxious about losing the order at the proposed firm price.

After the buyer has been provided enough time to express their frustration, the seller has an obligation to place a little attention-getting information on the buyer's lawn. They have a right to say things that will set the stage for maintaining a firm price and cause the buyer to hesitate about placing the order elsewhere. If this is not done with discretion, however, it will result in a more resistant buyer and a lost sale.

What follows are a few remarks which, if tactfully handled, will give the buyer good reason to consider your firm or almost firm price in a better light.

1. "You get what you pay for. Other suppliers may give you a better rate but you won't get the service from them that we've been providing you. We delivered the supplies to you immediately after the earthquake. Nobody else could do as well as we did in that emergency. You are a key customer."

2. "I'm not sure you fully appreciate our pricing. You're getting a very good deal. Our controller says that your account is a better deal for you than it is for us. I'll be glad to show you the analysis of your account. I believe you'll agree we are making very little for all that service." However, it is well to remember that the best defense starts with preparation and a dry-run in the privacy of your office before meeting the buyer.

3. "Here's what we are doing that the competition doesn't or can't do." For example, in the trucking business, the salesperson might say, "We can ship directly into areas

where you need fast deliveries. Our competitors have to transship to smaller carriers. That's what causes delays and lost goods in transit. You don't want that."

4. The salesperson might say, "Our truckers are trained and instructed to provide services on your loading dock which our competitors can't provide because of union rules. We help your people load and unload and that saves you lots of time and $30,000 a year."

5. "Your total cost is less when you deal with us. Let our people analyze your process at no cost."

Such remarks are guaranteed to win a buyer's attention and, to some extent, offset resistance to your price.

The Thirteenth Sales Defense – Use Win-Win Strategy to Maintain Your Price Position

One of the best ways for sellers to defend their price position is for buyer and seller to search for opportunities that benefit both parties. There is always a better way for them to do business together. The process of searching and finding joint benefits defuses the price issue.

To illustrate how win-win strategies can defuse difficult price problems, consider a hypothetical negotiation between a trucking company called ABC Freight and a manufacturing company named Acme Biotech. In the example that follows, the ABC Freight salesperson and the Acme Biotech buyer explore both-win opportunities:

1. Acme Biotech, the buyer, may gain a better price by offering to increase the total amount of Acme freight to be trucked by ABC Freight. Both would benefit. Acme would win a

lower price. ABC would increase its profit at the higher volume.

2. ABC truck drivers may deliver shipments and make pickups at a better time of the day. For example, 4:00 PM might be a slow period at Acme Biotech. If shipments arrived or were picked up at this time the truckers would face fewer delays and the shipper would enjoy more efficient freight processing. Both would benefit.

3. Their organizational and billing software could be integrated to streamline and improve their ability to track shipments and simplify billing. Both would benefit.

4. Minimum shipment size is a problem in the trucking business. The delivery and pickup of small shipments is costly. A joint analysis of small shipments is likely to yield a better cost/service balance that benefits both parties.

5. Important savings can be realized by improving the routing of freight and the consolidation of shipments. Better routing and consolidation would result in faster deliveries, and reduce storage costs. It would also minimize damaged goods in transit. These savings could be shared by Acme and ABC Freight.

In each of these situations the freight buyer and the trucker have jointly developed a better deal for both parties. The freight buyer may benefit by winning a better price and/or better service. ABC Freight would increase its profit by handling freight and paperwork more efficiently and by increasing its sales volume.

The important point to recognize is that both-win improvements are always possible. While the examples above involve the transportation industry, the same ideas are applicable in any relationship. The opportunity for mutual gain without loss to either party is one of the most powerful ways to defend your price and profit margin.

CONCLUSION

The key to defending a firm price lies in understanding that effective sales negotiators sell satisfaction as well as goods, services or prices. They show the customer how their package of benefits will help in ways which the competition cannot. Instead of being hooked into the buyer's emphasis on price, they demonstrate the added values, tangible and intangible, which they uniquely offer. They quantify and objectify their benefits whenever possible.

Defending your price in the face of intense competition will never be easy, but it can be done effectively. In this chapter we have developed an arsenal of defenses available to a seller who is under pressure to reduce price. These sales defenses serve one major purpose – to move the buyer's focus of attention from price and to redirect it to the full package of benefits and values offered by the seller.

THIRTEEN SUCCESSFUL STRATEGIES TO DEFEND YOUR PRICE

——— • ———

The 1st Defense   If Price Was the Only Reason People Bought Anything the Whole Economic World Would Be Different

The 2nd Defense   Don't Let Your Job Work Against You

The 3rd Defense   Woo, Woo, Woo, While You Sell Satisfaction

The 4th Defense   The Total Cost Approach to Holding the Price Line

The 5th Defense   Don't Be in a Hurry

The 6th Defense   Give Your Selling Price the Power of Good Backup

The 7th Defense   Buyers Do Not Expect to Win All They Ask for

The 8th Defense   Stop Discounting Your Benefits - Convert Them into Customer Dollars

The 9th Defense   Say "No" for a Longer Time Than You Usually Do

The 10th Defense   Give Buyers Time to Vent Their Frustrations

The 11th Defense   Make Concessions That Give Nothing Away

The 12th Defense   Don't Be Afraid to Throw Some Attention-Getting Information Litter on the Buyer's Lawn

The 13th Defense   Using the Win-Win Strategy to Maintain Your Price

10

The Strategy of Planning and Preparation

This may surprise you. Even when the stakes are high, people go into negotiation playing it by ear. Instead of doing the most rudimentary planning, they just hope for the best. The trouble is that the "best" doesn't happen unless you work and prepare for it.

Experiments confirm that planning pays off. Yet I challenge you to ask yourself how well you prepared prior to negotiating for the home or car you bought. If you are like most of us the answer was, "not much." Most people know that preparation is important, but they still don't do it. Can something be done to help them plan better? I believe so.

It's easy to advise someone going into an important negotiation to do their homework before talks start. That's good advice of course. But the trouble with "Do your homework" as a guide to action is that it begs the harder question: "What's the assignment?" In this chapter, we will look at the "Do your homework" assignment step by step. If we know what is to be done, we have a better chance of doing it well. The "Quick Planning Kit" which follows is a good place to start.

THE QUICK PLANNING KIT: THIRTEEN TIPS THAT HELP EVEN WHEN YOU DON'T HAVE TIME

In the give and take of bargaining there are occasions when you don't have time to plan. It shouldn't be that way, but it is. Here are thirteen tips that will help when time is short.

1. Before talks begin, write down your wants in order of priority. Distinguish between "must have" and "would like to have" wants.

2. Figure out what your opening offer and target will be on each issue to be discussed.

3. Determine what you will say after the other party says "no" to your opening offer. Remember, they are sure to say "no."

4. Make a list of things you will ask for in return if you have to make concessions later.

5. Choose the best time and place to meet.

6. Write down a few ways to make a win-win deal.

7. Build in a "lack of authority" and a "time to think" defense. This will help avoid being pushed into a premature "yes" decision.

8. Bring an associate who can help you listen better, ask good questions and say the right things.

9. Ask yourself, "What are some limits to their power?"

10. How will you support your position? What kind of backup should you bring along that will help persuade the other party to move in your direction?

11. Ask yourself, "What do they want that's under the 'iceberg'?" – things they want but can't ask for, such as looking competent to others or having less work to do.

12. What is our second choice if these talks break down?

13. Is there something you should ask for now that you'll wish you had asked for after the deal is closed? Examples would be training, return privileges, a larger order, or free delivery.

There is more to planning than the items above. Nevertheless, if you keep these quick planning points in mind, your bargaining position is bound to improve, even when there isn't much time.

THE POWER OF NEGATIVE PLANNING OR HOW TO STOP HOPING FOR THE BEST

The power of negative planning lies in recognizing that your plans will not work as they should.

Strobe Talbott, Deputy Secretary of State, once said:

> *The best laid plans are not sufficient to deal with situations as they actually develop. What you have to do in order to get it right is be flexible enough to deal with the world when it doesn't cooperate with your strategy. This is particularly true of negotiating where the other party is more intent on frustrating your plan than accommodating it.*

Two realities of planning deserve recognition here. First, the original plan you make will fall apart. Second, you will have to do more planning as the talks move toward agreement.

It's somewhat like what happens in basketball. Teams usually have a plan as they move from their back court toward the opponent's basket. Things go wrong largely because the opponent is intent on defending against the plan. An alternate plan based on the realities of the situation must be quickly developed by the offense to succeed in scoring. One big difference between the best teams and average ones is that in the best teams the coach and players are able to assess and cope with the ever changing realities on the court. Ordinary teams are less successful in doing so. The same is true in negotiation. The plan will have to change.

I am reminded of the football coach who was ready for the big homecoming game. He had a great game plan and two good quarterbacks ready to carry it out. The first string quarterback was a star. The backup quarterback almost as good. Every play was practiced a hundred times. The coach had a team of exceptional players ready to carry out the game strategy. Little was likely to go wrong.

The game started. On the first play the star quarterback sprained his leg. On the next play the backup quarterback snapped an ankle. What could the harried coach do? He had one quarterback left, a big, slow kid who didn't know any of the carefully worked out plays. So the coach did the best he could. He put the kid into the game with one instruction, "Run the ball three times then kick."

Things looked pretty grim. To everyone's surprise, on first down the new quarterback picked up 25 yards. On the second run he picked up another 12 yards. On the next he ran 18 yards. The coach looked on in wonder. They were on the opposing team's 20 yard line. It was first down. Things looked good. The other team was demoralized. A touchdown seemed certain if the right play could be called. Suddenly, before the coach could send in a new play, the kid kicked.

As we all know, plans have a way of not working out. I've seen people so disconcerted by a failed approach that they say or do something that actually raises the expectations of the other party. I've seen others so at a loss for words that they cave in all at once. Others become cantankerous when facing tough resistance, saying things they wish they hadn't. Like the coach in our story, they should have called time out to develop a new plan. What every negotiator should realize is that the other parties' "no" and their strong resistance are to be expected. It must be built into the plan. I suggest two courses of action.

First, before talks start, test your line of reasoning and your arguments through a "Devil's Advocate" defense. If it's a personal negotiation, the so-called "Devil's Advocate" can be your friend or spouse, or it can be an associate if it's a business transaction. The important thing is to have someone in your own organization take the role of the opposer.

The job of the Devil's Advocate is to frustrate your plans by doing two things. First, by forcing you to support your own position and second, by making you defend against the other side's difficult arguments – arguments that they are sure to raise in the course of later give and take.

Researchers call this the double defense: supporting your own arguments and rebutting those the opposer will bring up. Experiments in psychology have shown this to be the strongest defense preparation you can bring to the table.

My second suggestion also applies to any negotiation, be it personal or business. Learn to give yourself time to think by using frequent caucuses or time outs. This will permit a continuous review of the bargaining situation. As new developments come to light, you will be in a better position to make a revised plan and to adjust your strategy.

The process of negotiation is one of discovery. Strengths and weaknesses not anticipated beforehand will come to light. The regular use of a Devil's Advocate approach, combined with frequent time outs and better advanced planning, is the best way to anticipate the unanticipated.

NEGOTIATING – A FIVE ACT DRAMA: USING THIS NEW INSIGHT TO YOUR ADVANTAGE

A negotiation is much like a five-act drama. Viewing the give and take process this way provides insights and tools to plan effectively.

When he was Foreign Minister for Israel, Shimon Peres had a similar view of negotiation, but his metaphor was somewhat different. He saw the negotiation process as an airplane flight.

The plane enjoyed a smooth take-off. Before long it encountered severe turbulence as it rose through the dark and choppy clouds. Once above the clouds it proceeded in a smooth flight toward its destination. But to get where it wanted to go, it had to descend once more through the clouds. There the turbulence was worse than ever. Below these wild and treacherous clouds it encountered the normal difficulties of landing, never an easy task.

Peres expected that his meetings with the Palestinians and others would be difficult. By viewing the process in terms of an airplane flight he was better able to remain cool as others wavered when the clouds of disagreement grew dark. In a similar way, understanding negotiation as a five act drama will be useful as you prepare for your voyage through the ups and downs of the bargaining process.

The five acts of the negotiation drama are:

TEN NEGOTIATING DRAMA

ACT ONE
Before the Negotiation Begins

ACT TWO
The Bargaining Talks Begin

ACT THREE
Moving Toward Agreement

ACT FOUR
Hard Bargaining and Power

ACT FIVE
The Closing Stage

Act One – Before the Negotiation Begins

Act One takes place before the conference, sometimes long before. For a buyer of consumer, industrial or high tech goods or services, it starts as early as when the buyer first contemplates the purchase and considers the choices available. For the seller, Act One starts at first contact with the prospective buyer and ends when the parties begin to negotiate. For both buyer and seller, Act One is longer than the few days prior to negotiation which we usually think of as planning and preparation time. Act One in the real world of business may continue for days or, in some cases, for years.

Act One is when the seller can best learn about the buyer's needs and how dependent they are on the seller's service or product. The seller, at this early stage, can determine who in the buyer's business organization favors them, who the real decision-makers are, how the product or service is to be used and where the money to pay for it will really come from. It is far more difficult for a seller to get answers to these questions after talks begin.

Act One is also when the buyer can learn about the salesperson, how they are paid and given bonuses, how they are to be measured as individuals, and how they relate to others in their organization, such as the pricing or engineering departments. At this early stage, buyers can get cost and production information that would be unobtainable at the talks themselves – when both parties are wary of one another. Act One is when buyers can determine how badly the seller needs the business and what they will do to get it. Act One is off the record in most cases.

An alert buyer or seller can use this first act to reduce the tension of negotiation. They can iron out the tough issues before the formal talks begin and use the conference time itself to settle on terms and conditions of a less contentious nature.

It is interesting to note that this is what the Japanese do routinely in dealings between their buyers and sellers. They work so closely together during Act One that the negotiation which follows is, for the most part, ceremonial. Both parties in Japan know how to make Act One an important part of the bargaining process. We in America do not.

Act Two – The Bargaining Talks Begin

Act Two in our five-act drama begins when buyer and seller meet for the first time at the bargaining table. The act opens with pleasant introductions but is soon followed by turbulence and verbal fireworks.

One side or both open with positions that appear harsh or extreme. The large gap between them leads them to think that settlement will be difficult. Lots of smoke and fire are generated as they scramble to justify opening positions. They spend most of their time arguing about the validity of backup claims and numbers, posturing about what they must have, getting involved in peripheral matters and attacking each other's demands as unreasonable or unwarranted.

Act Two is not a pleasant stage in the drama. The clouds are dark and choppy as the participants rise through them. The settlement both parties want appears out of reach. The gap is large and the issues in conflict appear unbreachable. Neither side quite trusts the other. Act Two ends on a grim note.

Act Three – Moving Toward Agreement

Act Three consists of three parts that weave in and out. In this act the parties reconnoiter and narrow the settlement range, discover what each really wants, and jointly search for win-win ideas to make the deal better for both.

During Act Three the parties move away from fighting in the direction of agreement. Having gone above the turbulent clouds of the previous act, they now take real actions to close the gap. It is not easy sailing but far more peaceful than the verbal fireworks of Act Two.

Act Three is when the give and take of productive bargaining takes place. The adversaries become serious. They reconnoiter the settlement range in search of concession and compromise. Retreat from sham positions is slow but measured, and each listens to the other for subtle signs of willingness to give in. Negotiating goals and targets are adjusted as the parties introduce strategies and tactics to alter each other's expectations. Each party tests the resolve of the other on issue after issue. They push and pull, persuade and cajole, give and take, slowly closing the gap that divides them.

All through this act the parties seek to discover what the other really wants and needs, in contrast to what they say or do. They do so by observing and by listening to what is said and what is left unsaid. They test their assumptions and strive to alter the erroneous assumptions of the other side. They assess their power in relation to the other party.

What helps most in building mutual trust during Act Three is when the parties search for and find better, more creative ways to do business together. This is the win-win stage where they discover how to lower costs and improve the range and shape of products or services rendered. Values are added that neither party knew were possible before talks begin. The buyer/seller negotiating pie grows bigger and better.

Act Three ends on a high note. It now appears to both that an acceptable settlement is likely. But to land safely with such an agreement they must once again drop through the treacherous clouds. There are lots of problems ahead before the deal is closed.

Act Four – Hard Bargaining and Power

Now comes the hard bargaining and power stage of negotiation. Each side, prodded by its own organization to make the best deal possible, becomes self-centered. Each must decide how much to give in order to get what it wants. They know that if one gets more, the other will get less. Although the pie has been made larger by finding and applying win-win ideas, it still must be shared by hard bargaining and the application of bargaining power.

In the world of negotiation, power is rarely, if ever, equal. Although both sides have limits, one side is usually stronger than the other. Hard bargaining tactics are often used as the parties exercise their power to get what they feel they must have.
Such tactics are hard to handle for those who face them.

Some negotiators walk out to show strength and test the other's resolve. Others threaten. Some conduct "Reverse Auctions." Many say "Take-it-or-leave-it." Still others "Escalate" – taking back the concessions they made earlier. Needless to say, the hard bargaining stage is difficult to cope with. This is the crisis stage of negotiation: mutual trust diminishes and tempers often flare.

Act Five – The Closing Stage

Hard bargaining ends and the closure stage begins when the parties reconcile themselves to the fact that the deal they have worked so hard to achieve is better than no deal at all or is preferable to starting over again with someone else.

Closure is not easy for two reasons. One, because there are always loose ends that must be pinned down after the main points are agreed to. Second, because the agreement must be put in writing to assure that the parties perform as they said they would. Many a settlement has fallen apart at this point of landing.

When people negotiate, the words they speak are different from those that are written down. When words are written, ambiguities, omissions and different interpretations can be recognized more easily. The same is true when loose ends are settled and put on paper. As they say, the devil is in the details, and that's the Pandora's Box that opens as we pen the final agreement.

And there is one final problem. When an agreement has been submitted for approval, everyone with any interest in the deal has a chance to second guess the negotiator and pick at or improve any flaws they perceive. Lawyers are especially adept at this for reasons both good and bad.

The atmosphere once again becomes grim. The opposing negotiators find themselves in a strange new relationship; they become allies trying to save the hard-reached settlement from falling apart. In most situations, however, a few things are changed and the "improved" agreement is eventually signed. The play ends as the negotiators smile for the camera and celebrate.

Having looked at the negotiation process in a broader time frame, we are now in a position to consider the building blocks of planning in a systematic way.

THE PYRAMID OF PLANNING

Each block of the Pyramid of Planning represents a key step in the planning process. The next time you get into a bargaining situation, turn to the Pyramid and to the Planning Strategy Checklist at the end of this chapter. Between them you will have a step-by-step way of approaching any negotiation, large or small.

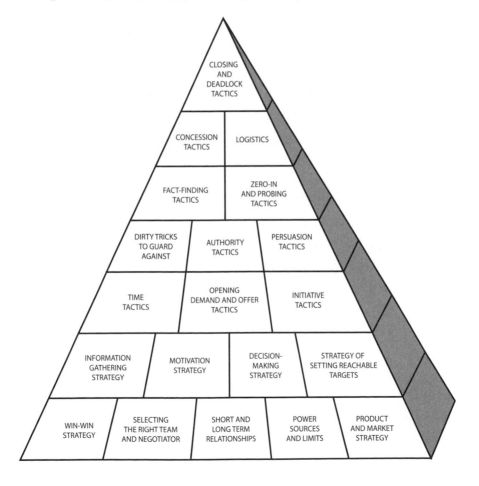

The pyramid is divided into two sections: strategy and tactics. Strategy is at the foundation because it is concerned with long-range goals and values. Strategy is also concerned with putting together the strengths one has to accomplish these goals. Tactics are the approaches, techniques, and other means to achieve the desired goals.

Our first step will be to look at the nine key building blocks of negotiation strategy:

I. Power Sources and Limits

II. Product and Market Strategy

III. Win-Win Strategy

IV. Short- and Long-Term Relationships

V. Setting Reachable Targets

VI. Selecting the Right Team and Negotiator

VII. Motivation Strategy

VIII. Information Gathering Strategy

IX. Decision-Making Strategy

It is well to note that each of these planning blocks applies as much to someone getting ready to buy or sell furniture or a boat as it does to negotiating a billion dollar contract.

For example, a couple buying furniture would try to understand the power they have and the limits on the merchant. They would give thought to what product they want to buy and whether it is to be used for many years or not.

To guarantee a long-term relationship and full satisfaction, they would select a merchant who not only provides a good warranty but will be around if things go wrong. They also need to decide what their opening offer will be and what their target price should be.

Who should negotiate is another important question to the furniture buyer. Should he negotiate, should she, or should they do it together? Also open to consideration is how to motivate the seller to make the sale at a lower price. We know that knowledge is power. How can they gain the information they need about furniture products and prices in order to make a better source selection and carry out a successful settlement? Notice how we have given consideration to many of the strategy blocks in the Pyramid of Planning in this relatively simple furniture transaction.

For those involved in complex negotiations – sales executives, purchasing managers or administrators in the industrial or financial sector – what follows is a series of detailed planning points for each strategy block of the Pyramid. Each point is designed to stimulate the kind of thinking and analysis that is essential to effective planning – the kind of thinking that will result in intelligent long-lasting agreements.

I. POWER SOURCES AND LIMITS STRATEGY

1. What rules or regulations are on our side? Theirs?
2. Are we prepared to work hard on this deal? Are they lazy?
3. What risks are we willing to take? What risks are they worried about?
4. What do we know that gives us strength? What don't they know about our weaknesses?
5. Have we selected the right negotiator and team? Have

they? Any weaknesses? Are we well-coordinated?

6. What are the time deadlines on them? Can the time deadlines on us be relieved?

7. How can we use the past (history, precedents, estimates, guidelines, or relationships) to add to our power base?

8. Have we got the best backup to support our positions?

9. What will happen to us if this negotiation breaks down? To them? What is our next best alternative? What is their next best alternative?

II. HOW DOES THIS NEGOTIATION FIT INTO OUR PRODUCT AND MARKET STRATEGY?

1. What are our near-future product and market needs and plans?

2. What are our far-future product and market needs and plans?

3. How should we go about moving from today's service (or product) and market to tomorrow's?

4. What are our present product and service needs?

5. What do we need to do to satisfy past commitments as we move to the future? How can this negotiation help us?

6. What are our priorities? List them.

7. How can we be sure that we will get what they agree to provide? How will we check? How will we measure both quality and performance?

III. WIN-WIN STRATEGY

1. Can we sell or buy more to get a better price?

2. What else can we buy (or sell) to them?

3. Will a change in specification help?

4. Can delivery be better coordinated with production to reduce costs?

5. Can transportation costs be reduced?

6. Can some parts of the production process be moved from their responsibility to ours?

7. Can payment terms us, them, or both?

8. Can we save on taxes?

9. Can risk be shifted through another contract type (fixed price, cost plus, not to exceed or incentive)?

10. Can inspection and quality costs be reduced for both parties?

11. How can the other party contribute to our sales and market strategy?

12. Should we form a partnership with them to expand joint win-win possibilities?

IV. SHORT AND LONG-TERM RELATIONSHIP STRATEGY

1. Do we want a short, or a long-term relationship? Is a real long-term PARTNERSHIP called for?

2. How will this negotiation affect future negotiations?

3. What can we learn from past negotiations?

4. What advantages have we gained from the past long-term relationship? How can we keep the gains and enhance the benefits?

5. What disadvantages have we suffered because of the past long-term relationship? Can we avoid these disadvantages?

6. Are our long- and short-term goals consistent with our tactics?

7. Should we do anything different in this negotiation?

8. Should we change the negotiator because he or she has gone "native" and now is too cordial to the other side's position?

9. Do we want to pay to create competition? A second source may cost more in the short run but less later.

10. Should we split our requirement between suppliers? Or should we reduce our supplier count to one?

11. How can we prevent being exploited later? How do we avoid being hampered by product or service changes later?

12. How much information (cost and other) should we give them? Why? What information should we get from them?

V. TARGET SETTING STRATEGY

1. What are the issues?

2. What are the "must" issues? The "give" issues? The "straw" issues?

3. What is our position on each issue?

4. What are the pros and cons of each issue?

5. What are our targets for each issue?

6. What are our opening offers for each issue?

7. Are our targets are high enough?

8. Can we trade "must" and "give" issues with them?

9. What is our fallback plan if we must move from our opening position to our target position?

10. What is our guess as to what they will settle for?

11. How can we find out how wrong our above guess is?

12. Why shouldn't we raise our targets on the basis of what they are saying or doing at the table?

13. How can we, in management, help our negotiators to commit to higher targets and to reach them?

VI. SELECTING THE RIGHT TEAM AND NEGOTIATOR

1. Who should negotiate?

2. Who should be on the team, if any? Why?

3. Who should be the official listener and note taker?

4. How many people on each side? What should each person do?

5. Are there any status or knowledge imbalances between negotiators which will intimidate our negotiator?

6. Do our people have the time to do a good job? Do they need more time?

7. Do our people get along well?

8. Is the chemistry between our people and theirs good?

9. What do we know about the opposing negotiators'

character, honesty, work habits, carefulness, knowledge and ability?

10. Every team has to have a leader. Who should be the leader in this situation? Why?

11. Is there enough time for the negotiator or the team to plan well?

VII. MOTIVATION STRATEGY

1. What do we think their organization wants?

2. What do we think their hidden, "under the iceberg" wants are?

3. What is our offer worth to them now? In the long run?

4. If we agree, who among those in the other organization benefits most?

5. If we disagree, who among them loses most?

6. Who pays the final price – the buyer, the buyer's customer, the government or some third party?

7. Who are the end users? Are they locked in? To us? To whom? Why?

8. What risks are they averse to taking?

9. Who makes the profit on the sale? How much?

10. Where is the real profit on the sale? Does it come now? In the long run?

11. Why are we important to them?

12. What cost-risk trade-offs are worth taking?

VIII. INFORMATION GATHERING STRATEGY

1. Write down what we want to know.

2. Where can we best get the information?

3. Who can best get it?

4. Who should act as our intelligence center?

5. Are there any moral or legal problems in getting information?

6. What don't we want them to know?

7. Where are the weak links in our intelligence? What are theirs?

8. Who is responsible for security?

9. What can we learn from past negotiations?

10. How can we help others in future negotiations?

11. How much business are we doing with them now?

12. How well are they performing on their present business?

13. How badly does the buyer need our offer of goods and services?

14. How badly does the seller need the order? Why?

15. What don't we want to talk about at this negotiation? Why?

IX. DECISION-MAKING STRATEGY

1. Who is their decision maker?

2. What is keeping him, her or them from making the decision we want?

3. Who is really in charge of their team? Our team?

4. What are their organizational conflicts? Who disagrees on what they want and why? How about us?

5. What can we do to help the other party's negotiator get

a "yes" answer from his or her organization?

6. How will this decision to agree affect the power structure in their organization? Who rises or falls?

7. How will a decision to deadlock affect their power structure and others in their organization?

8. How will a deadlock affect our organization and our negotiator? Why?

9. How will the decision to agree or deadlock affect decisions and future negotiations between us?

10. What actions (or inaction) can we take that will lead them to decide in our favor?

11. Are the tactics we have decided to use consistent with our long-term objectives?

CONCLUSION

There have been many experiments on planning. They show what we already know – that planning pays off. But they also indicate one thing that is dangerous. Most people do not plan in their personal or business negotiations unless they are forced to.

The cornerstone of good negotiating is strategic planning. None of us can afford the luxury of improvising a plan while we are actually in the session itself. The value of the questions we have raised is that they will force you to think in advance about some of the factors that will determine the outcome of talks. While you will never be able to find answers to all these questions, you will at least know what to probe and listen for as the talks go on.

The role of anyone associated with the person who negotiates is clear. Get involved with the negotiator in the planning process and help him or her do it well. Otherwise, it may not be done at all. It is far better to participate than to criticize the deal later.

In this chapter, we have developed a planning framework to help win favorable agreements. Later, we will have much to say about tactics and how they can make or break any negotiating strategy or plan.

PART II

NEGOTIATING TACTICS AND DEFENSES

VALUE GENERATING AND COMPETITIVE APPROACHES THAT GET RESULTS

11 | Powerful Demand and Offer Tactics

How demands and offers are made throughout the negotiating process can determine how talks will end. In this chapter we will discuss sixteen practical demand and offer tactics. Each has the power to change the outcome in your favor and, in many cases, also leave the other party more satisfied with the final agreement.

1. "GIVE ME YOUR BEST AND FINAL OFFER."

2. STRAW ISSUES – FILLING THE POT.

3. THE BOGEY APPROACH – A WIN-WIN TACTIC.

4. ALWAYS ASK "HOW MUCH" OR YOU'LL GET TAKEN.

5. TAKE IT OR LEAVE IT AS AN OPENING DEMAND.

6. THE REVERSE AUCTION – A VERY TOUGH TACTIC.

7. FROM THE ITALIANS – LEARN TO FLINCH.

8. THE IMPORTANT DIFFERENCE BETWEEN NEEDS AND WANTS.

9. THE PLANNING PURPOSE TRAP.

10 THE SALAMI SLICE APPROACH.

11. THE KRUNCH.

12. GIVE IT AWAY ON PAGES 1,2, 3 – TAKE IT BACK ON PAGES 4, 5, 6.

13. ESCALATION – A TOUGH OPENING AND MID-NEGOTIATION TACTIC.

14. "WHAT IF" – A GOOD PROBING TACTIC.

15. EVERYBODY LOVES A BARGAIN – HOW TO RAISE THE OTHER PARTY'S SATISFACTION LEVEL.

16. NEGOTIATING WITH A FRIEND OR RELATIVE – THREE WAYS TO APPROACH THE PROBLEM.

You have probably encountered many of these tactics and approaches before. They've been around for centuries. The better you understand what they are, why they work and what to do when they are used against you, the more effective you will be.

"GIVE ME YOUR BEST AND FINAL OFFER" – THE SHORTCUT APPROACH

There are buyers who use a shortcut approach to negotiation. They open talks with what would appear to most of us a naive question: "What's the least you'll take?" Sometimes they say the same thing in a different way: "Listen, I don't like to negotiate.

Just give me your best and final offer." They often get a better answer than they deserve.

Many sellers, anxious to close the sale come right down to the bottom line. This happens especially when the seller feels pressured by intense competition to win the order. The trouble with this approach is that the bottom line price rarely closes the deal. Usually the seller's offer just starts the negotiation at a lower price level. The buyer, having elicited the so called "best price" so easily, is wise to assume there are further concessions possible.

Why does a simple statement by the buyer such as "I haven't got time to negotiate. Just give me your best and final offer" work so well? Part of its success lies in the seller's natural desire to avoid the aggravation of negotiation and to close the sale quickly. They may also fear that by not responding they will be eliminated from further consideration.

The next time a buyer starts the negotiation by saying, "What's the least you'll take?" don't make the mistake of revealing your true bottom line. Recognize that the buyer is likely to negotiate for further concessions no matter what you say. The best defense is to respond by telling the buyer again and again what good values you are offering. Then, if you feel that a concession must be made, drop your price a bit, leaving room for the bargaining that will soon follow.

STRAW ISSUES – FILLING THE POT

In most negotiations, it's wise to give yourself room to make concessions if you have to. Straw issues are demands made specifically for the purpose of trading them away later to win something of greater importance. Straw issues have exchange value, but they are not crucial to the overall deal the negotiator seeks to close. They are demands that can be easily sacrificed.

Of course, the other party can rarely be certain that the straw issue demand is of less importance than others on the table. Like every other demand a negotiator makes, it creates a degree of difficulty for the other party. It becomes one more impediment that must be resolved before reaching settlement.

When surrendered during the course of negotiations, straw issues provide satisfaction to the other party in two ways. First, they give them something of value, a victory of sorts, to take home to their organization. Second, it provides satisfaction because just getting rid of the straw issue reduces the number of difficulties to agreement by one and therefore serves to bring settlement closer.

Union negotiators know from experience that the more they ask for the more they get. Even when times are bad, unions start by asking for extras they don't expect to win. They ask for improved pension and health benefits, special safety provisions, shorter work weeks, added holidays and easier work rules. These set the stage for a tough negotiation. History shows that most straw issues quietly fade away during the bargaining. They are traded for more important demands related to job security and wages.

When a buyer is dealing with a seller, it is usually wise to ask for things even when you don't need them. Asking for benefits like ninety days to pay, a higher credit limit, a low minimum order quantity, return privileges, special warranties or tighter specifications than required can be used for trading purposes. At best, you may be lucky enough to win some of these straw demands. If not, the seller will feel he or she has won something when you drop the demands.

From the seller's viewpoint, it's well to recognize that smart buyers create straw issues for four reasons: (1) to reduce the seller's level of expectation, (2) to assure others in their own organization that they are hard bargainers, (3) to provide room to negotiate and (4) to make it easier for the salesperson to explain why a lower price was accepted. When the salesperson tells management that he or she persuaded the buyer to remove some demands, everybody breathes a sigh of relief. It could have been worse.

Experienced salespeople know that buyers do not expect to get all they ask for. They know that with patience and persistence many straw issues disappear. Some vanish when buyer and seller talk frankly off the record. Some straw demands are dropped during sweeping trades of unrelated issues. Others disappear when the seller firmly declares that the buyer's demand is simply not acceptable or has never been granted to anyone before.

In their dealings with Western businessmen, the Chinese are not afraid to raise a large number of straw issues early in the talks. Then, in trying to win valued concessions later, they declare, "Why don't you be reasonable. We'll drop these four demands if you give us this one instead." The trouble for Westerners is that it's hard to determine whether the four issues they wish to surrender are merely a mask for the one they really value. There is nothing unethical about this Chinese approach to straw issues. It is a universal and time-tested negotiating approach.

THE BOGEY APPROACH – A WIN-WIN TACTIC

The Bogey ("This is all I've got") is a powerful tactic for getting more for your money. The beauty of it is that it is also one of the best both-win strategies a negotiator can employ. Most of us have used the Bogey, or had it used on us, without recognizing how and why it gets results.

Whether you buy or sell, the Bogey can help you make better agreements. You will see that the idea can be put to work in a wide variety of negotiating situations. Whether you are negotiating for a $300,000 house or investing in a sophisticated multimillion-dollar business computer system or buying a $20 toy for a child, the Bogey can save you money – lots of money where the stakes are high.

Imagine for a moment that a family decides to install rooftop solar panels. The wife solicits three competitive bids and selects for further consideration the one with the best package and track record. The solar panel installer submits a bid with a five-page specification and work statement at a proposed price of $41,000.

The trouble is that the family doesn't have enough money. They do have a $45,000 loan commitment from the bank to complete the entire project. But the solar panel bid of $41,000 does not include the purchase and installation of such essential items as the grid tie-in system, minor roof upgrades, and removal of light-blocking trees.

These are estimated at $10,000, making a total of $51,000 on the entire project. This leaves the family $6,000 short. What can she do to close the gap between the $51,000 she needs and the $45,000 loan commitment she already has?

My advice is that she build credibility with the seller by showing the solar panel salesperson the $45,000 commitment from the bank and then ask them what to do. By making the Bogey of $45,000 credible the buyer has said, "I want to do business with you, but this is all I've got. Please help me."

The solar panel installer will be pleased and frustrated at the same time. Pleased because they found a real buyer with money who wants to do business. Frustrated because the customer is $6,000 short.

For the salesperson, this is a common problem. They have helped others overcome such handicaps. Like most people who sell, the solar panel salesman knows more about his product than the buyer. He or she is in an excellent position to put their knowledge to work in solving the customer's dilemma and closing the deal at a nice profit.

The wife soon learns that many savings and alternatives are possible. She discovers that changes to the proposed electrical grid tie-in system can be made; that she can have her brother-in-law, an electrician, do the electrical work under the builder's direction; that the seller has connections with subcontractors who will do roof work and walks at a builder's discount and that the seller knows a place where smaller trees that don't block the panels can be bought at wholesale. These win-win suggestions help reduce the cost of extras from $10,000 to $6,000. This still leaves the bid of $41,000 for the installation of solar panels plus the $6,000 extras ($47,000) is $2,000 greater than the $45,000 loan commitment.

To close the $2,000 gap the seller does two things. He reduces the price by $500 (from $41,000 to $40,500) and accepts a $1,500 note from the buyer. And, closes the deal by throwing in a "delight factor," a handsome panel mounting salvaged from an earlier contract for only $50 extra.

The solar panel buyer in our example gained by saying, "This is all I've got." She learned more about solar panels than she knew before. She also avoided a financial squeeze, learned how to get things done at a lower price and purchased a better panel system and landscaping for less money. The salesman gained by finding win-win opportunities that benefited both sides and closing a difficult sale profitably.

Claiming "This is all I've got" does not always lead to a lower price. But in most situations it gives the buyer more information and a greater range of choices. These benefits may well prove to be more important than a lower price.

From the seller's viewpoint, lots of countermeasures can be taken to offset the buyer's Bogey. The salesperson can test the buyer's budget. Most budgets are flexible if both short and long-term options are explained. Or the solar panel installer can offer as an alternative a less expensive design or a lower priced but usable equipment package. These alternatives may help the seller in two ways. They serve to reduce the price and at the same time provide a higher profit margin than the original proposal. An alert seller can turn the buyer's Bogey into a seller's opportunity.

Or the seller may decide to test the buyer's $45,000 Bogey. He or she may stall for time before offering alternatives. In so doing, they may discover that the buyer has already decided to go ahead with their company and made other arrangements to get the additional money needed. The seller may also discover that the buyer has already decided to postpone the landscaping until next year when the family will have more money and do it themselves.

For buyer and seller, the Bogey is a legitimate approach to bridging the gap between what the buyer needs and the financial resources available. I like the Bogey approach because it brings out the knowledge and creativity of the seller in solving the buyer's problem. Whenever a buyer says, "Please help me!" he or she opens the possibility that both sides will benefit.

ALWAYS ASK "HOW MUCH" OR YOU'LL GET TAKEN

A generation of Americans were in France during the Second World War. Most knew little French but soon learned one word, *"combien"* – which means "how much." Of necessity, it became part of every soldier's vocabulary.

This word was essential in dealing with the French. Anyone who forgot to say *"combien"* paid dearly for that oversight. Americans who would not have dreamed of doing business in France without asking "how much" are, all too often, embarrassed to do so when purchasing services and products in this country.

There are reasons why people are reluctant to ask "how much?" Some are afraid that by asking, they will elicit a higher price than by not asking. Others wish to avoid the hassle that comes from negotiating if the price quoted is not suitable. Still others fail to get a front-end price because they do not wish to embarrass the other person by implying that he or she is not fair or trustworthy. None of these reasons make good business sense. Instead of clarifying the matter of price, those who fail to ask "How much?" leave themselves vulnerable to exploitation.

One of the surest ways to lose a good supplier is by being too timid to ask what a job will cost and what is included. This occurs principally when we deal with those who have provided satisfactory services in the past. For example, suppose that you have obtained a low bid of $1500 for painting three bedrooms. The next higher bids were $1800 and $2100. Soon after the low bidder starts painting, you decide to add a small closet to the job. Because the original price was reasonable, you are reluctant to ask how much the painter will charge for this relatively small increase in scope of work. You're in trouble.

When the work is done, don't be surprised to learn that the painter wants $500 extra for the small closet – a disproportionately high price compared to the $500 per bedroom original quote. You have trapped yourself into a "fait accompli." Now that the work is done, your options are to pay the bill or alienate a good painter by trying to negotiate retroactively. Had you asked "how much?" before the closet was painted, you might have been quoted a lower price. And even if the quote was $500, you would have been able to negotiate to a reasonable figure.

You are probably wondering: "Who would do a foolish thing like that – not ask for a price before the work starts?" My experience indicates that most of us have been guilty of this failure and lived to regret it. We hoped for the best and paid a premium when the bill came in.

The rule is simple. No matter how tempted you are to gloss over the question of price before buying, don't do it. Always request a price or a not-to-exceed limit whether you've done business with the other party for a long time or only since yesterday. It's the only way to avoid unpleasant surprises and to maintain good relations. The same rule applies to your dealings with doctors, dentists, lawyers and consultants of any kind. Ask "How much?" before telling them to go ahead.

By the way, a good way to practice asking "How much?" is in a restaurant. The next time a waiter tells your party of six about today's specials, ask the waiter how much one or two of the specials costs. If you can do this in front of your friends you'll be able to do it more easily when the stakes are far higher.

"TAKE IT OR LEAVE IT" AS AN OPENING DEMAND

"Take it or leave it" is a tough tactic. Many years ago, I saw it used to dramatic effect on two landscape architects who were dealing with a wealthy developer. That memory is still vivid.

The young architects were at the beginning of their careers. The developer offered them an opportunity to landscape a large office complex. It was their big chance. They designed an impressive set of plans and prepared what they believed to be a tight $200,000 proposal.

The developer invited them into his office to discuss the job. They brought along a large roll of drawings and were prepared to prove that they were offering a fine design at a relatively low price. To their surprise, the developer gave them no opportunity to discuss the plans. Instead, he put the pile of drawings on his desk, glanced at them for several minutes without a word, and then shoved them brusquely aside like a bundle of wastepaper. Then he asked bluntly: "How much?" They avoided answering right away and tried instead to draw his attention back to the plans. The developer merely repeated the question: "How much?" One of the men, unable to live with ambiguity, blurted out almost apologetically, "$200,000, sir, but look at what you are getting for the money."

The developer replied without hesitation, "Too much, I'll give you $100,000. Take it or leave it." As he said this he picked up the drawings and threw them helter skelter into a corner of the office. The landscapers were thunderstruck. They implored him to look at the sketches, but he would not discuss things further. He just told them to make up their minds within a week. The sketches remained on the floor as the young men were escorted out the door.

The architects spent the next week in anguish. They wrestled with the problem, reviewed the drawings, recomputed the bid, made a few small changes and then telephoned in an apologetic voice a bare-bone price of $150,000. The answer came quickly. A firm, "Too much! $100,000, take it or leave it."

What made it worse was that they sensed that the developer had not yet looked at the sketches. They were forced to assume that a strong creative design was apparently not a major motivating factor in the developer's mind. A few days later the unhappy architects capitulated by offering their services for bare-boned $110,000 provided that a few face-saving modifications were made. Only then did the developer review the plans with them and agree to the price.

The men executed the design to perfection. They even realized a tiny profit by working seven days a week. Long afterward they learned that the developer had recognized their talents from the beginning. In fact, he had praised their original plans to other executives. Had they called his bluff, he would probably have paid the full $200,000.

The developer achieved his objective but took a risk in handling the architects the way he did. He might have achieved the same result with less hostility by stating his position and by being willing to talk as long as the architects wished. Also, I believe he should not have used the phrase, "Take it or leave it." These words only inflame people. In this case they served to make the architects unnecessarily angry. Had he dealt with them without an openly hostile "take it or leave it" the negotiation might have taken longer and the price been slightly higher, but everyone would have been more satisfied with the outcome.

The two young men are now the busiest landscape architects in Southern California. They have the power to pick and choose their clients. They still work with their first client, but he pays more than other developers though he doesn't know it. People who feel that they have been used unfairly renegotiate when and if they can. In a sense, the landscapers are still renegotiating that original deal.

"Take it or leave it" is a powerful tactic that can win a good agreement for either the buyer or seller using it. The trouble with this approach is that it risks alienating the other party. The tactic also suffers one other major failing. It cuts off potential both-win possibilities. The better deal for both parties can rarely if ever be found with "Take it or leave it."

THE REVERSE AUCTION – A VERY TOUGH TACTIC

The reverse auction is one of the toughest tactics in a buyer's arsenal. It is used more often by European and Asian buyers than Americans. There is nothing unethical about the reverse auction. Whether you sell or buy, you will benefit by knowing how it works and what to do when it is used against you.

The buyer's aim in using the reverse auction is to get competing sellers to outbid each other in offering the best and most for the least amount of money. The reverse auction also permits the buyer to learn more about what he or she is purchasing and the options and risks involved.

We will illustrate the reverse auction in three purchasing situations: one quite simple, the next a little more complicated and the third fairly complex.

A simple example of a reverse auction is a friend of mine who was shopping for a new hybrid automobile. The first thing he did was to explore with two different dealers what the automobile could be bought for without much negotiation. He learned that it would not be hard to buy the hybrid he wanted, including specific accessories, for $54,000 - $8,000 under the $62,000 sticker price.

That's when he decided to carry out a reverse auction over the phone. He contacted dealers in Southern California. He called the first and told them that he was ready to buy if the dealer had the model, accessories and color he wanted. "What's your price?" he asked. "I can get it for $54,000." The dealer offered to sell for $53,000.

My friend called the second dealer, a woman, fifty miles from Los Angeles. She offered to sell for $52,000 after being told he had a $53,000 offer. Each of the four subsequent calls brought a reduction in price from $52,000 to $48,000 in about $1000 increments. At that point he decided to make two more calls. The next call did not result in a drop below $48,000. Neither did the next.

My friend bought the car for $48,000 without further negotiation.

When I asked why he hadn't called at least one more agency or negotiated further with the $48,000 bidder he told me that he was tired of the whole thing and wanted to get it over with. Having brought the price down from $54,000 to $48,000 he was satisfied with the reverse auction and its results.

Here is a second, more complicated, example of the reverse auction: A mail order executive has three printing companies bid on an order of one million high quality catalogs, each containing 50 pages. All bids are close together at $1.00, $1.03 and $1.04 each.

The buying executive invites the three suppliers to his office. Their appointments are scheduled fifteen minutes apart. He positions them in three separate offices adjoining the conference room. Each bidder knows the others are there because they have signed the visitors register and can see their competitors' names. The buyer tells each bidder that one will emerge with the big order today.

If you were the seller, would you stand for this? A few might not, but with the stakes so high, most would.

Soon the auction starts. With the best price at $1.00 each, the buyer tries to get one of the competitors to take 99 cents. When one seller offers 99 cents the buying executive moves to the next room to get a lower 98 cent offer. No funny money here. Each penny is worth $10,000 in real savings to the buyer and $10,000 less profit to the seller. The price moves down relentlessly. Each of the three sellers feels the pressure.

The buyer then moves to the issue of paper quality. One vendor offered a fifty-pound paper in the original proposal. He or she is induced to offer a heavier, glossier sixty-pound paper for the same price. The paper quality goes up even as the seller's prices move down.

One seller gives a discount of 1 percent for 10-day payment, another under pressure offers 2 percent for 10-day payment. Then the buyer asks for 45 or 90 days and a 2 or 3 percent discount for "prompt" payment in 30 days. Each seller's fear of losing the order drives him or her to offer better payment terms. And so the reverse auction goes. Each seller offers more and more for less and less money.

Before the auction is over, the winning seller walks away from the table having given the buyer the lowest price, the best quality paper, the fastest delivery date and the most liberal credit terms. Here is a third and more complex version of the reverse auction: A buyer uses the tactic not only to win the best package from competing sellers but to learn more about what he or she is purchasing.

Let's assume you're going to install a high performance heating and air conditioning unit in your home. You don't know much about the technicalities of heating or air conditioning installations, but you want to purchase a good system at the best price.

Three contractors bid. After studying the proposals you find that they are quite different. They offer different heaters, air conditioning units, duct systems, financial terms and delivery schedules. The choice becomes complicated. The system costs $20,000. If you make a mistake you will have to live with it for years. What can you do to make the right decision?

Start a reverse auction. Call the bidders and invite them to your home at various times of the day. Let them know that others are very interested in doing the job. Talk to them one at a time.

Seller #1 will tell you what's included in his or her offer and why it is best. They will also tell you things that will make you worry about the other sellers. You might learn that Seller #2 is using an inferior heater and that their ducts are not properly installed. You may also learn that there is a rumor afloat that Seller #3 is going bankrupt.

When you speak to Seller #3 later, he tells you that the others use inferior air conditioning systems which are now obsolete. Repair parts will be hard to get. Pretty soon you begin to learn things about air and heating systems you never dreamed of. You are better able to weigh and trade off the costs and risks associated with each choice.

In addition to this important gain in technical information, the buyer also applies pressure on each vendor to provide better equipment and well-insulated ducting. Before the reverse auction ends, the purchaser is likely to get a better system, lower price, an acceptable delivery date and favorable credit terms. Not bad for a day's work.

Some individuals and companies believe that the reverse auction is unethical. Others believe it to be unfair and therefore avoid it by policy. I do not believe it to be unethical or unfair. It is dangerous however. It has the potential to cause the buyer more problems than it's worth. An angry seller or one pushed to the wall will take advantage of changes or take shortcuts in labor or materials.

What can a seller do when confronted by a reverse auction? These actions help overcome some of the buyer's advantages:

1. Try to put yourself into a sole-source, noncompetitive position. You can do so by offering a both-win alternative which your competition is unable to offer.

2. Know who makes the buyer's decision. Try to determine where you stand with the decision maker. You may be in a better position than you think. The customer may already believe that you are the best supplier.

3. Make sure you have a well-thought-out bottom-line price. It will keep you from going down too far.

4. Use your best negotiator and field your best team.

5. Help the buyer make a better decision. The more help you give the more he or she will feel obligated to help you.

6. Bring along experts who make your assertions more credible.

7. Study your weaknesses. The other sellers are certain to bring them up. Know what you will say and do to overcome these negatives. Dry-run your defense before the negotiation. Use a Devil's Advocate to plead the case against you.

8. Customize and sell your strengths and benefits in terms of the buyer's specific needs.

9. Have some both-win suggestions available to keep the talks moving in your favor.

10. Recognize that the buyer is getting tired of the reverse

auction. He or she wants to get it over with and go on to something else.

11. Tell a story about a reverse auction that fell apart and got the buyer in trouble.

The Reverse Auction is one of the toughest hard bargaining tactics a seller will ever face. The eleven countermeasures suggested above will serve to relieve some of the intense pressure generated by this one-win "buyer take all" approach.

FROM THE ITALIANS – LEARN TO FLINCH

I never go shopping for anything expensive with Bill, my brother-in-law. He doesn't know how to flinch. I do like to shop with George, my Italian cousin. It was he who taught me to flinch like an Italian-with lots of emotion, gestures and arm-waving.

Italians are master bargainers. As early as the fifteenth century, the merchants and financiers of Venice were dealing on a worldwide stage. They did business with Marco Polo in the Far East, with Arabs and Persians in the Middle East, with Egyptians and Moors in North Africa and with the Spaniards and Greeks on the Mediterranean. Those who did business with the Venetians found them worthy negotiators.

The other day I bought a painting directly from a fledgling artist showing her work at the Laguna Arts Festival in California. George was with me and enjoyed negotiating with the painter on my behalf.

The conversation with the artist went like this. George asked her how much she wanted for the painting. "Fourteen hundred dollars," she said. "Wow" said George as he shook his head vigorously in apparent disbelief. To emphasize his surprise George gestured with his arms, shrugged his shoulders and brought his hands to his forehead. The artist soon began to explain why $1,400 was a really good price.

She provided the names of prominent people in the movie business who owned her work and proved to him that the same picture purchased through a gallery would cost at least 50 percent more. She showed him several favorable reviews she had received from prominent art critics.

It was almost five in the afternoon on Sunday. Other artists were closing for the day. George insisted he could not pay more than $800 for the painting. Cash. She countered with $1,100. George flinched again but offered $880. A deal was struck at $900.

Suppose George had not flinched as the negotiated price fell in stages from $1,400 to $900. The artist might have held firm at a higher figure, or having reluctantly agreed to $900 might have insisted that the price did not include $75 for the picture frame. Had he still not flinched she might have tried to add $25 for delivery and $20 for wrapping. Flinching served to lower her expectations. It kept her price down and discouraged her from asking for extras.

A good flinch may not guarantee a lower price, but it always provides the information you need to make a better decision. This is because the other party feels that they must relieve your obvious concern about the price by explaining why it is reasonable.

The reason I never shop with Bill is that, instead of flinching when the artist asks $1,400, Bill has the habit of saying, "My, all that work for $1,400." And then I end up paying extra for the frame, the delivery, the wrapping paper and sales tax on top of the full $1,400 price.

THE IMPORTANT DIFFERENCE BETWEEN NEEDS AND WANTS: A GUIDE TO ACTION

I once had dinner with a most unusual woman. Her name was Charlene, the world's most famous marriage broker. Charlene was a wise lady who knew a lot about life, love and negotiating. She taught me the difference between wants and needs.

When single men and women came to her seeking help in finding a marriage partner, she asked them what they wanted. All of them specified a long list of personality and character traits as well as social and sporting interests which they wanted in their prospective spouse.

When I asked Charlene if she met their specifications, she responded by saying, "My job as a marriage broker is to listen to what they want and then discover what they need. When I give them what they need, they forget about what they want."

I thought about it. Was Charlene being cynical? I don't think so. What she was doing was what we try to do when we negotiate.

In any fairly complex transaction, both parties start with all kinds of demands they would like to have met. Some are needs and some are wants. Needs, according to one of Webster's definitions, are an urgent requirement for something essential that is lacking, something that is indispensable to a particular end or goal. Charlene explained that few of her clients' list of wants were indispensable, most were just nice to have. It's much the same in negotiation, where our job is to discover what the other side says they want and what they really need.

If we can give the other party what they need, they will forget about many of the wants or demands they asked for at the beginning of negotiation. That's when both sides move toward agreement.

The negotiator who understands the subtle difference between needs and wants knows what to listen for at every stage of the bargaining process. He or she moves the parties toward an intersection of their mutual interests – an agreement that best suits their needs, not their wants.

THE PLANNING PURPOSE TRAP: "JUST GIVE ME A ROUGH IDEA OF WHAT IT WILL COST"

Often the salesperson traps him/herself into agreements that favor the buyer. All the buyer has to do is say little and enjoy the experience. Let me explain.

A friend of mine sells computer services to local businesses. He offers them consulting, programming, design and maintenance services. He has learned at great cost to himself that whenever a potential buyer says, "Give me a rough estimate of what it will cost me," he must be careful in answering or will later suffer the consequences.

The planning purpose trap works like this. A buyer tells the seller that, for planning purposes, he or she needs a rough idea of what some service or product required in the future will cost, emphasizing that the estimate need not be exact. The seller is encouraged to make a quick estimate because he or she will not be held to it. The buyer's words go something like this: "Just give me a ball-park idea of what it will cost. Don't worry, we won't hold you to it but we must have some idea of what we are getting into."

The salesperson, eager to be helpful, falls into the trap. Instead of being careful with the quote, he/she or the pricing department makes a quick estimate, generally on the low side – an estimate the seller feels the buyer wants to hear. The seller's planning purpose estimate is usually low enough not to frighten the customer into seeking additional bids from competitors.

For example, let's assume that the buyer has urged the seller, an accounting firm, to provide a planning purpose estimate for performing an audit for the year. The seller, anxious to win the contract, takes a quick look at the client's books and decides that a planning purpose estimate of $100,000 is appropriate. A month later the buyer, ready to place the order, asks for a formal quotation. At that point the accounting firm digs more deeply into the client's books and decides that it must bid $125,000 for the audit. That's when they realize they have trapped themselves.

The buyer responds to the seller's now accurate bid by protesting that the original $100,000 estimate has already been presented to management. The $100,000 expenditure was duly approved and is now fixed in the company annual budget. No change can be made in the budget without approval from the Board of Directors, and they only meet twice a year.

It is obvious that the seller's subsequent protests about the tentativeness of the original estimate will fall on deaf or hostile ears. The buyer tells the seller that the change from $100,000 to $125,000 has not only made things difficult for the company but has made him or her look bad personally. That's when the seller usually modifies the price downward to close the sale.

How can a seller avoid the planning purpose trap and, in fact, make an opportunity of it? The salesperson should approach the buyer's request for a "so called" nonbinding planning estimate this way:

1. Recognize that a "planning purpose estimate" is likely to be more binding than it looks.

2   Use the buyer's request for the estimate as a good excuse to better understand the work to be done and what problems are likely to be encountered.

3. Find out who the decision makers are and who has primary responsibility for seeing that the job is done correctly. Get to know these people before you make the estimate.

4. Don't just deliver the planning purpose estimate in person. Put it in writing and be sure to qualify it as much as possible. Don't make it easy for the buyer to say, "You said this or that and now you have to live with it."

5. Generally make your estimate on the high side. This helps to fix a higher price in the buyer's mind, and you can gain other concessions for lowering your price during the formal bidding. Whether your ball-park estimate should be as large as Yankee Stadium or as small as Fenway Park is a matter of business judgment. Lean toward Yankee Stadium.

6. Help the customer write their formal solicitation for quotation. The buyer's request for a quick planning estimate may allow you to communicate with those people in the buyer's organization most responsible for writing the final specification. I've seen many an order given to the seller who helped write the buyer's specification around the seller's product.

The next time you hear a buyer say, "Just give me a rough planning estimate. I won't hold you to it," watch out. Everything you say may be held against you. You may be in for a lot of price pinching later when the real negotiation begins.

THE SALAMI SLICE APPROACH

I like salami, especially the hard Italian variety that comes in a roll. When I buy it, my plan is to have it around for a week. I promise myself I'll cut a slice or two as a treat from time to time. The trouble is that it never happens that way. What happens is that I cut myself a slice as soon as I get home from the store. Then another little slice and then another. Before the day passes there is no more salami.

That's the way the Salami Tactic works in negotiation. A friend of mine is a big contractor. His negotiations are complex with lots of issues in contention. He would like to win them all at one time if he could, but the opposing negotiator rarely lets that happen. They don't concede the whole salami in one piece.

What my friend has learned is that most people in negotiation don't mind giving small concessions, a slice of this issue and a slice of that issue. They don't mind being flexible to keep the talks moving along. So what he does is try to get the whole salami, or most of it, slice by slice. A little here, a little there. With persistence he is able to win a nice chunk of the salami.

As a large contractor he deals with many subcontractors for such services as framing, plumbing and electrical work. In addition to obtaining at least three or four bids on every contract, he demands cost breakdowns from each bidder. Because competition is fierce, he usually gets good bids and detailed cost breakdowns. After the prices arrive, my friend negotiates with the low bidder for a still lower price using the salami approach.

In the following illustration, the bidder has come in very low at $581,900. The contractor, happy with the bid, has decided to use the salami technique to win further concessions. He is trying to get a mere 2 percent slice of salami on every element of cost.

SUBCONTRACTOR'S PRICE BEFORE THE SALAMI SLICES		SUBCONTRACTOR'S PRICE AFTER THE 2% SALAMI SLICES	
Labor, 10,000 hours		Labor, 9,800 hours	
at $20/hr	$200,000	at $19.60/hr	$192,000
Overhead 100%	200,000	Overhead 98%	188,238
Material	50,000	Material	49,000
Consulting	10,000	Consulting	9,800
Subtotal	$460,000	Subtotal	$439,118
Administration at 15%	69,000	Administration at 14.7%	64,550
Subtotal	$529,000	Subtotal	$503,668
Profit at 10%	52,900	Profit at 9.8%	49,360
Total	$581,000	Total	$553,028

The contractor has taken little salami slices of 2 percent from each of the subcontractor's cost elements: estimated labor hours, labor rate, material cost, consulting cost, administration and profit. Each slice in itself is quite small in contrast to the seller's bid of $581,900. But the small slices add up to a $28,872 saving, almost 5 percent. $28,872 buys a lot of salami.

THE KRUNCH

A buyer solicits three bids on a printing job. The three sellers are unaware that the prices bid are $5,000, $5,400, and $5,700 respectively. Anxious to bring the price below $5,000, the buyer tries an old negotiating tactic. He calls them individually and says, "You've got to do better than that." The odds are all three will come down, including the low bidder. Why?

Three factors contribute to making the Krunch effective. The first is that salespeople are sensitive to competition. They lose more jobs than they win and rarely learn exactly why. They perceive an invitation to "do better" as a "last ditch" opportunity to stay in the running by reducing the price.

The second point favoring the buyer rests on the fact that the typical salesperson tends to resent the price he or she is forced to offer the customer. Most are convinced that management sets prices too high and thereby makes their lives difficult. The third factor is the salesperson's discretionary authority. Salespeople usually have some freedom to lower the price in response to competitive pressure. These factors combine to make the Krunch so popular with buyers and difficult for sellers to resist.

Like all tactics, the Krunch has serious drawbacks. Lazy or immature buyers use this approach as a substitute for good buying practice. Professional buyers who resort to the Krunch as a regular practice come out poorly. Salespeople resent the approach and defend themselves. Once a buyer is identified as a Krunch user, sellers raise their bids to leave room to come down. Also, if pushed too far, they resist by skimping on quality, count or delivery. My advice to the buyer is that the Krunch be used primarily when it is essential – as when not winning a reduction in price will result in a significant loss to the buyer. It should not be used in a routine, day-to-day manner.

What should you do when you hear, "You've got to do better than that"? Don't panic. You may be in better shape than you think.

1. Don't drop your price until the buyer tells you specifically why you should. Ask the buyer in what specific way you must do better and why. Whenever you are faced with a general objection by the other party, make them be specific.

2. Don't drop your price quickly. Keep selling your added values and benefits.

3. Never assume that the final buying decision will be based on price alone. It rarely is. Product, service, terms, delivery, and quality are major decision criteria.
4. Ask for something in return when you make a concession.

5. Calibrate the buyer based on their history of negotiating. Do they back down if you don't? Many buyers ask for a lot and are willing to settle for far less.

Finally, there is another precaution that can easily be taken. The next time you are invited to the buyer's office to discuss a bid, ask yourself in advance, "What will I do if the buyer says, 'You've got to do better than that'?" A bit of forethought can help make an opportunity out of the Krunch instead of a problem. You will be better able to accentuate the positive aspects of your proposal rather than cave in to the buyer's generalized "do better" demand. With forethought you may be able to do better by getting the buyer to increase the order size or by finding other creative win-win ways to make a better deal for both parties.

The Krunch is a tough tactic to cope with, especially for less experienced salespeople. I am reminded of a negotiation in the garment business involving the Krunch. The garment business is very competitive. Manufacturers will give almost any discount to win a large order. Garment buyers use the Krunch to win additional discounts on prices that are already quite low.

A young saleswoman under severe price pressure called her boss. "Mr. Johnson," she said, "The buyer just told me that we have to do better than that. It's a $300,000 order and our price is already heavily discounted. How much would you take off?"

Mr. Johnson's answer came quickly, "Everything but my socks."

That's the way the Krunch works for the buyer most of the time.

GIVE IT AWAY ON PAGES 1, 2,3 – TAKE IT BACK ON PAGES 4, 5, 6

Movie people have a reputation for being tough negotiators. No tougher, however, than the Oklahoma farmer once encountered by an oilman from Phillips Petroleum. They were negotiating an oil lease and this is how it went.

The old farmer began the talks cordially. Early in the bargaining, he granted the oilman point after point. The oilman wondered if the old man had all his wits about him. When they recessed for the night, it looked like clear sailing down to the last line. Elated, he called his boss to tell him that all was going well.

The next morning they met again to iron out several still outstanding issues of moderate importance. It was then that the farmer really began to negotiate. What he had given away on pages 1, 2, 3 of the contract, he took back with interest on pages 4, 5, 6.

Three things conspired to put the oilman on the defensive. The first was that he found it difficult to say "no" to the farmer after having won such easy concessions the day before. The second was the farmer's persistence. The old man insisted like a broken record that he would never have made the earlier concessions if he had any doubt that his later demands would not be granted. The third problem facing the oilman was that he had locked himself into making the deal when he told his manager at headquarters that the agreement was all but settled. In the end, the farmer won a very good contract by giving things away on pages 1,2,3 and taking them back on pages 4,5,6.

The tactic is used much the same way in the movie business. I know of a promising young actor who was solicited by the studio for a good part in a film. He is told that the big budget movie will propel him to stardom. The producer invites the actor and his agent to his lavish studio office to settle on contract terms.

The talks open with the producer granting most of the actor's major demands. He agrees to pay the actor $2 million for twelve weeks work on the film. One million in advance and one million after filming is complete. Having never earned one-tenth that much, the actor is delighted. All that remains to launch his great career is writing the contract. This the studio promises to do as soon as possible.

For two or three weeks the actor is in a state of euphoria. Variety leaks a story of the pending agreement. He is interviewed by a famous movie columnist. His friends, his banker, his agent and even the maitre d' at the fancy French restaurant treat him with deference. For him, this is the ultimate ego trip – the American Dream come true.

A month later, still without a word from the studio, the actor becomes apprehensive. His agent assures him that such delays are normal considering all the approvals required. Convinced that there is no need to worry, the actor continues to enjoy the limelight and begins to search for a modest house in Bel Air near other stars. Before long, a $900,000 cottage comes along requiring a small but manageable down payment. Although the monthly payments are high, the actor goes ahead on the basis of the million dollar advance he is soon to get. To go with the house, he treats himself to a used Masserati at $80,000 on credit.

Months pass and still no contract. The actor, by now, is on the verge of a nervous breakdown. If the deal falls through, he'll be bankrupt. At last, however, the long awaited call to sign the contract comes. Each side brings its lawyer.

Everything discussed earlier is as it should be on pages 1, 2, 3. Then come pages full of terms and conditions which had never before come up. On these pages, the payment is spread out over four years, the actor is excluded from appearing on television, he is tied to the studio for his next three pictures and is told that he will be billed as supporting actor rather than star.

Fear grips him. If he walks out, his dream will be shattered. There will be debts and lengthy, expensive legal battles. And what about his chance for stardom and fame? The negotiation now proceeds in earnest. Finally, after much hand-wringing and anguish, a contract is signed. The studio has its way even on the advanced payment issue. They agree to give the actor an $800,000 advance line when filming starts. All he will receive in addition is $900,000 over the next four years. He feels better. At least he can pay some of his bills and get on with his life.

The movie producer and the old farmer shared a secret. They knew that the person with whom they dealt was psychologically conditioned to close the transaction. Both understood that what they gave away on page 1, 2, 3 they could take back with interest on 4,5,6.

ESCALATION – A TOUGH OPENING AND MID-NEGOTIATION TACTIC

Escalation is one of the most powerful tactics in negotiation. It sends a clear message to the other side that they have gone as far as they can go.

Sooner or later in business or personal affairs you are certain to run into "escalation." On a personal level, it will probably take place in one of the larger transactions of your life, such as when you buy or sell a house or boat. The penalty is costly for not understanding and preparing for escalation when the stakes are high.

In this section, we will cover two examples of escalation. The first involves a business negotiation between an office maintenance company and the owner of an office building. The second, the sale of a home.

Suppose that you, the seller, have proposed a package of IT services for the buyer's multi-national firm at $100,000 a month. You've priced the services at rock bottom and left almost no room to negotiate. As an experienced supplier of IT services you are convinced that your offer is competitive. Your proposal provides good references and assurances that IT personnel will be carefully screened to guarantee a high level of performance and honesty.

Like most people, the buyer expects some concessions on the $100,000 a month proposed fee. What can the seller do to show the owner that there is no give in the price?

You can escalate. If you go into the negotiation and demonstrate credibly that your proposed price of $100,000 a month was actually miscalculated and must be revised to $110,000, everyone on the buyer's side will be shocked.

Sellers are not expected to raise their proposal price. Normally they make concessions that lower the original bid. Before the escalation, the buyer made plans to drive the $100,000 price down. Now the buyer is faced with a completely different problem. She will have to spend time and energy bringing the new asking price of $110,000 back to $100,000.

Of course, this approach involves risk. The buyer may throw the seller out or act as though the $110,000 revised proposal had never been made. The buyer may rant and threaten, but if the escalated proposal is credible, the buyer will treat the higher proposal seriously. When the parties settle at the original $100,000 price, the buyer will be well satisfied. They will reason that it could have been worse. Paying $100,000 per month will look like a bargain. The seller has used escalation to convince the buyer that she has proposed a very tight price.

Escalation has another role in negotiation. It can also serve to discourage additional demands made by the other side. The following example concerns the sale of a home to a buyer who makes demands that the seller feels must be resisted.

Some years ago a friend of mine was selling her house in Los Angeles. Negotiations for her $900,000 home were going smoothly. The parties had already settled on a price and other matters. What was still at issue were extras like a fine chandelier, a nice fireplace fixture, removable draperies and the interest rate on a small $50,000 second mortgage. None of these issues appeared difficult.

As the talks continued, the buyer asked for and was granted the fireplace fixture and draperies, neither of which would have fit well in the seller's new home. The trouble was that the buyer, encouraged by winning these easy concessions, asked for a low interest rate on the second mortgage. The buyer also insisted that the chandelier be thrown into the package. My friend, anxious to get it over with, granted the mortgage request and asked only $1,000 for the chandelier, a very low price. Tired, both parties agreed to meet next morning to close the sale.

Early the next day, the buyer opened talks with a surprise request for a Persian rug in the seller's bedroom and a longer payback period on the second mortgage. Neither issue had been raised previously.

The seller handled the new demands by escalating. She told the buyer that she had made a mistake the prior day by conceding the fireplace fixtures and the low interest rate. She also proved to him that the chandelier was erroneously priced at $1000 since it would cost $3000 if purchased at a store. On that basis the seller raised the chandelier price from $1000 to $1700. It was a risk, of course, but it sent a message to the buyer that he had little chance to get the rug or anything else.

In the end she sold the Persian rug to the buyer at a good price, received $1200 for the chandelier and let the interest rate stay low on the unchanged second mortgage. Had she not escalated her demands the buyer might well have asked for even more. The seller had every right to change her mind on prior concessions made before the final agreement was signed. It was the buyer who kept the deal open with ever growing demands.

Escalation can be difficult to deal with. To cope with it, take the actions suggested below:

1. Call the other person's bluff. He or she may be as unwilling to start over again as you are.

2. Caucus. Give yourself time to think. Don't react right away.

3. Counter escalate. Consider changing your offer or demand in response to the escalation.

4. Give consideration to walking away from the deal. This will test the escalator's resolve. There is a good chance that she will back off.

One more way to minimize the likelihood of escalation is to do as the Iranians do. They write a memorandum of agreement on each matter settled as it happens. Both parties sign the memorandum. Then, if the opposing party decides to change their mind later, they are confronted by the signed memo. This makes it harder for the escalator to back away from prior agreements on an issue. The Iranian approach does not guarantee that escalation will be prevented. It only serves to make it less likely to occur.

"WHAT IF" – A GOOD PROBING AND WIN-WIN TACTIC

"What if" is a powerful negotiating technique for getting information that the other party might ordinarily not wish to reveal. Few would disagree that a buyer who knows more about the cost structure and needs of a seller is apt to make a better agreement.

Equally important, "what if" opens the way for both parties to find a better way to do business than either thought possible to start with. Few approaches to bargaining yield as much information and opportunity for win-win as "what-if." The following example applies to an international business situation, but the ideas are directly applicable to personal buying or selling as well.

Suppose an American buyer of laptop sleeves from China wishes to purchase 20,000 sleeves to bundle with specialized laptops for engineers in the United States. Instead of just asking for a quote on 20,000, she asks for prices on 5,000, 10,000, 20,000, 50,000 and 100,000. Once the Chinese bids are in, the buyer and her cost analysts are in a position to determine the seller's material and labor costs, their setup costs, and to make estimates about their marginal pricing and efficiency.

The buyer is then in a good position to negotiate the price on 20,000 units. Knowing what the costs are on a 50,000 run, the buyer can drive the unit price for 20,000 down closer to the 50,000 level.

Is "what if" an ethical tactic? Was it right for the buyer to ask for so many bids when only a 20,000-unit purchase was contemplated? I believe it was. Her role was to make the most sensible decision she could based on the information available. "What if" is a good way to get price and cost information as well as to learn something about the seller's pressure to sell.

In dealing with the Chinese manufacturer, other "what ifs" like those below might have opened opportunities for both-win:

1. What if we give you a two- or three-year contract?
2. What if we supply the material?
3. What if we lend you money for the machinery? (Or buy the machinery for you?)
4. What if we buy sleeves and computer bags?
5. What if we buy your total factory production?
6. What if we change the laptop sleeve design to include a stamped logo?
7. What if we give you advance payments or cash on delivery?
8. What if we pay you in German marks? Any of these "what ifs" could have provided an insight into the seller's motivations not otherwise available. They can, with some creativity, lead to win-win trade-offs and benefits. Trade-offs which neither party could have anticipated had "what if" not been considered.

EVERYBODY LOVES A BARGAIN – MAKING OFFERS THAT RAISE A BUYER'S SATISFACTION

Everybody loves a bargain. I've seen very rich men purchase a used sports car for $70,000 when the going price was $90,000, then boast as though they had made a million in the stock market. People buy all sorts of things they never use because they are on sale. Rich or poor, we have a need to validate our self-esteem. Getting a bargain seems to satisfy that need to a surprising extent.

There are two points to recognize about bargains from a seller's standpoint. The first is that a bargain is a state of mind. It mayor not have anything to do with the price the buyer paid or is being asked to pay. It is not the amount of money involved but the satisfaction the buyer receives or is likely to receive from the agreement. The second point about a bargain is that it makes sense to package your offer of goods, services and added values in such a way that the other party perceives it as a bargain. If the seller does not present the offering as a bargain, it won't be perceived as such.

The twenty-four bargains which follow, if incorporated into your offer, are likely to leave the buyer with a higher level of satisfaction:

1. Getting something somebody else wanted.

2. Getting a better price than they thought they would pay.

3. Winning a better price than was asked.

4. Reaching an agreement they had to work hard to get.

5. Being told by others that they got a bargain.

6. Getting something personal thrown in for goodwill.

7. Getting the service or goods when they thought they might lose them.

8. Getting more "bang for the buck" by receiving superior performance for every dollar they spend, even if the price is high.

9. Purchasing something which has a low risk of dissatisfaction later.

10. Recognized evidence of good taste by others.

11. Discovery of subtle hidden virtues not easily seen by others.

12. Purchasing something that has a high probability of future satisfaction.

13. An unexpected dividend – something free thrown in like extra samples or services not anticipated.

14. Being envied by others.

15. Winning a good price compared to what was paid last time.

16. Seeing that others (associates or friends) are pleased with the results of the purchase.

17. Not being aggravated after the purchase is made and the goods or services are in use.

18. Discovery that a mistake (however small) has been made in their favor.

19. Getting a chance to look good to others in their organization later.

20. Getting a chance to win something or to gamble on something significant at low personal cost to themselves – a free million dollar lottery ticket thrown into the deal as a "delight factor."

21. Getting a third party to absorb part of the cost.

22. Seeing supportive advertising on television after they buy the product.

23. Purchasing a product or service with recognized conspicuous consumption or snob appeal.

24. Getting first class work done at the going rate for average performance.

There is another type of bargain people are responsive to. Some years ago, I read an essay called, "The Value of Unchosen Alternatives." The author claimed that human beings place a disproportionately high value on options and extras they are unlikely to use. They pay for the availability of services they will rarely if ever need, for accessories they will hardly ever use, for performance characteristics they are unlikely to require, for magazines they will barely read, and for warranties on breakdowns that will happen only in rare circumstances.

Recently, I saw a cartoon in a magazine which showed two New Yorkers in Central Park. One was holding a leash that led into the bushes; the other was a well dressed businessman. The man with the leash tells the businessman he has an elephant for sale at the bargain price of $1000. The businessman looks astonished and says, "What would I do with an elephant in New York City?"

The seller responds by offering the elephant for $600. The business man replies by saying that the discussion is ridiculous because even if he had an elephant there is no place he can keep it.

At this point, the man with the leash offers the elephant for $400. The businessman, slightly interested, says, "What's the point of talking. I don't want an elephant."

"All right," says the man with the elephant, "I'll make nothing on the sale, but I'll give you two elephants for $600." At that point the businessman gets a big smile on his face and says, 'Ah – now you've got a deal."

This cartoon is not farfetched. I know a man who actually bought a gigantic old Catalina cruise boat for only a few thousand dollars. He couldn't pass up the deal, though he didn't know a thing about boats. Ten years later, after enormous expense keeping the boat moored safely in the harbor, he paid a fortune to have it destroyed. Like the businessman in the cartoon, he loved a bargain.

Negotiators on the selling side who package their offers as bargains will get the attention of buyers and close more sales. Almost everybody is responsive to a bargain.

NEGOTIATING WITH A FRIEND OR RELATIVE – THREE APPROACHES TO THE PROBLEM

There is an old Russian saying, "The best way to lose a friend is by bargaining with him." Those who have done so can testify how difficult it is to deal with friends or relatives. In this section, we will consider three approaches to this tricky problem.

A good example is a friend of mine who retired to Florida. He was selling his home in New York and decided to dispose of the furnishings. Before doing so, he offered them to his two nephews and his niece. The relatives, married and in their late twenties, were interested in some pieces but not all. Like others their age, they had little money. Each dealt with the uncle in a different way.

The first used an "arm's-length" approach. He negotiated with the uncle as though he were a stranger. This resulted in hard feelings because the uncle, though he was fond of the nephew, resented being put into a bargaining position. It proved uncomfortable for both of them.

The second nephew took another tack. He said to his uncle, "You put a price on the item and I'll pay that price." Oddly enough, the old man also felt uncomfortable with this seemingly fair arrangement. The problem was how to put a value on used furniture and bric-a-brac, some of which was quite expensive, without appearing to take advantage of a family member. The uncle was not wealthy and was torn between charging what he believed to be a fair market price and letting his nephew enjoy a bargain. It placed the uncle in an awkward position.

The niece used another approach. After deciding which pieces of furniture she wanted, she shopped around to determine what the articles were worth. She then placed a price on each item, explaining to the old man what she was willing and able to pay in terms of her budget. After committing to purchasing the articles at the stipulated prices, she urged the old man to put them up for sale for whatever the market would bear.

In the end, the niece did best in terms of maintaining good relations and purchasing what she could at prices she could afford. The old man was pleased because he retained the discretion to sell or not sell selected pieces to outside customers. The niece's approach permitted the pressures of price, needs, financial resources, friendship, generosity and the market place to reach their own level in a gracious yet businesslike way.

CONCLUSION

Demands and offers – and the strategies for presenting them – are an essential part of the negotiating process. Learning to defend yourself against tactics used by the other side will help you reach your objectives in any bargaining situation, be it personal or professional.

The demand and offer tactics and defenses presented in this chapter are powerful negotiating tools. An understanding of these tactics is essential for anyone who intends to be a successful negotiator.

POWERFUL DEMAND AND OFFER TACTICS

———————— • ————————

1. "GIVE ME YOUR BEST AND FINAL OFFER"

2. STRAW ISSUES - FILLING THE POT

3. THE BOGEY APPROACH - A WIN-WIN TACTIC

4. ALWAYS ASK "HOW MUCH" OR YOU'LL GET TAKEN

5. TAKE IT OR LEAVE IT AS AN OPENING DEMAND

6. THE REVERSE AUCTION - A VERY TOUGH TACTIC

7. FROM THE ITALIANS - LEARN TO FLINCH

8. THE IMPORTANT DIFFERENCE BETWEEN NEEDS AND WANTS

9. THE PLANNING PURPOSE TRAP

10. THE SALAMI SLICE APPROACH

11. THE KRUNCH

12. GIVE IT AWAY ON PAGES 1, 2, 3
    TAKE IT BACK ON PAGES 4, 5, 6

13. ESCALATION - A TOUGH OPENING AND MID-NEGOTIATION
    TACTIC

14. "WHAT IF" - A GOOD PROBING TACTIC

15. EVERYBODY LOVES A BARGAIN - HOW TO RAISE THE OTHER
    PARTY'S SATISFACTION LEVEL

16. NEGOTIATING WITH A FRIEND OR RELATIVE - THREE WAYS TO
    APPROACH THE PROBLEM

12 | Time Pressure Tactics and Defenses

Once I worked for a manager who believed that the best way to negotiate was to get it over with quickly. He saw no point in wasting time with useless talk. "Why not just come to the point?" he would say. "Tell the other person what you want, find out what they want, and settle somewhere in the middle."

Years later at the University of Southern California, I was able to test his advice under experimental conditions. It turned out that quick deals were dangerous because they tended to be extreme. One side did very well at the expense of the other. The research convinced me of something I had already observed: time is a critical element in negotiation. How you use it and how you react to it has a great deal to do with the final settlement. Time has the power to exert hidden pressure on those who bargain. In this chapter we will cover twelve time tactics. Each has the power to influence the outcome of any negotiation, whether it is between nations, buyers and sellers, husbands and wives or friends and neighbors.

1. NEGOTIATING OVER THE TELEPHONE: COSTLY MISTAKES WE ALL MAKE IN PERSONAL AND BUSINESS DEALINGS.

2. WAYS TO GIVE YOURSELF TIME TO THINK UNDER PRESSURE.

3. HURRY UP AND WAIT – HURRY UP AND WAIT.

4. CHOOSING THE BEST TIME TO NEGOTIATE AND MAKE OFFERS, DEMANDS, AND CONCESSIONS.

5. MARATHON SESSIONS – FOR AND AGAINST LONG TALKS.

6. THE POWER OF PATIENCE IN GETTING THE STORY AND PAVING THE WAY FOR A WIN-WIN DEAL.

7. BUYER AND SELLER DEADLINES THAT GET RESULTS.

8. ACCEPTANCE TIME – HOW TO GET THE OTHER SIDE ACCUSTOMED TO YOUR VIEW-POINT.

9. HOW BODY TIME CAN MAKE A GOOD NEGOTIATOR INTO A POOR ONE.

10. THE 90-10 RULE: CONTROLLING TIME AT THE TABLE.

11. WHEN IS IT WISE TO BUY NOW AND NEGOTIATE LATER? IS IT BETTER FOR THE BUYER OR SELLER?

12. TIME AND WORK DIFFERENCES AROUND THE WORLD: HOW IT AFFECTS NEGOTIATION.

NEGOTIATING OVER THE PHONE: COSTLY MISTAKES WE ALL MAKE IN PERSONAL AND BUSINESS DEALINGS

Most negotiations take place over the phone and increasingly by email, not face to face. The trouble is that people make costly mistakes over the phone. Mistakes that can easily be avoided with just a bit of effort and forethought. The tips and techniques in this section are certain to save you a lot of money and heartache in your future phone dealings.

The first thing to recognize is something we all know: It pays to be prepared. Nowhere is preparation so valuable as before negotiating over the phone. The reason is that a phone conversation gives neither party enough time to think or to get ready for the unexpected. The person who benefits most when dealing over the phone is the one who knows what she wants to say and has prepared her arguments in advance.

Telephone negotiations are efficient but dangerous. They are of far shorter duration than even the most simple face to face talks. Too much information is exchanged in too short a time for people to absorb it all. The pressure of discussion leads to mistakes in reasoning and even simple arithmetic. Negotiators leave out points they wanted to cover, sometimes important points. As a manager, I've had some of my telephone salespeople get off the phone with a happy smile and a newly closed agreement. Only minutes later, when I congratulated them and asked what the price agreed to was, they couldn't remember. That's what phone negotiations can do. Mistakes, omissions, memory lapses and poor note-taking are inevitable.

Telephone negotiations are not as effective as face-to-face talks for two other reasons. First and most important, it is much harder to conduct win-win negotiations over the phone. There is simply not enough time to search for and develop innovative ideas that will benefit both parties.

It is also hard, if not impossible, to "read" the other party over the phone. The only clues you can get to their reaction to your demands, your arguments, or your concessions is through what they say and the way they say it. In face-to-face discussions you can observe their reactions. Indeed, I've been at face-to-face sessions where the team leader on the other side screamed wildly that what we offered was unfair, while others on his team actually looked so pleased with our offer that we thought we had made a mistake by giving too much. We could not have perceived this on the phone.

The question of whether to deal over the phone deserves careful consideration. If the stakes are high, face-to-face talks are usually best. If the issues are complicated and the potential for win-win creative approaches large, then the phone is not the best communication medium. Business can be conducted in a variety of ways: by letter, by phone, directly in person or through intermediaries. Don't let the form of the negotiation just happen without forethought. Choose the media that best meet your needs.

The Telephone Negotiation Checklist on page 262 is designed to help you before and during the talks. Discipline yourself to go through it point by point. For example, Item #1 raises a commonly forgotten issue: 'Ask about quantity price breaks." Even if you only want to buy one tire, ask the merchant what he would charge for two, three, or four. If you want 10 yards of a material or fabric, ask what he would charge for 12 or 24 yards. The price break for a larger quantity may surprise you. Sometimes the price falls by half or more.

I know a couple who, when purchasing a condominium, asked about the price for two and learned that a 15 percent discount was available. This gave them a clue that the developer was more flexible than she appeared. Another acquaintance found, when buying land, that he could purchase 40 acres for $200,000, although the owner was asking $100,000 for ten. In both cases, the fact that they asked for different quantities resulted in useful information, information which led to discounts they didn't expect.

Each point on the checklist is a mind-jogger that will help reduce your future cost or aggravation. For example, I have found that Item #13, 'Any hidden added costs?" can reduce my vulnerability to unpleasant extra costs for transportation or installation. Item #21, "Kinds of tooling or art work: who owns it?" has proved an invaluable reminder that if there is tooling necessary to do the job, I better make it clear that we retain legal ownership rather than letting the other party keep the tools after the job.

TELEPHONE NEGOTIATION CHECKLIST

Name _____

Phone No. _____ Order No. _____

Item	Yes	No	N/A	Subject	Notes
1				Quantity price breaks	
2				Reschedule delivery trade-offs	
3				Transportation (FOB) costs considered	
4				Spec QC upgrade/downgrade trade-offs	
5				Payment cash discounts taken	
6				Can other items be added for leverage?	
7				Payment and cash flow trade-offs	
8				Contract type - T&M, FP, CPFF, lease	
9				Packaging specifications	
10				Storage and inventory trade-offs	
11				Inspection services included or not	
12				Accessories standard equipment or not	
13				Any hidden costs?	
14				Are options available at no cost?	
15				Can spares be priced now for future delivery?	
16				Maintenance and warranty alternatives	
17				Can surpluses be returned for full credit?	
18				Special legal terms and clauses	
19				Can work be shared to lower costs?	
20				Can material or equipment be furnished?	
21				Kinds of tooling or art work; who owns it?	
22				Extra drawings, manuals, samples	
23				Previous price history considered	
24				Does order affect past/future relationship?	
25				What are limits of opponent's power?	
26				Are calculator, records, note-taking available?	
27				Was confirmation sent?	
28				Check competition	
29				Tax implications considered?	
30				How good is their track record?	
31				Why shouldn't the deal be made now?	
32				Is more information/analysis needed?	
33				Check corporate agreements for price break	
34				Have time limits been considered?	
35				Are price/cost breakdowns available?	

The salesperson or buyer who places this checklist next to the phone and uses it regularly will be in a better position to make comprehensive and intelligent agreements. Also, if you keep the following ten suggestions in mind, your bargaining results are certain to improve even more.

1. Talk less and listen attentively. Don't try to do something else while on the phone.

2. Before the call is made, write down what you want in priority order.

3. Take notes to avoid misunderstandings. Repeat all understandings reached to reduce the likelihood of later conflict.

4. Dry-run the call beforehand. Use a "Devil's Advocate" to act as the other party in making arguments against your position.

5. Have your backup papers and a calculator at hand before the call. Have a pen and lots of blank paper or preferably a bound notebook to write on. Think about how many times you answered an important call and weren't ready for it.

6. Have the courage to resist being pushed into a quick concession or decision on something you do not sufficiently understand. Don't shoot your answer from the hip. People on the phone often do and regret it later.

7. If you are not prepared when the other person calls, tell her you'll call her back. Get prepared before you do.

8. If, as a salesperson, you are asked for references, have good ones at your side, including current addresses and phone numbers.

9. If, after hanging up, you discover that a mistake was made, something left out or you do not understand some part of the phone agreement, have the courage to call right back. Clear the matter up. Don't wait.

10. If you want to avoid a "no" answer, negotiate face to face. If you want to give a "no" answer, the phone is a good way to do so.

In the future global marketplace, only the most important negotiations will be held face to face. Most will be by telephone or video conference and supported by email. The possibilities for error, omission, and misunderstanding will multiply as we deal with people who speak different languages and live in other cultures. The cautions we have suggested will be all the more important in the 21st century.

GIVING YOURSELF TIME TO THINK UNDER PRESSURE

All of us have said, "If I only knew then what I know now!" It's remarkable how clear things are in hindsight. The trick is to change hindsight to foresight.

There are two ways to make wiser decisions about the future. One is by planning ahead and the other by giving ourselves time to think in the heat of events. Planning has been covered in Chapter 10. In this chapter we will consider ways to give yourself time to think under pressure.

First: Go into negotiation with people at your side. My experiments confirm that people who are accompanied by partners take longer to plan, longer to recess and longer to settle than those who bargain alone. The old adage "two heads are better than one" certainly applies here. What one fails to consider, the other will. What one fails to observe or listen to, the other will often pick up.

Second: Take frequent caucus breaks during discussions.

Short sessions followed by long recesses are better than long sessions and short breaks. Use the time to review your notes. Plan your responses and adjust your strategy. Don't just relax, even though you'll want to. Frequent caucuses should be part of your planning strategy.

Third: Let the other party present their position and demands before you do. Whenever possible, have the other side complete their presentation before a natural break period such as lunchtime, the end of the day or before a weekend. When dealing, for example, with a tax agency on an income or assessment problem, try to arrange the session in two separate phases. In phase one, have the agent layout her position before closing time on Friday afternoon. Make your presentation and defense on Monday. This will provide you an opportunity to study the agent's position, rebut her arguments and counter with your own.

Diplomats over the centuries have developed sophisticated and well-tested rituals to do the same thing. They raise a question one week, have it answered the next and present a counter-position still later. Demands and offers are made in writing to give the parties time to weigh the impact of each word and to respond sensibly.

Two other common approaches are employed to buy time to think: change the negotiator and use interpreters where language or technical barriers exist. Both serve to slow the negotiating process. Although Chinese and Japanese negotiators are generally quite fluent in English, they prefer to bargain through interpreters in order to build a time buffer between thought and response. These techniques of diplomacy are applicable with little modification to the less complex negotiations in our daily life.

There are other approaches which, though simple, provide you time to think under pressure if you don't repeat them too often:

- Having to make an urgent phone call.
- Running to the coffee truck.
- Forgetting some important backup data and searching for it.
- Bringing so much backup data that it cannot be sifted, absorbed or found quickly.
- Going out to dinner suddenly at 3:00 PM, 3:00AM or some other strange time just because.
- Having people on the team going in and out of the conference room to attend to emergency problems and taking time out for these interruptions.

The key issue from a bargaining standpoint is that a negotiation is too important to be treated like a ping pong match. When the other party asks a question, there is no rule that says you must respond with a prompt answer. When they want you to make a quick decision, there is no law that says you must. The best defense against dumb answers and decisions you will later regret lies in recognizing that it takes you and everybody else time to think. Build time buffers and caucuses into your planning. It will make your agreements more intelligent and less aggravating.

HURRY UP AND WAIT – HURRY UP AND WAIT

Some years ago, I was doing research on how other cultures negotiate. One technique used time and again by the Chinese was "Hurry up and wait." It drove Westerners, anxious to penetrate the billion-person Chinese market, half-mad.

Today, Beijing is not the most comfortable place to spend a long period of time. Only a few years ago it was worse. Poor air conditioning, strange food, a decrepit phone system, language barriers and being away from home combined to make it difficult for Americans to work there.

When a Chinese demand for goods or services becomes known, business people from all over the world descend on Beijing to win the order. The Chinese urge them to make proposals quickly and they scramble to respond. After proposals are submitted the Chinese do nothing, often for months. The Western executives don't know what to do next. On the one hand, they are desperate to return home. On the other, they have to hang around in the hope that a call for more information or some bargaining will be forthcoming.

When a call for more information does come, months later, all competitors respond frantically. After a week or two of direct communication with the Chinese, activity again slows to zero. This often goes on for a year or two, with the pace fluctuating between a "hurry up" phase and a "wait" phase. By the time it is over and one company wins the contract, all the Western executives involved are close to a breakdown.

A Boeing executive who lived through this hurry up and wait

cycle for two years wrote about how it affected his team. He described how their beards grew and their clothing took on a Chinese look. They were haggard from the unremitting tension of doing nothing for long periods of time. In the midst of doing nothing came frantic calls to answer difficult questions and to prepare changed proposals on short notice. It was unlike any experience they had ever faced before.

As for the Chinese, "Hurry up and wait" served a purpose. Although they actually ordered few airplanes and were limited by meager financial resources and a less than adequate understanding of Western specifications, they were convinced that the approach helped them win better prices, products and terms than would have been achieved otherwise.

"Hurry up and wait" is not employed in the Western world as frequently as it is in Asia and the Middle East. Where it is used, the tactic has the power to disconcert salespeople and drive a wedge between them and their organization. It is a change-of-pace approach that functions here much as it does in China.

In our society, a number of sellers are called to the purchasing office and asked to provide prompt quotations on a requirement. Some time after the quotes are received, the buyer begins discussions with several of them. Each expects that the order will soon be placed. That's when the buyer begins the "wait" cycle.

The purchasing agent is suddenly in no hurry. The pace slows. He or she becomes inaccessible. During the anxious period which follows, competing sellers imagine that someone else has the inside track on the job. A month later, the buyer quickens the pace once more, this time demanding special concessions not asked for before. These are easily won because each seller is delighted at the opportunity to land a piece of business already thought lost.

"Hurry up and wait" is effective because it creates anxiety in both the salesperson and his or her organization. One day management is led to expect that the sale will close any day now. The next day it appears lost. This swinging back and forth from elation to depression leads those in sales management to lose faith in the salesperson. It also causes salespeople to lose confidence in themselves. Everyone concerned wonders if further concessions should be granted to make the price attractive to the buyer.

There is nothing inherently unethical about using "Hurry up and wait" to achieve your budgetary objectives. When the stakes are high, it is worth considering. Like all negotiating approaches the danger lies in overdoing it. Those considering this tough tactic should recognize that business people in most cultures would not hesitate to employ it to win better prices and terms.

For salespeople facing a hurry up and wait situation on a substantial order, the best defense is to get ready for it. Resign yourself to the fact that the journey will be long and unpleasant with sporadic periods of euphoria and despair mixed in. Above all prepare your organization for frustrations likely to come. If they realize what they are likely to face, they will continue to support your sales effort, your mounting expenses and your constant requests for more information and additional proposals. Of course, if you are in a strong competitive position you can use that leverage to urge the buyer to act quickly rather than lose access to your services or pay a higher price due to the delay.

CHOOSING THE BEST TIME TO NEGOTIATE AND TO MAKE OFFERS, DEMANDS, AND CONCESSIONS

There is a right and a wrong time to negotiate, just as there is a correct time to bring up any subject with your children, your boss or your friends. Time has a language of its own that can improve the chances of agreement or plunge a discussion into the morass of deadlock and emotions. A good negotiator is sensitive to time and how it affects results.

For example, when you sell your home, you probably already know the best time of the day to have the negotiation take place. If your house is like mine, there are times of the day like six or seven in the early evening when traffic subsides and the back yard looks most tranquil and attractive. That's the best time and place for getting a "yes" answer.

A large number of Vietnamese have settled in California's Orange County, a conservative community. Californians rarely bargain when shopping at a supermarket, but the Vietnamese do. They were brought up in a bargaining culture. When they first arrived, it seemed quite natural to them that the local supermarket would be flexible in its pricing. They were disappointed when the market maintained a fixed price policy on canned goods and packaged products purchased in small quantities.

Ever alert for bargaining opportunities, the Vietnamese soon learned that some store managers gave discounts on case and half-case orders. As time went on they discovered that they could also receive concessions on time-dated groceries and bakery products. Best of all they found success in the produce department. At 9:00

AM on Saturday bananas were 80 cents a pound, but by 5:00 PM, just before the store closed for the night, the Vietnamese succeeded in buying bananas for 15 cents a pound. Now, I am told, some native Californians have followed suit. Late Saturday afternoon is now bargaining time in many Orange County produce departments.

Important decisions are made because the clock says so. April 15, Christmas and the last day of the year have caused many an order to be signed and many a piece of property to be sold or bought. Time speaks with a loud voice in every business. There are slow and busy periods. There are times when inventories are large. There are slow and fast pay periods. There are seasons when new models emerge and old ones are discounted.

The right time to negotiate is as important as where to bargain. If a seller is constrained by meeting a monthly quota or by booking an important sale to meet the demands of an annual stock report, the alert buyer will try to negotiate close to the end of the month or year. Tax deadlines or changes in the tax law can send advantageous signals for those who sell or buy. The right time can help settle an otherwise difficult negotiation.

A good sales negotiator pays attention to time and knows when to negotiate. When the buyer says, "Come in at 9:00 AM on Tuesday," and you think that's a bad time, find a reason for changing the meeting to a better time. The buyer may be more flexible than you think.

The timing of an offer can be critical. An opening offer or counteroffer made too quickly can signal weakness. A quick concession can send the message that lots more will be made. A last and final offer made too soon may not be credible, but one made after considerable discussion may be perceived as firm.

Time talks and few know it better than insurance companies in personal injury cases. But even they make mistakes occasionally. The Los Angeles Times recently reported that an insurance company executive agreed to pay $500,000 at the exact moment that a jury was returning with a verdict. The insurance company executive said afterward that the fact that the jury had been deliberating for five days convinced her that a two or three million dollar verdict was in the offing. Instead, the jury returned a "not guilty" verdict. It was too late for the company executive to back out of her "last minute" $500,000 offer.

What amazes me is that so many people are insensitive to time in their relationships. They plunge ahead with what they want to say or do as though time were not a factor. It is. The right time can make something happen. The wrong time can make an otherwise simple difference of opinion appear irreconcilable.

From now on, say to yourself, "Have I picked the right time?" before deciding when to negotiate with the other person or when to make the next concession. The time of day, day of the week, and month of the year can make a big difference.

MARATHON SESSIONS – FOR AND AGAINST LONG TALKS

Marathon sessions lead to agreement. All night meetings between labor and management are common in industrial bargaining history. Many of the great mergers and billion dollar deals we read about in the Wall Street Journal result from close-quarter talks that go on uninterrupted for days. Marathon negotiations have always played a critical role in diplomacy and international trade talks. To see how they influence results, we will now consider one of the most unusual marathon negotiations in history.

In 1979, two world leaders, arch enemies for most of their lives, tried to reach agreement on issues that had divided their people for centuries and had resulted in three bloody wars in less than thirty years.

The leaders were Anwar Sadat of Egypt and Menachem Begin of Israel. The world did not believe that these two men could possibly reach agreement. They had openly reviled each other for so long. Their negotiation was one of the longest and most unusual face-to-face marathon sessions in diplomacy.

To facilitate agreement, President Carter of the United States tried something which had never been done before on such a high level. He brought the two heads of state to the United States and kept them together in a marathon session. Twelve uninterrupted days later these ancient enemies emerged from the isolation of Camp David with a settlement few imagined possible. A great share of credit for the phenomenal Camp David success belonged to the three participants, but part of it lies in the chemistry of marathon sessions.

When people spend long hours together – when they sweat and strive, play and laugh, drink and relax together – there is a good chance they will get to know each other. By working together and sharing a common emotional experience, Sadat and Begin became, in a sense, partners. I'm sure they revealed to each other the constraints they faced at home and the risks they were subject to. What the marathon did was reduce the abstractions and stereotypes of national conflict to the manageable reality of person-to-person give and take.

The Camp David talks worked because there is a hidden ingredient in every negotiation – how people feel toward each other as individuals. This is the "attitudinal" dimension of negotiation. An agreement is hard to reach if the chemistry between the parties is not right. What is required is a commitment to mutual satisfaction, a feeling of trust that they will do as they say and if trouble arises help each other over the rough spots.

The marathon worked for another reason. When two parties negotiate they are isolated, at least to an extent, from those they represent. It becomes "us" (those in the conference room) against "them" (those in both organizations outside the room). A long uninterrupted session increases the likelihood that such feelings of solidarity against outside forces will develop. Both parties have a chance to talk off the record.

Lest we get carried away with the Camp David success, the same strategy could easily have led to disaster. Sir Francis Bacon cautioned against such meetings between heads of state for fear they would lead to prolonged deadlock or war. Two men together for twelve days might well have learned to hate one another even more. For corporate presidents or kings, summit meetings are "iffy" things.

Long sessions do have a place in business dealings. I am in favor of all night uninterrupted sessions under these conditions:

- When the impetus toward agreement already exists and a long session can help guarantee that outside influences will not raise new questions or otherwise deflect a settlement.

- When the parties have repeated the same arguments to the point that they are themselves tired and ready for compromise.

- When the negotiators respect each other.

- Both parties have the stamina to handle the stress of long sessions without suffering physically or mentally.

- When discussions have progressed to the point where divergent issues and positions have a reasonable likelihood of being moved toward agreement.

On balance, a negotiator is better served by short sessions with long breaks than vice-versa. Marathon sessions lasting to early hours of morning are most dangerous to those who lack stamina and whose goals are not clear. That's when big mistakes are made.

THE POWER OF PATIENCE IN GETTING THE STORY AND PAVING THE WAY FOR A WIN-WIN DEAL

Every negotiation has a story behind it. As the wise old furniture dealer in Arthur Miller's play "The Price" observes, "If you don't understand the viewpoint you can't understand the price." Patience allows the story to unfold.

Patience is a supertactic of negotiation. It makes it possible for the parties to best resolve their differences and to find creative win-win possibilities in their relationship. I do not believe that anyone can be an effective negotiator without patience.

Only with patience can negotiators discover what the other person really needs. It allows them to understand the issues, weigh risks, test strengths, find weaknesses and change expectations. Patience gives negotiators and their organizations time to accept the idea that what they wish for must be reconciled with the realities of what is possible. Negotiation is the art of the possible in reconciling differing desires and viewpoints. That takes time.

Patience, with its partner persistence, can work for you. It can test the will of the other party like few other approaches can. It can also help in seven additional ways:

1. It can lower the other side's expectations.
2. It can divide their organization.
3. It can lead to concessions being granted by them to get things going.
4. It can bring new issues to the surface.
5. It can allow third parties to mediate or make suggestions.
6. It can allow outside forces to be organized or to come into play on your behalf.
7. It can change the balance of power.

Most of ail, patience is the only way that the two sides can search for better ways to deal with one another. Both-win solutions are not possible in quick deals. Like good wine, both-win takes time to mature well.

BUYER AND SELLER DEADLINES THAT GET RESULTS

Not long ago, I caved in to a deadline demand over the phone. To this day I don't know if it was a deliberate tactic or not, but I do know that it caused me to act. Here's how it happened.

I wanted to rent a video player and four television sets for a seminar in New York. After calling several companies, it became apparent that prices and services varied a great deal. It was late Friday afternoon. Most rental companies were closed for the weekend, and it was imperative that everything be in place on Monday morning at 8:00 AM. Time was running out.

One company quoted a price which was 20 percent higher than usual, but they got my order anyway. This is how the salesman did it. After giving me the high price he hesitated and said, "Pardon me, I'd better check to see if we still have any." He put the phone down. Then, I heard him ask, "Hey Charlie, I've got a customer who wants one player and four TV's. Have we got any left?" Loud and clear I heard the answer, "We've only got one player and five TV's left." By time the salesman came back to the phone I yelled, "I'll take it." By implying that they might be out of stock at any moment, they had created a credible deadline. Later, I wondered if they always answered the phone by playing this "out of stock" scenario.

Was it any surprise that participants in my experiments became anxious and made large concessions as deadline approached? I don't think so. Given sixty minutes to bargain, most reached agreement in the last minute or two. I prescribed sixty minutes and they accepted it. Only one participant out of the more than a hundred in the experiment asked for an extension.

Buyers employ deadlines as well as sellers. The following are some buyer imposed deadlines which induce a seller to close.

- The money to buy won't be available after December 31, the end of our fiscal year (and this is December 31).
- If we can't agree, I'm going to have to place the order elsewhere tomorrow.

- Bids will not be accepted after June 1.
- Please give me a ball-park estimate of your price. I must have it this afternoon.
- I won't be responsible for buying this item after Friday. If you want a higher price, you'll have to talk to the new buyer next week.
- My boss has to approve, and he's leaving for Europe tomorrow.
- Here's my production schedule. If you can't meet it, we'll have to take the order elsewhere tomorrow.
- The buying committee meets on Wednesday. Shall I tell them you want the order at this price or not? I have to let them know.
- We are being reorganized any day now.
- We are willing to buy it now at this price. If we can't do it now, we'll have to wait until next year to see what our budget can stand.
- I'm leaving the company on Friday for a new purchasing job.

Salespeople likewise know that deadlines can lead buyers to make a decision, even when they aren't ready. The following statements are designed to nudge a buyer toward closure:

1. The price goes up July 1.
2. The offer is good for fifteen days.
3. The option expires June 30.
4. Inventory is subject to prior sale.
5. If you don't send us more money tomorrow, we'll have to stop work.
6. If you don't give me the order (or the specification) by June 1, I can't deliver by June 30.
7. It will take eight weeks to get it through our production

plant, and you need it in eight weeks.

8. Better place the order immediately to assure the availability of long lead-time items.
9. The cargo ship leaves at 2:00 PM. Do you want space on it?
10. If we don't get your deposit tomorrow, we can't hold it.

The best defense against deadlines is cautious skepticism. Test deadlines imposed by the other party. They are probably negotiable. A deadline should be viewed as just another bargaining issue like price or delivery. Don't let deadlines hypnotize you into making premature decisions. Yet in the real world, some deadlines are real. That's where good business judgment comes in.

ACCEPTANCE TIME – HOW TO GET THE OTHER SIDE ACCUSTOMED TO YOUR VIEWPOINT

As a buyer, I once suffered the shattering experience of having a price raised by 25 percent in one jump. For a year I had been purchasing 10,000 fancy plastic jewelry boxes a month at $20 each and barely meeting my cost control target. Now, after the increase to $25 each, my company would have to incur an un-budgeted expense of $50,000 a month. Not surprisingly, the marketing people and the controller's office were up in arms about this large loss in profit margin. Since I was the bearer of bad news, they blamed me for not warning them earlier.

The seller supported the $25 price by showing that they had lost money on previous plastic molding orders. They provided cost records to prove that the new price was warranted. While that didn't relieve the problem, it did reduce my hostility a bit. Nevertheless, my boss and I were still disturbed. We swore that we would never do business with this company again and immediately began searching as far away as Taiwan for other sources.

Twenty-four hours later we were still angry, but a sense of reality began to settle upon us. We had to admit that we were getting good service from the vendor and that they had always proved reliable in meeting our growing commitments. They were located close to our manufacturing plant, so we could easily check their progress and quality whenever we wished. This helped us maintain smaller inventories and assure higher quality. They were one of our best "just-in-time" suppliers.

By end of the week, we were reconciled to the idea of paying $25 each on at least one more order. We felt that it was wise to make the transition to a new source carefully. Taiwan by now seemed further away.

The next thing we did was ask for the seller's help in reducing the price by finding both-win alternatives. They were helpful in suggesting design modifications which could quickly be incorporated to save money. These changes reduced the price gap by $1 a unit. Next they reduced the increase by 40 cents as a token of goodwill. We were now down to $23.60 a unit ($25.00 less $1.00 less $0.40) which seemed by then, if not a bargain, at least better than $25.00.

Within a month, the marketing department reacted to the loss of profit margin by changing the sales discount structure on the box and the costume jewelry that went into it. This had the effect of raising prices charged to our customers by about a dollar. At the same time the production department followed through on the cost cutting program by finding new methods to assemble the package. This resulted in an additional saving of 35 cents a unit. We were by then getting close to making up for the large price increase.

A year later the company had fully absorbed the entire $5 increase. Acceptance time and its partner, "making the best of things," had done their work.

Acceptance time gives people a chance to adjust in a gradual way to new circumstances. People go into a negotiation with a set of wishes. The process of bargaining converts wishes to reality. For example, the family that wishes to buy a home for $200,000 shops around and finds that inflation has forced prices up to $220,000. They reconcile themselves to paying that much. Then they see a house they really like for $250,000 but learn in the process of negotiating that the seller will accept no less than $240,000. Again acceptance time goes to work. Within a relatively short time they begin to adjust their budget, their mortgage and their life-style to the new reality. The $240,000 price becomes incorporated into their thinking as they learn to live with this new reality. That's how acceptance time works.

The concept of acceptance time has profound implications in negotiation. It means that when you, the seller, make your original proposal of $1000 a unit, the buyer is likely to resist it if they expected to pay $800 a unit. After considerable discussion and resistance by the seller, acceptance time will do its work. The buyer will begin to adjust to having to pay more than they thought they would.

Similarly, when the buyer makes an offer to pay $800 each in response to the seller's demand for $1000, it is likely that the seller will be highly resistant to the low offer. After acceptance time does its work, the $800 offer will appear to be more reasonable to the seller. The seller's new perception of reality may lead them to take less than they originally hoped for. For the buyer in negotiation, it takes time to get used to how much the seller is asking. For the seller it takes time to get used to how little the buyer is offering.

"Time brings things by slow degrees," say the Chinese. When you ask a person to change new ideas for old, there is bound to be initial resistance, especially when the new ideas are unpleasant. Negotiation is a process by which the other party must exchange some of their old ideas for new ones of yours. It would be foolish to believe that they will do so without acceptance time. Give them the time to adjust to the differences between your position and theirs. Factor acceptance time into your bargaining strategy.

HOW BODY TIME CAN MAKE A GOOD NEGOTIATOR INTO A POOR ONE

Howard Hughes was known to negotiate at weird times and in strange places. Once he summoned the president of the giant Lockheed Aircraft Corporation to a conference at three in the morning at a crossroad in the middle of the Mojave Desert. Can you imagine how that high level executive felt when the phone woke him with an invitation to do business under such bizarre conditions? Three in the morning was surely not his finest hour.

It was, however, a definite part of the Hughes approach to bargaining. He chose to conduct business when others normally slept because he knew that people did not function well when their body time was disrupted.

Human beings are governed by natural rhythms that determine how they think, feel and react at different times of the day. Research into the influence of time on behavior is relevant to negotiation. The following recent findings are worth keeping in mind the next time a Howard Hughes type calls you:

1. Performance is tied to body rhythms. People perform best between 8:00 AM and 7:00 PM and worst between 2:00 AM and 6:00 AM.

2. People suffer serious mental discomfort when their work schedules shift. They become confused and accident prone. They develop ulcers and begin to suffer from hypertension.

3. Jet travel has introduced special stress problems. Doctors have reported premature aging among pilots flying east to west runs. They also find that it is easier to fly west than east.

4. One doctor studied crew members on a long flight and found that senior pilots had learned to cope with jet lag by staying on their own "at home" time. If they fly from Los Angeles going eastward and arrive at midnight in Rome (noon in Los Angeles) they try to function as though it were noon in Rome. It also helps them to preserve their biological and psychological stability by eating the same foods in Rome as they would have eaten in Los Angeles.

In her book Body Time, Luce Gay observed that "businessmen may be negotiating with a body whose heart rate indicates a state more like sleep than waking." Those of us who have negotiated at nine in the morning in New York after flying all night on the "red-eye" from Los Angeles know how hard it is to pay attention or to add simple numbers. We fall victim to the triple threat of west-to-east travel, a changing sleep routine and a mixed up work-eat schedule. Time has a profound impact on performance. To get the most out of yourself, pick the time that best suits your body.

Body time is especially important when we negotiate in Europe or Asia. Research indicates that it takes a person approximately one day to adjust for jet lag for every time zone flown through en route. While it is rarely possible to take so much time to adjust, a sensible rule would be to give yourself a full day or two before engaging in serious business overseas.

It is never wise to go into a negotiation without considering body time in your planning. Neville Chamberlain, Prime Minister of England in 1938, made the mistake of dealing with Hitler after traveling long and far to meet him. Hitler was fresh, Chamberlain exhausted. Hitler won Czechoslovakia and World War II started a year later. The verdict of history agrees that Chamberlain got the worse of the negotiation. His disorientation contributed to the results. Tired negotiators make poor agreements.

THE 90-10 RULE – CONTROLLING TIME AT THE TABLE

The 90-10 rule can help you in two important ways. It can allow you to leave enough time in the talks to adequately cover the issues of value to you, or it can allow you to leave little time for those matters you do not want to talk about.

Ninety percent of the time in bargaining is spent on matters that have little importance. We talk of this or that at the table, and only a small part of what we say is directly relevant to the issues in contention. As little as ten percent of conference time deals with key matters.

If you want to avoid talking about an issue or position that is difficult to defend, remember the 90-10 rule. Spend lots of time discussing other things – the weather, the other person's little dog or the World Series. There won't be much time left in the session for the issues you want to avoid.

Conversely, if there is some crucial issue that must be covered in great detail, recognize that the "90-10 Rule" says that you won't have time unless you shorten the chit-chat.

I have participated in real estate negotiations for office buildings in which lots of time was spent arguing the cost of garden and maintenance services, items which didn't matter much, and little time was left to talk about existing tenant lease issues that mattered a great deal. For the buyer of the office building, it was a big mistake. He didn't leave enough time to see how good the leases were and what kind of vacancy rates he could expect in the future.

The "90-10 Rule" can help you make more of the time you have at the table. It can allow you to direct the talks away from what you don't want to talk about or toward what you want to cover in detail.

WHEN IS IT WISE TO BUY NOW AND NEGOTIATE LATER? IS IT BETTER FOR THE BUYER OR SELLER?

Does it ever make sense for a buyer to authorize a seller to start work before an agreement is reached? The answer is not "yes" or "no." In most cases, it's a matter of business judgment.

In a typical "buy now – negotiate later" arrangement, the buyer needs something started quickly and asks the seller to begin immediately on what is usually a time and material basis. Limited funds are allocated to keep the work going. The parties agree to negotiate and finalize a contract later.

Such an arrangement poses serious negatives from the buyer's standpoint. The buyer gets locked in to the seller as a sole-source. There are always technical, scheduling, financial and psychological reasons why it is hard to change suppliers in midstream. Aggressive sellers find it easy to exploit these buyer disadvantages. They can use their solesource power position at negotiation time to charge as much as the distressed buyer can bear. Not all sellers are so aggressive, but the potential for a buyer to pay dearly is real when they have to negotiate after they have authorized the seller to proceed.

Despite these disadvantages, it is sometimes in the buyer's best interest to negotiate after work is started or even after it is done. "Buy now-Negotiate later" may be called for under the following conditions:

1. When there is no time to negotiate. An example would be when a pipe in your house is leaking and the basement

is flooded. The plumber has to do something quickly. He has to act before he knows what exactly is wrong. Once the water is stopped a good estimate of the entire job may be made.

2. When the buyer wants to find out if the seller knows what they are doing. Doing part of the job may reveal the seller's competence or lack of it.

3. If the seller is willing to commit to a "not-to-exceed" dollar amount. In that case the buyer is aware of the most he or she will have to pay.

4. When the seller's history shows that they are unlikely to exploit customers. The smart buyer asks for references and checks them. Reliable sellers have no trouble providing good references.

5. When the job cannot be estimated until enough work is accomplished to provide visibility. For instance, a contractor repairing termite damage to a foundation might not be able to make a realistic estimate until the extent of the damage is uncovered.

6. When a specific performance point on the job can be reached after which competition can be introduced. In the flooded basement example above, competition could be introduced after the leak was stopped and the basement water pumped out.

7. When the buyer believes the seller's price is heavily loaded with problems and probable costs that are unlikely to

occur. In that case it may be wise to negotiate later or to let the seller complete the job on a time and material basis.

8. In the rare situation where the seller's bargaining position will be worse later. This may occur when the seller is afraid to lose the job in process because they need it to keep their people working.

For the seller, "buy now – negotiate later" is usually advantageous, but not always. A seller may be better off saying no to "buy now – negotiate later" because they may get a better price before the work is started than after it is completed. The "call girl-call boy" principle says that the value of services is greater before they are rendered than after.

SOME TIME AND WORK DIFFERENCES AROUND THE WORLD: HOW IT AFFECTS NEGOTIATION

There are twenty-four time zones in the world, four of which fall in the continental United States. Anyone who has lived in Los Angeles and played phone tag with businesses in New York knows how difficult it is to deal with just four time zones.

Most of us office types work from nine to five. By the time we in California get to work at nine, our counterparts in New York are going to lunch. When they go home at five, it's only two in Los Angeles. Our communication window is only two hours. Less if they take breaks during the day.

We now live in a global economy. Americans do business with people in China, Pakistan, Greece and Great Britain. Germans do business with Russians across six time zones. Italian cloth is sold in Singapore and Beverly Hills. Can you imagine all the telephone tag that's going on as people negotiate with each other over 24 time zones?

It's even worse than that. Lunch starts in Spain at three, in Germany at one and in Norway at eleven. The Norwegians start work at eight, the Swiss at seven, the British and Turks at nine thirty, the French at seven or eight. The Germans go home at four, the British at five thirty and the Italians at two – but they work on Saturday.

The Greeks used to take three-hour lunches, but they recently passed a law reducing it to two. However, they are still entitled to 30-minute snacks. Negotiating with the Greeks is not easy, even if you can find them. It's not easy to deal with the Italians either. They don't take calls in the afternoon.

The Irish say, "God made plenty of time." Those in the Islamic world believe that things will get done when Allah wills. Americans say, "Time is money." Time means different things around the world.

When we add twenty-four time zones into this witch's brew of cultural differences, we have the makings of a communications nightmare. New technology will help, but not enough.

What can be done? We can become expert at maximizing our use of video conferencing and email to maintain personal contact across time zones and cultural barriers. We can train our people to waste less time. We can go on the metric system and promote international work standards. We can try to develop an international commercial code to settle disputes.

None of these improvements will be easy. For a long time we will have to continue to do business as we are already doing it. The likelihood of mistakes, omissions, misunderstandings and misinterpretations in international bargaining will surely increase until we get a better handle on time and work differences.

CONCLUSION

Time is money. Few people are more aware of this than Americans. They rush from here to there making the most of the time they have. But there is a problem. In negotiation the expression "time is money" means something else. It means that the more time you give to a negotiation, the better both parties are likely to do, and the better you will do.

When Americans go into a bargaining situation, they want quick results. Other cultures take lots more time. They seem to know better than we do what "time is money" really means as it relates to the negotiating process. They know it means taking the time to get the story and making a both-win deal.

THE TIME PRESSURE TACTICS AND COUNTER-TACTICS

———————— • ————————

Approach #1 Negotiating over the Telephone: Costly Mistakes We All Make in Personal and Business Dealings

Approach #2 Ways to Give Yourself Time to Think under Pressure

Approach #3 Hurry up and Wait - Hurry up and Wait

Approach #4 Choosing the Best Time to Negotiate and to Make Offers, Demands, and Concessions

Approach #5 Marathon Sessions - for and Against Long Talks

Approach #6 The Power of Patience in Getting the Story and Paving the Way for a Win-Win Deal

Approach #7 Deadline Pressures That Get Results

Approach #8 Acceptance Time - How to Get the Other Side Accustomed to Your Viewpoint

Approach #9 How Body Time Can Make a Good Negotiator into a Poor One

Approach #10 The 90-10 Rule - Controlling Time at the Table

Approach #11 When Is it Wise to Buyer Now and Negotiate Later? Is it Better for the Buyer or Seller?

Approach #12 Some Time and Work Differences Around the World: How it Affects Negotiation

13

Authority and Lack of Authority Pressures

HOW TO COPE WITH THEM

An article in the Times once caught my eye. The headline read, "$200,000 Offered for House and She Turned it down." It was years ago, when $200,000 for an old home in a rundown part of Los Angeles was a tremendous sum.

The opening sentences read, "The nuns have quit phoning. They no longer stop two or three times a week to offer Mary Gianetsas huge sums of money for her house." What followed was a fascinating story of how authority or the lack of it works in negotiation.

The Church had been planning to build a new medical center near Mary's property for many years. Now, since they were ready to build, they began to negotiate with her. She had bought the house and land for $20,000 in 1945.

Mrs. Gianetsas, an immigrant from Greece, explained the negotiation this way: "I'm sorry for the sisters. Mother Superior say, 'pray to God,' every time she make new offer. I told her, 'OK, Sister I pray to God.' But every time I pray to God, God tell me same thing – 'Don't sell. Don't sell.'"

The Mother Superior returned time and again to ask the same question, "Did you pray to God, Mary?" Each time Mary replied, "Yes, I pray, Sister. I get same answer – 'Don't sell. Don't sell.'"

The article went on to say, "Just before redesigning the new hospital, the sisters raised the offer for the house $10,000 a month. Through it all Mrs. Gianetsas continued to say, 'God tell me, "Don't sell."'"

The negotiation between Mary Gianetsas and the nuns was a classic. Mary carried the limited authority approach to its extreme. How could the sisters deny her the right to seek the ultimate in higher approval? How could they argue against God's admonition, "Don't sell. Don't sell"? All they could do was test the resolve of the Lord once more by raising the offer $10,000 a month and hope for the best.

Well, Mrs. Gianetsas never did sell. Knowing property values in that area today, I'm quite sure the old house would now sell easily for over a million dollars. The Lord's good advice and the power of limited authority prevailed.

Most of us have used or been abused by authority tactics in one form or another. In this chapter we will consider the full gamut of such tactics – from full authority to no authority. We will learn in the eight sections which follow what these approaches can do for us and how to defend against them.

1. NEGOTIATING WITH NO AUTHORITY – WHY IT'S WISE.

2. NEGOTIATING WITH FULL AUTHORITY – WHY AND WHEN IT'S NOT SO WISE.

3. LIMITED AUTHORITY – FOUR GOOD LIMITS THAT WORK:

    I) Organizational limits.
    II) Structural limits.
    III) Financial limits.
    IV) Government regulations and their limits.

4. CHALLENGING A REGULATION, A POLICY, OR A PROCEDURE – AN UNUSUAL APPROACH.

5. MISSING PERSON AUTHORITY – WHAT IT CAN DO TO YOU.

6. ESCALATING AUTHORITY – A VERY TOUGH TACTIC.

7. HOW TO DISCOVER HOW MUCH AUTHORITY THE OTHER PERSON REALLY HAS.

8. AUTHORITY TO NEGOTIATE: SOME CONTRASTS BETWEEN CULTURES – FRENCH, GERMAN, CHINESE, JAPANESE, AMERICANS.

NEGOTIATING WITH NO AUTHORITY –
WHY IT'S WISE

People who negotiate with no authority are surprisingly effective. First, we will consider the strange, almost hypnotic power of no authority. Later, we will discuss the advantages and disadvantages of negotiating with various levels of authority – from limited to full authority.

Would you negotiate with a person who could make no concessions? Your first reaction is probably "no." But when you think about it, most salespeople you deal with when shopping at an electronics merchandiser such as Best Buy cannot deviate any further from their company policy, price or terms than the sales engine at Amazon.com. Most have no apparent authority to change anything. Yet, despite this absence of authority, we do business with them as though they had it. If in the course of the transaction you decide to negotiate for a better deal, you have to start with them.

The reason we deal with those who lack authority is that they perform a necessary negotiating function. They serve as conduits to those with authority. Although they cannot grant concessions, they listen to our arguments, supply information and carry our viewpoints to their management.

As a buyer, I have dealt with salespeople who, though they did not themselves have authority to change price or terms, knew how to get around obstacles in their organization on my behalf. In a sense, they acted as my agent by urging their sales managers to make significant exceptions and concessions to their offerings.

Often these concessions were granted by the sales managers, not so much to help me, but to show their own salespeople that they were willing to do all they could to help close the sale. Some of these people did a better job of getting a "yes" answer from their own organization than I, as the buyer, could ever do.

As a manager of both sales and purchasing activities at different times in my career, I have found that there are significant advantages gained by sending someone into bargaining without authority. It changes the negotiation from a "give and take" to a "take and take" affair. If, for example, your negotiating representatives are personable, here are some benefits they are likely to win without giving much if anything in return:

1. They can win some price concessions.
2. They can discover what the other party wants and the priorities they place on getting those wants fulfilled.
3. They can find new both-win ways for the sides to mutually benefit.
4. They can learn about the other party's decision-making process, who decides and on what basis.
5. They can find weaknesses in the other party's position or arguments.
6. They can gain an insight into the minimum concessions higher authority must make to close the deal.

Try a new approach at your next negotiation. Send someone to the table who can give nothing away. Your representative may be a friend, a lawyer, a cost analyst, an engineer, an accountant or anyone else who understands the issues and can present your case. He or she will rarely come back empty handed. Then you or someone else can start the negotiation at a more favorable level.

NEGOTIATING WITH FULL AUTHORITY – WHY AND WHEN IT'S NOT SO WISE

Full authority is a booby trap we set for ourselves, especially in our personal dealings. Think about how many times you have bought a car, sold a piece of property, contracted for urgent plumbing repairs or negotiated for a bank loan with less than full authority. Probably never. Like most of us, you represented yourself in dealing with others. As far as negotiation is concerned, you were making a big mistake.

From a strategic standpoint, you are better off with limited or no authority rather than full authority. There are good reasons for this.

The trouble with full authority is that it boxes you in. When buying a car, it's the salesperson who retains the flexibility of asking the boss's permission to give or not give this or that concession or extra. It is she who finds it easier to change her mind while you, having full authority, feel constrained to live with what you've said. She has a built-in, face-saving way out. You don't.

It is the car salesperson who has time to think, while you feel pressured to say yes or no. She can more easily ask for advice from others, while you, being fully in charge, have nowhere to go. The fact that you have full authority skews the process of give and take in her favor.

Those with full authority should recognize that they are at a disadvantage and compensate for it. They should build time to rest, to think, to check facts and to touch base with others into the planning process. They must feel free to ask dumb questions and to say "I don't know" as often and as casually as other people do.

Above all, the key to negotiating with full authority is to avoid pressuring yourself into a quick decision, even though you have authority to do so. Unfortunately, that's exactly what most people with full authority do. They coerce themselves into acting sooner than they would if they had less authority. It was no accident that, in my experiments, one-on-one negotiators with full authority took less time to plan and settled sooner than those who had others at their side.

An acquaintance of mine, Sid, is president of a large consumer electronics company and has full authority to commit his organization to business deals. I asked him how he escapes from full authority when he wants to. His suggestions are applicable to those who buy or sell on a personal level as well as those who are titans of industry:

- Sid is unafraid to tell the other party that, although he has authority to make an agreement, he wants to check with his vice-president or lawyer before doing so.
- When financial issues are involved, Sid buffers his full authority by stating that he feels obligated to clear the matter with the controller or the bank loan committee. Whenever a major buy, sale or merger is being negotiated, Sid says that he has to talk to a money person.
- Sid often limits his authority by hiding behind company policy and procedures as a reason for delaying a decision or holding out for further concessions.
- Sid also disciplines himself to confer with other executives in his company who will be responsible for executing the

agreement. This is important because they understand the ramifications of the agreement better than he does from an operational level. He recognizes that he cannot be boss as well as engineer, production head, financial genius and sales expert at the same time. Sid never lacks for others he must consult with.

The reality is that Sid recognizes the dangers inherent in full authority and compensates for it. His ego is strong enough to surround himself with credible limits. These are usually accepted by the other side as reasonable. Imposing these limits on himself helps Sid make intelligent decisions under pressure.

LIMITED AUTHORITY –
FOUR GOOD LIMITS THAT WORK

Limited authority is a source of strength. The ability to say, "I can't agree to your offer because the manager won't let me or because company policy doesn't permit it" is a face-saving way to say "no" and an effective way to find out how hard the other party is willing to work to win a better agreement.

There are four good ways to limit your authority and gain power at the same time. Each of the following makes it more difficult for the other party to resist your demands or to gain concessions:

I. Organizational limits
II. Structural limits
III. Financiallimits
IV. Government regulations and legal limits

1. Organizational and Personal Limits of Authority

It is easy to limit a negotiator's authority by imposing organizational constraints. For example, some years ago when 1 was buying a painting, I used an organizational limit to delay my final decision and leave room for further bargaining on price. I said to the artist, "I would like to talk to my wife and have her see the painting." How could the artist resist such a reasonable and face-saving limit to my authority?

Organizational constraints to authority are common. Each of us has encountered such limits and accepted them without much resistance. The next time you want time to think or to try for further concessions, tell the other party that you have to discuss the matter with one or more of the following people in your organization:

- Your boss.
- Your partner.
- Members of the "committee."
- One or more of your subordinates.
- One or more of your peers.
- The controller or accountant.
- Your lawyer.
- The banker who lends you money.
- Your spouse or friend.
- Executives in other departments like manufacturing, quality or sales.
- Your customer. Your supplier.

Most people who negotiate feel uncomfortable with organizational constraints to their authority. My advice is that you welcome such constraints rather than reject them. They will make it easier to push for the agreement you want.

II. Structural Limits That Give You Leverage

Another powerful limit to authority is what I call structurallimits. Company policies, procedures, specifications, union restrictions and even job descriptions can prove useful to a person who wants to say "no."

When I worked at Hughes, a very large corporation, it was understandable that the other side might retreat when I said, "Our policy at Hughes prohibits us from doing that." They could see that I didn't make policy for such a big company.

What amazes me now that I have my own business is how often people accept the statement, "Sorry, I can't do that. Company policy won't permit it." They tend to honor the limit, even though I personally have a large role in making policy and have a good deal of authority to change it on the spot.

The ten structural limits to your authority which follow provide a face-saving way to defend against the other party's demands. Arm yourself or your negotiators with these subtle tools of power and they will deliver better agreements:

1. Company standard terms and conditions.
2. Procedures for approving changes.
3. Rules against revealing cost and other information.
4. Liability to third parties.
5. Methods for handling payments and billing.
6. Quality control standards and testing procedures.
7. Types of contracts permissible.
8. Insurance coverage requirements.
9. Limits on changing specifications.
10. Special committee limits such as purchasing, standards,

material review, sales, pricing, source selection, negotiation review. If the committee says we have to do something a certain way, that's what I tell the other party.

The interesting thing about these structural limits is that, though they are self-imposed, they tend to hypnotize the other side into accepting your preferred viewpoint.

III. Financial Authority Limits That Move Others Toward Agreement

Everyone and every organization, no matter how rich, including the United States government, suffers financial limits. It is this fact which makes such limits credible. When a buyer says, "I can't pay more than $10 each because that's all there is in the budget," or a rich man says, "I can't lend you the funds at this time because my money is tied up," we tend to understand because all of us have suffered budget and cash flow problems at one time or another.

Howard Hughes, a brilliant and farsighted businessman, was a billionaire when only a handful of people had attained that distinction. Like many wealthy men and women, Mr. Hughes' personal dealings were far different from his business ones.

Hughes imposed few financial limits on himself when it came to his personal life. Noah Dietrich, Mr. Hughes's highest level executive officer, wrote in his book, *The Amazing Howard Hughes*, that when Hughes wanted a yacht he usually paid the asking price without bargaining. What mattered to him was having the yacht available for a weekend date with a starlet. He didn't seem to care a bit about the thousands he might easily shave off the then exorbitant asking price of $135,000.

Where business was concerned, however, Hughes ran his multi-billion dollar empire with a dollar limit so low that even a small businessman would have found it cumbersome. Dietrich, who was in charge, had to approve every purchase order over $10,000. Can you imagine how often Hughes buyers used this authority limit to playa part in bargaining with vendors?

Many a transaction at Hughes was settled below the magic $10,000 limit just to avoid the delay and uncertainty of waiting for Noah Dietrich's approval. The approval limit played another role as well. Not only did it affect how a buyer would deal with vendors but how they would explain their purchasing decision to management. Every buyer who negotiated an order greater than $10,000 had to be careful to document their decision, knowing that they would be reviewed by Mr. Dietrich, a stickler for detail.

Although the $10,000 limit was absurdly low for a business of this size, the principle of setting a financial limit was important to Hughes. He believed that a company should structure its financial limits to conform to its purchasing and management control strategy. These limits were designed to provide its negotiators with tools to make it easier for them to say "no" or to delay a decision when such delay was desirable. They were also designed to allow better management surveillance over a buyer's decision.

Below are financial limits that I, as a negotiator on the selling, buying and management sides of business, have been glad I had when dealing with others:

- Budget limits.
- Standard cost limits.
- Capital versus expense limits.
- Small purchase limits.

- Petty cash limits.
- Credit amount limits.
- Credit time limits.
- Advance payments limits.
- Progress payment limits.
- Quantity discount limits.

Financial authority limits are a source of negotiating power. They provide a credible buffer against making hasty decisions and help increase a negotiator's resistance to the other party's demands. Such authority limits also serve to escalate the bargaining to higher executive levels whenever management chooses to do so. Few Hughes suppliers wanted to take on Noah Dietrich in person. They knew how tough he was.

IV. Government Regulations and its Limits

The most formidable authority limit is a government regulation. If you want a powerful friend who will rarely let you down, bring to the table a set of rules and regulations from a government agency. The thicker the better. The moment the other party meets your friend, their expectations will drop. They will realize that the problem is bigger than both of you.

A good example of the power of government regulations is a run-in I had with the Motor Vehicle Department. Some years ago I requested what appeared to be a simple change. "Please change the registration on my car from my name to a charitable organization. I am making a gift of it," I told the official at the desk.

Seems easy enough, doesn't it? I soon learned, however, that I needed a number of notarized documents to make the free exchange. They had to be sure that I was the real owner and that the charity really existed. "Why do you need a notarized statement?" I asked. "Because the State needs a notarized statement. That's why," replied the clerk behind the counter. I complained, but it didn't help. I began to sense that the quicker I got to a notary, the less time I would waste. The State regulation made it easier for the official to tell me in a face-saving and polite way what had to be done.

The problem of confronting a government statute is that there is no one to talk to. A person can be persuaded, a team can be convinced, but a regulation is impervious to argument or short-term change. Trying to argue and win your point against an array of unseen foes soon appears too difficult and not worth the enormous effort required.

Yet all is not lost. While government regulations are a source of leverage, there are limits to its power. The outcome of a negotiation is not related solely to the legitimacy of the rules or regulations. Regardless of how firm they appear, they are subject to pragmatic good sense. They can be bent to fit the best interests of both parties, but, as we shall soon see, it will take a lot of hard work and patience to do so.

CHALLENGING A REGULATION: AN UNUSUAL APPROACH – "BUT IT DOESN'T APPLY IN THIS CASE"

There is a an unusual defense against regulations for those with the courage to use it. I learned the technique from an old contract administrator, Bill Van Allen, who had done battle with the government for years. He called it the "But it doesn't apply in this case" approach.

When a government bureaucrat said to my friend, "I can't grant you this or that term, condition or benefit because the regulation prohibits it," he would, after a considered pause, say, "Yes, but it doesn't apply in this case." A perplexed and stunned silence usually followed. When the other party said, "It does apply," my friend would counter, "Just read it carefully and you'll see that it doesn't apply in this case."

This tactic usually forced the government representative into carefully reading the regulation, usually for the first time. These statutes are invariably hard to read and understand. If, after rereading the passage in question, the representative said, with considerably less assurance, "but I think it does apply in this case," Bill would pick some ambiguous or difficult section and read it out loud. He would then insist that his reading of the regulation made sense in the specific situation being discussed. His viewpoint did not always prevail, but it did more times than even he expected. There were good reasons.

Government regulations, laws and rules are vulnerable to argument because they are themselves products of a negotiation.

The published regulation represents a compromise among the people who analyzed, wrote and reviewed it. Each participant had a somewhat different viewpoint. The final version always represents a compromise involving many factors.

What Bill Van Allen taught me was that the limits imposed by regulations and laws are often subject to negotiation at the table. Whatever the regulation says is subject to challenge. The bargaining situation in which one finds oneself is always different from the original scope of the regulation. The issues and conditions covered by the regulation may be out of date, smaller or larger, or of greater or lesser complexity than those on the table. Political and social forces may have changed. When people search for exceptions to rules and regulations, especially complicated ones, they find them – but it takes persistence, time and effort.

Gladstone said, "Good laws make it easier to do right." He did not say, "Good laws make people do right." From a negotiating standpoint, arm yourself with the best governmental regulation limits you can find. If the other party has them on their side, proceed to discover why they do not apply in this case.

Let Thomas Jefferson be your guide. When asked about the suitability of laws in changing times, he replied, "We might as well require a man to wear still the coat which fitted him as a boy." Your task is to demonstrate to the other party that the limiting rule or regulation which they confront you with doesn't fit the current situation.

MISSING PERSON AUTHORITY AND WHAT IT CAN DO TO YOU

Howard Hughes was the ultimate missing man of negotiation. For over twenty years only a handful of people knew where he was or, as he grew older, what he looked like. His isolation was so great that I suspect he could have walked the corridors of the Hughes corporation and no one would have recognized him. Yet thousands of deals were made in his behalf, a number of which were aborted because he wasn't there and could not or would not be found.

Howard Hughes was the person with final authority. When subordinates made agreements which Mr. Hughes wished to improve, he would disappear from sight. Since nothing could be done until he returned, and nobody knew when or if he would, enormous pressure was put on the other party to close the deal if they had something to gain. Tensions would build as time passed. Finally, in order to induce him to approve, the opposing side would make further concessions.

The "Missing Person" authority approach works in the same way. The person with final authority suddenly goes abroad or leaves on vacation before she can sign off on the agreement her subordinates made. The reality in most cases is that the person in charge does not want to sign the agreement for one reason or another. The other party is usually stuck with waiting or making additional concessions to reach a settlement.

There are lots of reasons why negotiators use the missing person approach. For some, it allows time to make a better deal elsewhere or to lower the expectations of the other party. For others, it's because they want to retain the option to close without actually signing off on the deal. For still others, it creates time to search for alternatives or to tie the other party up while they wait. Missing persons have a way of showing up when their own best interests are involved. Therein lies the key to dealing with this borderline approach. Putting a time limit on your proposal or offer helps. Making it known that you are doing business with or negotiating with other people during the waiting period can often help ferret out the missing person. Walking away should also be considered.

When the other party begins to pull the missing person maneuver, there is one thing you must do or your troubles will only grow. Be sure that your boss and all concerned with the negotiation are prepared for a long delay. If you don't let them know what is going on, they will put pressure on you for not anticipating the tactic and avoiding it – pressure which will add to your burdens and aggravations at closure.

ESCALATING AUTHORITY – A VERY TOUGH TACTIC

In this section we will cover a tough authority situation which most of us have already encountered in our business life. We will illustrate ESCALATING AUTHORITY in three situations: an individual buying a piece of used furniture, a business selling a copy machine system and a producer negotiating a contract with a movie star.

Escalating authority typically works like this. An agreement is reached between two opposing negotiators who have apparent authority to make the deal. Then, one of them says that he has to show the agreement to his manager for routine approval. That's when the first surprise occurs. The manager rejects the agreement as being insufficient. She demands further concessions to make it acceptable. A renegotiation granting these concessions then follows to settle the almost closed deal.

I have seen such escalations go to not one level of authority but to two or three levels. Each level demands and wins further concessions to reach final agreement. Do people tolerate such behavior on the part of the other side? They do more often than they should.

Escalating authority is common in the auto sales business. Why do car buyers tolerate this borderline tactic? They do so because they have already done so much work selecting the car they want. They are, at this late stage, reluctant to start negotiating over again with another car agency. Having made up their minds, they want to get on with other matters.

When, at the last moment, the sales manager says to the car buyer that the deal is not good enough, the buyer is psychologically disposed to give a little more even if she resents it. The escalation in authority from salesperson to manager chips away at the buyer's expectations and leads her to make concessions she would not have made originally.

I recently encountered escalation when I was buying an unusual, almost new couch at an upscale estate sale. The asking price was $5000. After some bargaining with the woman handling the sale, we agreed on a price of $4300. I left a deposit of $200 and promised to have it picked up the following day, at which time I would give the seller a certified check for the balance. The couch was exactly what we had been searching for. We were satisfied that the price was probably about right, perhaps a bit high.

To my surprise, next morning I received a call from theowner himself. He told me that the woman who had made the agreement at $4300 had no authority to go below $4600 for this fine couch. He explained the virtues of the furniture, its fine material and workmanship, and told me that he would be glad to return my deposit. I told him I would call back.

What do you think I did when I called back? After discussing the matter for fifteen minutes with my wife, I decided to buy the couch anyway. When I called back I tried to get him to come down to $4400. We settled at $4500. Did I feel angry about paying the higher price? Yes, for a short while. Then, when I saw the couch delivered, I was once again pleased. The long search for the right couch was over.

Should I have tested the price further? Yes. Should I have walked away from the deal? Perhaps. Why didn't I test the price harder or walk away? Because, having talked myself into the fact that $4300 wasn't too bad a price, $200 more wasn't so bad either. Besides, we'd already done more than enough work.

Escalating authority is an equal opportunity borderline tactic. Buyers use it as well as sellers. Last year my company decided to sell our old copying system and invest in a more sophisticated one. As we grew in size, we were customizing more negotiating programs for customers. Many were now receiving a tailored workbook in addition to our standard one. The customization of the program and workbooks required printing and collating capacity not needed before.

The copying machine to be sold was old but in excellent condition. Our advertisement in the newspaper listed it at $8000. We expected to sell it at about $6800 to $7000. An exact market price was hard to determine.

After several ads and considerable time spent talking to prospective buyers, one came along and offered $6000. We accepted $6500 with a $300 deposit check and waited for several days for them to pick it up. When they didn't, we called. That's when the owner himself, not the person who made the deal, talked to us. He told us he could not go ahead at the $6500 price. The original offer of $6000 was all he could afford.

We sold it to him for $6200 a day later because our new copying system was due in any minute and we didn't want to wait any longer.

When it was over, I wondered if the escalation in authority was deliberate. Some are deliberate and some develop in a natural way from an organization's decision-making process. The problem is that you, the victim of the escalation, will never know unless you have enough information to determine in advance whether the other party habitually resorts to this approach. If they escalate others, they are likely to escalate you.

Escalating authority is common in the movie business. Life Magazine reported how it was done by the three Skouras brothers who were then big Hollywood producers. Life wrote that when a movie star negotiated through his agent against the Skouras brothers, he was in for a difficult time. The first person the agent faced was the youngest Skouras brother. After the parties reached agreement, the next older brother was asked to approve the deal. He would not approve and would then proceed to renegotiate to get the actor to take a lower price than before. When the actor and his agent then agreed to a lower price, old Spyros himself started all over again. Few actors could resist this escalation in authority. Actors who were unsure of themselves or needed work badly usually caved in to the Skouras brothers.

Escalating authority calls for firm countermeasures when directed at you. One thing you can do is walk out and take the risks that go with it. If you are a buyer, you might counter by lowering your offer. Either approach on your part may cause the other party to drop its escalated demands. After all, they have also spent lots of time negotiating and don't want to start over again.

One thing that will help you resist escalation is to keep your organization aware that it may happen. If you are careful not to arouse the hopes of your organization that a deal is almost closed, it will be easier for you to stand fast later when the other party employs escalating authority tactics.

Remember, you have more power than you think. If the escalation is deliberate, the other party expects an easy victory. If the stakes are high enough, it's worth testing their resolve by holding fast or walking out.

HOW TO DISCOVER HOW MUCH AUTHORITY THE OTHER PERSON REALLY HAS

When I was a purchasing director, it was important to know whether the person I was talking to had authority to make the deal. I didn't want to waste my time negotiating with salespeople who could not reach a firm agreement.

The trouble was that many suppliers played games with authority. Some sent in people who were bird dogs without authority. Their job was to ferret out my basic wants. Some sent in strong salespeople who lacked authority but were good at arguing their position. Others sent in high level executives with little authority to do anything more than zero in on my bottom line.

I didn't like being exposed to these authority tactics, which were designed to gain information and reduce my expectations. Naturally I preferred dealing with salespeople who could make the final decision, but it was never easy to tell who had authority and who did not.

While there is no perfect defense against those who want to play authority tricks, the ten countermeasures suggested below are designed to help cope with hidden authority tactics on the part of those who oppose you:

1. Ask the other party whether she has the authority to negotiate. Pin down her limits as clearly as possible. Do

not accept evasive answers. This advice is a lot easier to execute as a buyer than as a seller.

2. Know the history of the company and person with whom you are dealing. If they have a history of fooling around with authority, you can expect a problem.

3. Understand the other party's decision-making structure.

4. Get the other party's boss to tell you if any authority limits exist. Make the boss commit herself, either off the record or on the record.

5. Find out in advance how long it takes to get an approval cleared. Have them layout the process you will have to go through.

6. Find out if those who must approve will be available when and if agreement is reached. You don't want to wait until they return from Europe.

7. Get a clear list of all documents required for approval. The absence of a single form, certification or document can often delay decisions by months.

8. Do not state your own authority unless pressed to. Do not be too clear about it unless you have to.

9. Keep your people informed that the other party may use such tactics. Don't let yourself present arguments prematurely to those who do not matter in the negotiation. If you do, you'll find yourself saying the same thing to different people over and over again.

10. If you are a buyer, an effective tactic is to tell the opposing sales manager that you refuse to deal with Charlie, the salesman, because he did not have authority at the last negotiation and wasted your time. The sales manager probably won't send Charlie, but if she does, Charlie will probably have the authority to close the deal this time.

These countermeasures will not work all the time. They will not guarantee success against those who want to play games with authority. Sometimes nothing will work but the courage to call the other side's bluff and a willingness to walk away and start over again with someone else.

AUTHORITY TO NEGOTIATE – SOME CONTRASTS BETWEEN CULTURES: FRENCH, GERMANS, CHINESE, JAPANESE AND AMERICANS

In this section, we will contrast the differences between North American negotiators and those of other cultures in their approach to authority. While there are large variations within each culture, my studies indicate that each society has a "stream of tendency" in the matter of authority styles.

North American negotiators tend to have broad authority to close agreements. In contrast, French negotiators have considerably less. The French management system places greater emphasis on central decision-making and authority rather than individual freedom to act. They are more bureaucratic in structure. Greater constraints are placed on their negotiating teams. This often leads the French to escalate authority to higher executive levels before a final agreement is signed.

British and German negotiators resemble the North American authority style more closely than the French. While limited authority tactics are employed in all cultures, the tendency in the United States, Great Britain and Germany is for negotiators to enjoy broader authority to reach agreement than French men and women in business.

In contrast to North American negotiators, Chinese negotiators have virtually no authority to make final decisions. They begin the talks by saying that they have full authority, but it soon becomes apparent that this is not so. Authority in China, especially when you are dealing with the government or large enterprises, is buried in the bureaucracy and hard to identify. Non-Mainland Chinese business people also bargain with far less authority than North Americans. Chinese decision-makers are rarely at the table, in contrast to Western negotiators, who usually have the power to make decisions on the spot.

Compared to North American negotiators, the Japanese have very little authority to negotiate. The Japanese place great emphasis on consensus building and commitment to targets rather than individual freedom to act. If Japanese salespeople are under pressure to lower a price or change the terms of sale, they are expected to form a new consensus and receive higher approval. The decision-maker is rarely, if ever, at the table and is usually hard to find.

The cultural differences we have discussed in this section are not absolute. They represent, at best, a "stream of tendency" with respect to authority. Differences within each culture are perhaps as great as they are in ours.

CONCLUSION

In every society it takes a lot of homework to know who really makes the decisions in any organization. Things are often not what they appear to be. The same is true of authority limits. Negotiators are like politicians when it comes to defining the authority they have. When they want to be, they can be very hard to pin down.

As far as authority limits are concerned, a history of what a company did last time you negotiated with them is the best guide to what they will do next time. That's one reason it pays to maintain a negotiation history file when you deal with someone. In that file should be a record of how the other party negotiated, how they opened, how they moved from their opening positions, how they closed and whether or not their negotiators had final authority to make agreements. Like the Skouras brothers, they will tend to repeat the authority tactics that worked for them before.

AUTHORITY AND LACK OF AUTHORITY TACTICS – HOW TO COPE WITH THEM

———————— • ————————

Tactic #1 Negotiating with No Authority - Why and When it's Wise

Tactic #2 Negotiating with Full Authority - Why and When it's Not So Wise

Tactic #3 Limited Authority - Four Good Limits That Work
    I. Organizational Limits
    II. Structural Limits
    III. Financial Limits
    IV. Government Regulations and its Limits

Tactic #4 Challenging a Regulation, Policy, or Procedure - an Unusual Approach

Tactic #5 Missing Person Authority

Tactic #6 Escalating Authority - a Very Tough Tactic

Tactic #7 How to Discover How Much Authority the Other Person Really Has

Tactic #8 Authority to Negotiate - Some Contrasts Between Cultures

14

Gaining and Maintaining the Initiative

EVEN WHEN THINGS ARE NOT GOING WELL

Maintaining the initiative under adverse conditions is a common but difficult problem in negotiation. People are taken aback by unfavorable statements and arguments from the other side. Most become reluctant to assert themselves when caught in a mistake or when aggressively challenged by another person. Few like to be contradicted and confronted in daily life. Unfortunately, negotiation is one part of life fraught with contradiction and, all too often, intense confrontation.

This chapter offers practical advice on how to gain and maintain the initiative in negotiation. Eight approaches to maintaining the momentum will be covered. These will help negotiators become more assertive when things are not going well.

I. THE NEGOTIATOR'S BILL OF RIGHTS.

II. KEEP TALKING – KEEP TALKING.

III. TAKE THE HIGH GROUND.

IV. THE HAIRY HAND APPROACH.

V. WHERE TO NEGOTIATE AND HOW TO SET UP THE ROOM.

VI. HOW THE DEVIL'S ADVOCATE, CAUCUS, AND PLANNING CAN MOVE THINGS YOUR WAY.

VII. PERSUASION IDEAS THAT MOVE OTHERS TO YOUR VIEWPOINT.

VIII. MAINTAINING CONTROL – SOME TIPS AND TECHNIQUES INCLUDING WIN-WIN.

I. MAINTAINING THE INITIATIVE – THE NEGOTIATOR'S BILL OF RIGHTS

People are too hard on themselves. Research shows that they want to impress not only those they represent but those who bargain for the other side. This works against them. In striving to look good to others, they often become less assertive than they should and end with poor agreements.I would like to propose a "Negotiator's Bill of Rights."

Its purpose is to help negotiators feel more comfortable in situations that normally threaten their self-esteem and cause them to retreat rather than advance their viewpoint. The seven amendments of the "Negotiator's Bill of Rights" follow. Taken together, they tell you to not take yourself too seriously in negotiation. If you accept the fact that you're not perfect, you'll do better.

NEGOTIATOR'S BILL OF RIGHTS
The Seven Amendments

1. You Have a Right Not to Understand.

2. You Have a Right to Be Wrong.

3. You Have a Right to be Indecisive.

4. You Have a Right to be a Broken Record.

5. You have a Right Not to Answer Questions.

6. You Have Right to be Somewhat Illogical.

7. You Have a Right Not to be Liked.

"THE FIRST AMENDMENT"
You Have a Right Not to Understand

In negotiation, too much happens too quickly for anyone to understand all of it. The other party can be counted on to say things that are confusing and to present numbers and evidence that are not clear or accurate. They use supporting arguments for their positions that are often vaguely illogical and usually self-serving.

To absorb and analyze all that is happening, you have to be quick thinking and take lots of time. The trouble is that few of us are as brilliant as we would like to be or have the time to process what is going on at the table. If we are to achieve the best deal possible, we must determine what the other side really means and what to do about it under the pressure of the moment. Negotiation is in many ways the most demanding work we do in business. Too much happens too fast.

So what is to be done? The person who has enough courage to say, "I don't understand," until they do will do better. Their persistence will give them a better understanding of the situation and, in my opinion, win them respect for their self-assurance.

You have a right not to understand, and, if the other party's explanation doesn't clarify the matter, you have a right to ask the question over and over again. I know it takes courage to repeat your question, but it pays to do so. In negotiation as in life, being somewhat dumb is often smart.

"THE SECOND AMENDMENT"
You Have a Right to Be Wrong

People make mistakes when negotiating. It is understandable because there is so much pressure. They say things they shouldn't and make concessions that are not warranted. They sometimes present statistics and data to defend their position which the other party discovers to be wrong or irrelevant. That's the natural order of things in a heated negotiation. You will make errors which the other side will be overjoyed to point out.

From now on, when you make a mistake and are confronted by the other party for doing so, fight the tendency to become passive.

Accept the fact that negotiators under fire are less than perfect. The final outcome will have less to do with your mistakes than with the many other factors involved.

Sometimes in the tension of bargaining, you will make a concession and discover afterwards that you made a mistake. You have the right to change your mind. You have the right to back off at any time before the agreement is closed and signed. Don't be embarrassed or passive about exercising this right.

You even have the right to correct mistakes after the negotiation is over. When you discover that you have made a mistake, you have the right to ask the other party for help. Whether they will grant relief at so late a stage may be in their hands, but the right to ask for relief is yours.

The next time you make a mistake of any kind, say to yourself, "I've got a right to be wrong." Nobody is perfect. Continue to be assertive in presenting your viewpoint. Be like the first President Bush, who proclaimed while making a speech several years ago: "I hope I stand for antibigotry, anti-Semitism, and anti-racism." The audience gasped. Bush recognized his error, smiled a bit and went on speaking. He had a right to be wrong and so do you.

"THE THIRD AMENDMENT"
You Have a Right to Be Indecisive

Don't force yourself into making a decision under pressure of deadline or deadlock. My research has found that people panic as a deadline approaches. They make very large concessions. A psychiatrist friend of mine is convinced that most personal decisions made under stress are wrong. The same appears to be true in bargaining.

You have a right to be indecisive. In fact, it is not a bad position from which to negotiate. In my experience, the indecisive party in a negotiation has something of an advantage in one regard. If the other party wants to settle, they will do something to make the indecisive person make up his or her mind. At a minimum they will provide more information. At best they will make concessions to move things along.

You have a right to be indecisive as long as you want to. I personally find it difficult to deal with indecisive people. My impatience to make them decisive leads me to make concessions I later wish I hadn't.

In a strange way, indecision requires strength. Because it teaches us to live with the ambiguity of being neither here nor there, it can work for us in bargaining.

"THE FOURTH AMENDMENT"
You Have a Right to Be a Broken Record

Sooner or later people run out of new things to say in negotiation. At that point some are embarrassed to say again what they said before.

My advice is, don't be afraid to repeat yourself. Many experiments confirm that an audience will retain more of what the speaker says if it is repeated. The more the speaker repeats, the better it is remembered. When you do not know what to say next, say what you said before. Say it again and again and again.

I was once in a negotiation with an Iranian manufacturer who sold industrial lighting fixtures. What I remember most about him was that he was the most persistent broken record I ever met.

Even when I repeatedly said "no" to the many things he asked for, that didn't stop him.

He would return again and again to the same issue after talking about something else for a while. He made the same arguments over and over again as though I had never heard them before. He was the perfect "broken record."

After the negotiation was over, we became friends. I asked him why he repeated himself so much. He laughed and said that it was common in Iran and also worked well for him in the United States. I have since found it easier to be a broken record. When I don't know what to say next, I shamelessly say what I said before, said before, said before.

"THE FIFTH AMENDMENT"
You Have the Right Not to Answer Questions and You Have a Right Not to Know the Answer

People who feel that they should know the answer to every question asked of them place themselves in a difficult position. They deprive themselves of the right to say "I don't know" or "I will try to find out."

The negotiator who thinks he must know almost everything about the subject at hand usually talks too much and, in so doing, is likely to damage her position rather than help it. If you are lucky enough to run into someone who is so insecure that he feels he must answer every question you ask, be patient. He will soon tell you more than he should.

You have a right not to know the answer to a question. You also have the right not to tell what you know if you do know the answer. You have a right to give half an answer or none at all. You have a right to say, "I'll look into it," rather than shoot from the hip with a quick statement.

A negotiation is not a test. The right answer may be a partial answer, a delayed answer or no answer at all.

"THE SIXTH AMENDMENT"
You Have the Right to See Things Through Your Own Eyes and to Be Somewhat Irrational or Emotional

In negotiation there is no judge or jury, no teachers and pupils, no grades or tests to be passed. You have the right to reject the other person's viewpoint without good reason. You have the right to be illogical and to express your emotions. You do not have to agree with the arguments and the facts presented to you, however correct they appear. You can be illogical or partly logical or even irrational in interpreting what the facts mean and what they leave out. You have a right to say 2 + 2 does not equal 4 in this case – for whatever reason occurs to you.

The trouble is that it is hard to be illogical or emotional if that's not your style. The more logical and emotional you are in business situations, the more difficult it will be to exercise the rights we have just expressed. Nevertheless, try being illogical once in a while. If you are angry or passionate about an issue, don't be afraid to express your feelings. They will help convince the other side that you are committed to your position.

"THE SEVENTH AMENDMENT"
You Have a Right Not to Be Liked

The Russians have an old saying, "If the person you are negotiating against likes your representative and has good things to say about him, your negotiator is not doing a good job for you."

The person with a need to be liked will find that the other party plays to that need. They may patronize the needy person by providing warmth and comfort in exchange for gaining their objectives. Or they may make the needy party uncertain in front of others by withholding approval, causing him to be less assertive in defending his position. Most normal people have a need to be liked, but those with too deep a need will have a harder time at the table.

Negotiation involves conflict. Conflicting values, ideas, and issues must be reconciled. What you say, what you do, and what you demand will not be welcomed by the other side. Charming or not, they will find it hard to love you if you do your job well. Negotiation is no place to win a popularity contest. You have a right not to be liked.

People tend to demand too much of themselves when bargaining. We are overly sensitive to every mistake we make, to everything we don't understand and to every attack made on our position and its shortcomings. This puts us on the defensive too quickly and too easily.

The Negotiator's Bill of Rights allows us to recognize our imperfections in a negotiating setting. It allows us to laugh at ourselves and our imperfections rather than retreat in the face of them.

II. MAINTAINING THE INITIATIVE – KEEP TALKING, KEEP TALKING

One of the great mergers of the Twentieth Century was between TCI, the cable giant, and Bell Atlantic, a huge telephone and communications company. How they reached agreement after talks broke down was reported in Time Magazine.

The Chief Executive Officers of both companies met on a large yacht. They negotiated for hours but could not agree. Finally they decided to give up and head for shore.

At that point, however, a mechanical problem arose on the yacht. The ship's anchor could not be raised. It was stuck on the ocean floor. No amount of power or pulling helped. After quite a while the crew recognized that a professional diver was necessary, so they radioed for one. It took hours for the diver to get to the yacht.

Having nothing else to do, the two CEO's started to talk again. They talked and talked while waiting for the diver to clear the anchor. They went over old ground, came up with some new options, changed the price, and worked further on possible terms, conditions, and controls. Before reaching shore, many hours later, they had arrived at an agreement both had thought out of reach.

Talking has a momentum of its own. It carries the parties along like the current in a river. Long talks reveal hidden needs, unseen alternatives and potential benefits not previously thought possible or relevant. When talks bog down, a good way to keep things going is to continue the discussions in any way you can.

As to the Tel-Bell Atlantic story, the agreement hammered out on the stalled boat didn't sail in the end. About six months later the deal between them was called off as a result of severe price gyrations in the stock market. Perhaps they will start talking again.

III. MAINTAINING THE INITIATIVE – TAKE THE HIGH GROUND

The best way to maintain the initiative in negotiation is to take the high ground. It is easier to control the flow of the bargaining process if your position is supported by credible facts and logic. While facts and logic will not help in every case, in most situations they allow you to present your position in the best possible light – and add to your confidence in doing so.

What constitutes the "high ground"? High ground is the supporting backup brought to the bargaining table. Supporting concepts or documents serve as a guide to discussing each issue, to strengthening one's arguments and to persuading the other party. Five types of backup are most effective in reaching high ground:

REACHING FOR THE HIGH GROUND FIVE TYPES OF BACKUP TO SUPPORT YOUR POSITION

---

1. GUIDING PRINCIPLES.
2. GUIDING HISTORY OR PRECEDENTS.
3. GUIDING LOGIC OR CONCEPTS.
4. GUIDING STANDARDS OR NORMS.
5. GUIDING RULES, REGULATIONS AND LAWS.

Each of these high ground support areas are designed to give credibility and legitimacy to assertions or to demands and offers.

The more guiding support you bring to the table, the more likely the outcome will favor your viewpoint.

1. Guiding Principles

Guiding principles serve to focus the discussions on the merits of an issue rather than the details. For example, if our position is that 10 percent is a fair profit for the seller, it would be wise to open the negotiation by having both parties agree on the guiding principle that the seller is entitled to a fair profit. This should not be too difficult.

Once agreement is reached by buyer and seller on the "fair profit principle," the matter to be negotiated next is whether 10 percent, 25 percent or 5 percent is a fair profit and why. Your next task is to find guiding principles that support your 10 percent goal rather than 5 percent or 25 percent in this specific situation.

The important thing is to employ guiding principles that support your strategic objectives. Examples of some principles that can be used to guide negotiation are fair profit, the right to stay in business, the right not to lose money, the right to a fair warranty, the right to get paid in a timely fashion, the right to a usable product or service, the right to a safe product, a fair wage, the right to protection from inflation, protection from changes in currency values, the right to change how we do business if circumstances change radically, the right to equal treatment and the right to conduct our affairs without undue interference.

Negotiation from guiding principles allows the bargaining to proceed on the high ground rather than getting mired down in details. Agreement on details is made easier when an agreement in principle has been achieved. When talks on details break down later, the opposing negotiators can maintain momentum by returning to the principles previously agreed to.

2. Guiding History or Precedents

Before going into negotiation, buyers should bring with them history cards of prior purchases of the same or similar goods or services. Such history is most useful when it lists the prices paid, quantities bought, who negotiated, and problems encountered by the buyer in the course of the seller's performance.

The salesperson can also use history wisely. For example, good current references build credibility. It is amazing how many sellers provide the names of references who have died or who are no longer in business. Some are even careless enough to provide references from dissatisfied customers.

A salesperson who maintains a history of relations with the customer and their customized needs can better deal with a buyer's arguments during negotiation. By knowing past prices paid, quantities ordered, promises fulfilled, special favors rendered and payments made late by the buyer, the seller can handle the negotiation in a more assertive and intelligent way.

A salesperson smart enough to take notes about a buyer's tactics during a negotiation is in a better position to deal with the buyer's bargaining style next time. Armed with this history, the seller can anticipate the other party's demands and concession pattern as well as what they will do as they move toward agreement.

Yogi Berra once said, "It's hard to make predictions. Especially about the future." Despite that, the sales manager who asks her salespeople how the buyer negotiated last time and insists on written history files of past bargaining will get better results in future dealings.

3. Guiding Logic or Concepts

It's hard for me to negotiate against anyone who is very logical. My problem is that when the other party is logical, I find myself guided by the power of their reasoning. I tend to go along, even when I don't want to. They gain the initiative and move me in their direction.

A salesman attending one of our seminars told me a story about a price negotiation with an angry buyer. The seller's company policy was to charge on a per unit basis depending on the size of the order. For example, one to 12 units were $100 each; 13 to 24 units were $90 each; and 25 or more were $80 each. Lower prices for larger quantities makes sense.

The customer was angry because the salesman had quoted $90 each on 17 units ordered in accordance with the price list. He insisted that the price should be $80 because this was the third order in two months – prior purchases were 23 units and 35 units at list price. "Now," said the buyer, "I won't pay more than $80. It's not fair or logical. I've given you two orders for 58 units and here's 17 more for a total of 75 in two months. You're ripping me off at $90 each for the 17 I now want."

The buyer's logic was good and the seller responded by looking at the price structure, averaging the three orders, and giving the customer the $80 price. Furthermore, the practice of averaging orders over a three month period became company policy. Logical negotiators, like this determined customer, find it easier to persuade others.

4. Guiding Standards or Norms

Few things in negotiation carry as much weight as well thought-out standards and norms. Negotiators who can back their position with objective standards take the high ground in a negotiation.

Cost standards lend legitimacy to the buyer who says to the seller, "We've got to buy it within my standard cost guidelines. This is all management has allocated for this part." If the buyer shows the computer printout for standard costs to the salesperson, the bogey becomes doubly credible.

From the seller's standpoint, standards can guide the buyer to a "yes" decision. The salesperson armed with standard price lists, standard terms and conditions, standard warranties and standard discounts holds the high ground. In a strange way, the seller's standards make it easier for the buyer's organization to accept the proposal offer.

Before going into your next negotiation, ask yourself whether there are any standards or norms that will help your viewpoint prevail. There probably are.

5. Guiding Rules, Regulations and Laws

At one time or another, most of us have been kept from doing what we felt to be reasonable because some company policy or computer program prohibited us from deviating from its constraints. For example, there were many occasions when I, as a seller, had to provide the buyer with cost breakdowns I didn't want to give. This cost information was submitted because government procurement regulations said I had to. If they represent your viewpoint, rules, regulations, policies, procedures, and laws make it easier for your position to prevail, but they can be a real problem if they work in favor of the other side.

From now on, put the power of legitimacy on your side. Before going into a negotiation, search for the high ground in your own company policies and procedures. Even better, see if there are government regulations, rules or statutes that support your position. These guides to action make it easier for the other party to say "yes."

In this section we have covered five types of backup that provide a negotiator with high-ground support. These guidelines help move the other party and their organization in your direction.
These guidelines and standards serve another subtle but crucial function. They help negotiators marshal the support of their organization behind their bargaining position and arguments. This benefit should not be overlooked since it reduces the impact of those who would criticize the agreement later.

IV. MAINTAINING THE INITIATIVE – THE HAIRY HAND APPROACH

Norman Rockwell, the famous painter of mid-twentieth century Americana, once told this story of the "hairy hand." As a young artist, he earned a living making portraits and full-body paintings of people. Almost invariably, his early clients were picky about the paintings. No matter how good they were, clients found fault with something.

Rockwell tried to keep them happy, but it was hard to do. Many drawings required tedious reworking to correct the flaws his clients believed they could see. It took a great deal of time and kept him from doing the work he wanted to do as a creative artist.

Rockwell finally learned how to handle the problem from an older portrait artist. "Just put a lot of hair on the hand," said the old artist. "Then, when the client sees the portrait his attention will be directed to the hairy hand. He won't bother you about anything else."

Rockwell discovered that people get a great deal of satisfaction from finding flaws. Sometimes they overlook more important factors in their pleasure at appearing to be discerning. From that time on, Rockwell deliberately placed a "hairy hand," or its equivalent, in every portrait. When the client discovered it, Rockwell graciously conceded the point and efficiently removed it. Everybody was happy.

I know negotiators who deliberately put hairy hands into their proposals and presentations. They build in flaws which can easily be detected by the other party. I've seen proposals in which projected material costs were inflated far beyond reason. Their purpose was to focus the talks on material costs, not on the high labor estimates where the big profits were.

The "hairy hand" is also present in personal dealings. Real estate agents go to great lengths to point out minor flaws in the rear bedroom of a house in order to keep prospects from noticing that the brick lining of the fireplace is falling apart. Used car sellers prefer to highlight small defects, like a stain on the rear carpet or a window that won't roll up easily, rather than have the customer discover that the air conditioner is noisy and may soon need replacement.

The purpose of these negotiating hairy hands is the same as that of Rockwell's. They are designed to be discovered by the customer and to direct the discussion away from vulnerable areas. In that way, the salesperson or negotiator maintains greater control of the talks.

V. MAINTAINING THE INITIATIVE - THE CONFERENCE ROOM AND SEATING ARRANGEMENT

The setting of a negotiation can affect the outcome. The Italian dictator Benito Mussolini preferred to deal with others in his palatial office. People coming to see him had to walk a long distance across a huge, almost empty room. To talk to Mussolini, they had to sit on a small chair in front of his gigantic desk. Is there any doubt that the portly dictator in his bemedalled uniform held the high ground?

In planning for a negotiation, attention should be directed to the conference room and its setting. Overlooking this detail may concede the initiative to the other side. A few cautions are appropriate. Never allow the other party to place you in an uncomfortable chair or one facing the sun. The shape of the table is important. Seat your people around the team leader in such a way that they can maintain eye contact and direct communication with each other. Both teams are better off if there is symmetry of positions between their respective specialists, leader to leader, lawyer to lawyer, and expert to expert sitting opposite one another.

The size of the room should be scaled to the size of the meeting. A small group in a large area is intimidating. A large group in a small area makes it difficult to concentrate or work in. Each side should have enough room to spread its papers and documentation. It is essential to have nearby conference rooms to allow each side to discuss strategies in private. Having lunch and dinner facilities close by is helpful. Each side should be able to choose a place to eat away from the other if they wish to.

Finally, a few tips are useful to help make an effective presentation in the conference area. Choose a setting that will permit you to easily direct the other side's attention to your presentation materials. Assure yourself of access to high-speed internet service, data projectors for laptop presentations, laser pointers, high-resolution screens and whiteboards, flip charts, fax and copy machine access, and paper. If you fail to plan ahead for these items, you will not have them when the need arises. Check in advance whether the lighting and audio aspects of the room are adequate.

Oh yes, don't forget what I once forgot. Tell your people in which city you are going to negotiate. I once forgot to tell my pricing specialist in Los Angeles that we were negotiating in New York. He never showed up because he assumed we would negotiate in Los Angeles. Logistics are an important but often overlooked factor in maintaining the initiative, especially when you are far from home. Someone should be put in charge of hotel arrangements, travel coordination, backup materials, charts, calculators, computers, and other aids and comforts. This will allow the negotiator far from home better control of the bargaining process.

VI. MAINTAINING THE INITIATIVE - HOW THE DEVIL'S ADVOCATE, CAUCUS AND PLANNING CAN MOVE THINGS YOUR WAY

Former Secretary of State Henry Kissinger once said, "My job as a negotiator is to know what I want and to discover what the other party is capable of giving me." This requires planning.

Planning is essential to move talks in the direction you want. Common sense indicates that the better you understand what you need, the better your chances of saying and doing those things that will get you there. A good plan is like a compass setting. The winds of negotiation are bound to change from time to time. You cannot anticipate every storm and every obstacle. Without a plan, the best you can do is react to the other person's moves and arguments. To succeed, you have to know where you want to go and how to get there. What makes a good plan is covered in Chapter 10 of this book.

One aspect of planning is especially important in maintaining the initiative. One person on your side should play the Devil's advocate and act as the opposing party. For example, if you are buying a car, let your spouse or friend play the role of the car salesperson. Go through a practice negotiation with your associate. Present your reasons for a lower price, additional services, and free or lower priced accessories.

Afterward, let your associate rebut your reasons, just as the real salesperson is sure to do. Then come back with further reasons and actions in response to those objections. This approach is sure to help you anticipate the opponent's arguments and improve your own as the talks progress.

One more thing that will help maintain the initiative throughout the negotiation is to caucus frequently. As the discussion moves toward agreement, differences heat up. Demands, offers and options are presented which require careful analysis. There is rarely enough time to think things through at the table. Under this pressure, the key to moving the talks in your direction is to spend less time in talks between parties and more time in caucuses with your own people.

VII. MAINTAINING THE INITIATIVE – PERSUASION IDEAS THAT MOVE OTHERS TO YOUR VIEWPOINT

Negotiators who are skilled in the art of persuasion do better in supporting the positions they take. The persuasion tips which follow are worth remembering:

1. It is better to start talks with easy-to-settle issues than with highly controversial ones.

2. Repetition of a message leads to learning and acceptance.

3. The more you show that you understand the other party's position, the more trust and cooperation you'll get.

4. When you anticipate resistance on a point, diffuse it in advance.

5. Agreement on controversial issues is improved when they are tied to less troublesome issues.

6. The "Wooing Principle" says that people want others to want them. They want others to actively pursue them, to be especially friendly toward them, to say and do nice things, to go out of their way for them, to listen attentively, and to display ardent interest in ways large and small.

7. People tend to believe numbers and statistics published by reputable (and sometimes not so reputable) sources. However, don't be seduced by such data and numbers. They are almost always subject to interpretation and negotiation. They are always self-serving.

8. A message that asks for a greater change of opinion is likely to produce more change than one that asks for less — within reason of course.

9. Learning and acceptance are improved if emphasis is placed on similarities of position rather than differences.

10. It is more effective to present both sides of an issue than just one side.

11. People tend to want what's hard to get.

12. If you get people angry, they will get even by rejecting your message, even when it is good for them.

13. Write down the arguments in favor of your positions before you go to the table.

14. The Chinese say, "Time brings things in slow degrees." The skilled persuader starts early and lets acceptance time, repetition, and logic do the job by slow degrees.

15. People are disinclined to argue with those of higher status or expertise.

16. When two messages must be sent, one of which is desirable and the other undesirable, the most desirable one should be sent first.

17. Agreement is facilitated when the desirability of agreement is stressed.

18. A message that first arouses a need and then provides

information to satisfy it is remembered best. However, when a need-arousal message is severely threatening, the listener tends to reject it.

19. The believability of a message is enhanced if it is given by someone not involved in the negotiation.

20. People are more inclined to be for an idea if they are unaware of important people who oppose it. That's why it's wise to sell some ideas off the record or one on one.

21. Most people can't pass up a free deal. Given something free, they will open their minds to a persuasive message.

22. When pros and cons of an issue are being discussed, it is best to present the communicator's favored viewpoint last.

23. Listeners remember the beginning and end of a presentation more than the middle.

24. Listeners remember the end better than the beginning, particularly when they are unfamiliar with the arguments.

25. Take the time to be right about what you present. Accuracy in backup details builds credibility.

26. Commitment to an idea is enhanced by words, involvement, or logical processes in favor of the idea.

27. Conclusions should be explicitly stated and summarized rather than left for the audience to decide.

28. There is a Russian saying, "It's not the horse that pulls the grain. It is the grain that pulls the horse."

VIII. MAINTAINING THE INITIATIVE – GENERAL TIPS AND TECHNIQUES TO MAINTAIN CONTROL INCLUDING WIN-WIN

In every negotiation there is a time when neither party knows what to say next. They feel that everything relevant to making an agreement has been covered not once but many times. The following tips and techniques are useful in moving things along during this awkward part of the bargaining process:

One: The Win-Win Way – Find a Better Deal for Both Parties

One of the best ways to gain the attention of the opposing party is to say, "Let's find a better way for both of us." It's the way I often reduce the stress of bargaining and come up with creative both-win ideas. Chapters 3 and 4 have many hints on where and how to discover innovative win-win possibilities. Such mutually beneficial ideas are guaranteed to keep the talks going, even when the parties are half asleep or ready to walk out.

Two: Take the Path of Least Resistance

When you find agreement difficult on an issue, jump to something more agreeable. For example, if you cannot reach settlement on price, move to delivery or payment terms. Don't hang up on tough issues. Move from point to point. Return later to the difficult issue.

Three: Maintain a "Yes" Mode

Hold some easy "yes" issues in abeyance for use when things

bog down later. They may be of minor or major significance. These "yes" issues may be used as trading chips or as goodwill concessions to move the talks toward agreement.

Four: Negotiate a Good Agenda

In diplomacy, as in business and life, those who control the agenda are in the best position to hold the high ground of negotiation. Agenda is the key to gaining and maintaining the initiative because it controls what will be said, when it will be said and, perhaps more important, what will not be said.

The negotiation agenda is a program of things to be covered at the meeting. It is the first test of the party's relative bargaining power and motivations. A good agenda can create a climate which minimizes conflict and supports win-win solutions. It helps keep talks on track and promotes a patient exploration of facts and logic. It can also allow you time to present your position in the best possible light.

Whether you are negotiating a budget with your wife or friend, dealing with the Japanese on a trade treaty, or closing a sale with a tough customer do your best to agree on an agenda before talks begin.

Five: Be Ready to Change the Subject from Business to Personal Matters

Negotiation creates tension for both parties, especially when conflicting positions begin to harden. That's whenit's smart to change the subject from business to personal matters such as family, sports, politics or movies. When things cool down, you can return to business issues. Something else that works: When tensions rise, enjoy a coffee and donut break together.

Six: Rephrase Your Proposal and Offer Many Times and Never Assume the Other Side Has Read Your Proposal or Fully Understands Your Offer

Many sellers hesitate to repeat what they have written so carefully in their proposals. That's a mistake. My advice is that you repeat verbally all that you proposed in writing. There is a good chance that nobody on the other side read the whole proposal. There is even a chance that some people at the table read none of it. Never assume they know what benefits you are offering or why your price is good.

As the negotiation goes on, don't be shy about rephrasing your offer as often as necessary in slightly different ways. In the rephrasing, especially when things are bogging down, you may deliberately choose to make a small change or even a small concession. The other party will listen attentively to your rephrased offer in the hopes of finding some sign of concession, accommodation, or agreement. They may respond with a conciliatory gesture of their own to move the slowed talks along.

Seven: Do Something All the Time

To move things along in a negotiation, it's useful to take actions all the time. Take notes, put data into your laptop computer, punch your calculator, start writing a clause, get more information out of your attache case, or make a dinner reservation for both sides.

Movement and action can also result from events you initiate. For example, making a date early in the day to meet the other side for dinner at a good restaurant can help ensure that talks go on for the rest of the day, even if things get rough in between.

Eight: Under Severe Pressure Resist Like Water

When water is under pressure or made to flow into unfamiliar channels, it falls back. Then, in its own good time, it seeps back bit by bit. Eventually it reaches its level. In the face of strong pressure, resist like water. Fall back, listen, think, and then move forward slowly.

Nine: When a Deal is Close to Agreement Stay With it Until It's Done

When agreement seems near keep the session going until it's done. I have seen too many negotiations that were close to settlement late on Friday fall apart Monday morning when the parties met again. Had they worked together Friday evening, an agreement could have been reached. Over the weekend "Monday Morning Quarterbacks" in both organizations had the opportunity to pick apart the details of the agreement. By Monday morning, the agreement – so close at hand earlier – was further away because neither side was willing to follow up with the small concessions necessary.

The best thing to do when agreement is close is to put it over the goal line. It may not be possible tomorrow morning.

CONCLUSION

In this chapter we have presented eight approaches which lead to gaining and maintaining the initiative. When things are going well, these approaches will make your position stronger. When things are not going well, they will help you fight the tendency to become defensive or passive.

In negotiation you will someday find yourself facing someone making a very strong argument in favor of his or her position. When that happens to a friend of mine, he follows the example set by William Jennings Bryan.

A century ago Bryan was known as the "Great Orator"; he loved to argue and debate on any subject. One day a friend heard that he was going to debate something about which he knew almost nothing. He asked Bryan, "How can you possibly talk about that?" Bryan countered, "I shall take the negative. You don't have to know anything to oppose a proposition." Politicians, like negotiators, haven't changed much in a hundred years.

GAINING AND MAINTAINING THE INITIATIVE

———— • ————

I. The Negotiator's Bill of Rights - You've Got a Right to Be Somewhat Dumb, Indecisive, and Wrong

II. Keep Talking - Keep Talking

III. Take the High Ground

IV. The Hairy Hand Approach

V. The Conference Room and Seating Arrangement

VI. How the Devil's Advocate, Caucus and Planning Can Move Things Your Way

VII. Persuasion Ideas That Move Others to Your Viewpoint

VIII. Maintaining Control - Some General Tips and Techniques Including Win-Win Negotiation

15

How Others May Try To Intimidate You and What to Do About It

One of the best selling books of the 1980s was called Winning Through Intimidation. The author believed that the best way to get ahead was to intimidate those you do business with. Many people are convinced that this approach is effective in negotiation. I am not.

This chapter is concerned with tactics of intimidation, tactics you are sure to encounter in your business dealings. When the other side uses these strategies, they are trying to place you in a defensive position. The purpose of this chapter is to heighten your awareness of what to do about it. Eight types of intimidation will be covered:

1. LEGAL INTIMIDATION.
2. INTIMIDATION BY EXPERTS.
3. INTIMIDATION BY RAISING THE STAKES.
4. THREAT AND ITS INTENDED AND UNIN-TENDED CONSEQUENCES.

5. STATUS INTIMIDATORS.

6. INTIMIDATION BY TAKING FINANCIAL AND OTHER TYPES OF HOSTAGES.

7. PHYSICAL AND ENVIRONMENTAL INTIMIDA-TORS.

8. EMOTIONAL, NUISANCE AND EMBARRASS-MENT INTIMIDATORS.

LEGAL INTIMIDATION AND HOW TO HANDLE IT

It's regrettable that the legal profession is held in such disrepute. Newspapers are full of stories about lawyers who abuse their clients and charge unconscionable fees. It is no surprise that so many people wonder if the legal system and its army of lawyers is out of control. Lawyer jokes, like those that follow, say much about the frustration people feel.

• • • • •

There's the one about the lawyer who said to a client, "Before I can represent you I have to get a $5000 retainer." The client was surprised and wrote a check for $5000. "Thank you," said the lawyer. "That entitles you to two questions." "What! $5000 for only two questions? Isn't that awfully high?" asked the client. "Yes, I suppose it is," said the lawyer. "Now, what's your second question?"

• • • • •

Another is about the Pope and a lawyer who were both killed in the same car crash. When they met St. Peter at the Pearly Gates, St. Peter told the Pope to wait until he took care of the lawyer.

While the Pope looked on, Peter took the lawyer to a beautiful mansion and said, "From now on this is where you can live. If you need anything else just ask." Peter then took the astounded Pope to another residence, a one-bedroom apartment on the ground floor. The Pope was surprised but said nothing. Several days later, one of the Pope's assistants got up the courage to ask why the lawyer had gotten a mansion and the Pope only a small apartment. The Pope, after all, had spent his entire life doing God's good work.

St. Peter answered, "We have 188 Popes in heaven but this is the first lawyer we've ever seen. We want to encourage them."

• • • • •

Some years ago, the head of the American Bar Association asked the press to stop repeating lawyer jokes because they demeaned the profession. It didn't help. Lawyer jokes are more popular than ever.

Almost everyone is afraid of getting involved in legal battles. A century ago, Charles Dickens wrote about people whose lives were ruined and whose estates were decimated at the hands of lawyers. Four hundred years ago, Shakespeare wrote, "Let's kill the lawyers." Disdain for the legal profession is pervasive. As a business friend of mine put it, "Lawyers are like enemas. You hate them until you need one, then you still hate them."

People are intimidated by the threat of legal action, and for good reason. In an extended legal battle opposing lawyers are certain to expose weaknesses in your procedures, policies and judgments. They can cause the most competent and self-respecting executives to lose confidence in themselves. Even the smallest character flaws are brought to the surface and exaggerated. In a lawsuit, business secrets may be exposed. Mistakes you thought you had put behind you are opened to scrutiny. I have known competent medical doctors reduced to tears during testimony – their egos deflated under a barrage of "legal search and destroy" tactics. Is it any wonder that we are intimidated by lawyers and lawsuits?

In addition to the stress of going through a lawsuit, we have to consider the huge costs involved. Lawyers charge an average of $350 an hour. Top lawyers earn $1000 an hour. It's easy to run up a bill of two or three hundred thousand dollars on even a simple matter.

So you are sued and call a lawyer. They get paid to do the work, don't they? Nonsense. It's likely that you and your family or associates will have to do an enormous amount of the work it takes to provide your lawyer with the documentation needed to defend you. Endless hours will be spent looking through records to prove or disprove details your lawyer deems necessary for your defense.

Forget the daily work that earns you a living. The lawsuit must come first. Defending yourself will soon take all your time and energy.

OK, so it costs a lot, but it's worth it. Justice prevails and the good guys win. Or do they? Some years ago I worked for a company of good guys, honorable in every way. Nevertheless, they spent a million dollars preparing a case for trial. Just before the trial began, the other party admitted wrongdoing off the record. They offered $100,000 in a cash settlement and a loosely worded letter that said they would discontinue the behavior we objected to.

We laughed at the offer until our attorney told us that the trial would probably cost an additional million dollars and that a favorable jury verdict was by no means certain. The good guys settled for a more clearly worded letter and an additional $50,000 to sweeten the bad guy's offer.

Why? Because we wanted to get it over with and return to normal life. Sure we wanted more, but by that time we had reason to believe that the bad guys had hidden their assets in Swiss bank accounts. Even if the jury awarded us a big settlement, we could have recovered little or none of it. Bad guys with good lawyers do better than they should.

Legal intimidation does influence negotiation. One of the parties may be afraid of the legal process. One may have the resources to pay high legal costs, while the other does not. There are people in business who budget legal action into their competitive strategy, knowing that others will run from it. The possibility of a lawsuit is often a hidden factor in determining the outcome of negotiations.

What can be done to reduce the impact of legal intimidation? These countermeasures can help:

1. Few threats to sue end in lawsuits. When the other party threatens, don't overreact. They may talk big but be unwilling to pay the costs or do the work that goes with legal action. Keep talking.

2. Because we live in a litigious society, it's wise to build the cost of legal action into your overhead and pricing strategy. Legal intimidation is less effective when you have the cash to defend against it.

3. Build mediation and arbitration into your business relationships. It reduces the tendency toward legal adventurism. Japan has one-tenth the lawyers we have in the United States. Almost all disputes are settled through mediation or arbitration.

4. It pays to put an attorney on retainer, or to hire one for your staff if business warrants. It will help avoid legal pitfalls before they arise. If legal problems are allowed to fester, the cost of protecting yourself will rise. Getting good legal advice early on pays for itself.

5. When a serious lawsuit threatens, use the services of the best law firm you can afford. The difference between a good firm and a mediocre one is enormous.

I once met the manager of a medium-sized oil company with forty lawyers on staff. He told me that the owner of the company was convinced his financial success was a direct result of the size of his legal staff. He hired them not only to protect his legal interests but to help negotiate better deals. Everyone who dealt with that corporation knew they would be in for costly battles if a dispute was not settled by negotiation. The size and aggressiveness of the legal staff intimidated the other party without a word being said at the bargaining table.

INTIMIDATION BY EXPERTS

It's hard to negotiate against an expert. People are reluctant to assert themselves when dealing with those who are authorities in their field. Experts are a source of power. They serve to move settlement in their direction.

Almost all of us have been intimidated by experts at one time or another. There is probably some room to negotiate a mechanic's proposed price to repair your car, or a dentist's price for working on your teeth. Yet the moment we try to bargain, we find ourselves confronted by the language of expertise – a foreign tongue beyond our understanding. All we can do is make a feeble attempt to bargain and hope they will be kind enough to give us a break.

The same is true when buying a diamond ring. You know there is some fat in the price. But no sooner do you try to negotiate than the jeweler starts talking in the technical language of his profession. Words like color, cut and types of imperfections are thrown at you. Your eyes cross. You feel like an idiot trying to bargain about something you know nothing about. The jeweler's expertise is his power. He senses your weakness, and if you're lucky he sells you a good diamond at a slightly reduced price. If you're not so lucky, you buy a poor diamond for a lot of money.

That's the way expertise affects bargaining. It conditions us to be passive.

Does this happen in business negotiations? Yes. I have been in sessions where our engineers, normally forceful during planning sessions, said little to defend our position when confronted by the other side's superior experts. Of course, it often worked the other way also; our lawyers or computer experts intimidated their counterparts to our advantage. Most negotiators take respectful cover when dealing with those they perceive as experts. They ask fewer questions, do most of the listening and become less assertive in expressing their viewpoint.

In the world we live in, you must expect to be confronted by experts again and again. What can you do to protect your position?

The first thing is to recognize that every expert has limits. The best of them may know a great deal about one thing, but they are rarely masters of a broad area. They are apt to know less and less as the area of knowledge required becomes greater. Also, it iswell to recognize that their expertise in one area makes it unlikely they will be credible in another. For example, an expert in fabrics is not likely to be an expert in interior decorating. By the same token, a software developer is probably not an authority on marketing the products she creates. The trouble is that we have a tendency to accept the person's speciality in fabrics or product development and attribute that expertise to interior decorating or marketing as well.

Trial lawyers are generally less intimidated by experts than most of us. They know that for every expert there is an equal and opposite expert. In negotiation, the best thing you can do when confronted by an expert is to get one of your own.

Research in psychology indicates that people who are introduced as experts have greater credibility. It's important that you give your experts all the credibility and prestige you can muster. It will help them influence the other party in support of your position.

There is one more crucial point about experts that deserves to be made. A negotiation is not a jury trial. The outcome will not be determined by whether a jury believes the expert. There is no jury. The result will be determined by the balance of power, the skill of the bargainers, their motivations, the creative both-win alternatives they can jointly develop and the expectations they bring to the table. The "Negotiator's Bill of Rights" grants you the right to disagree with the experts for any reason you choose, be it right or wrong, intuitive or scientifically rational.

INTIMIDATION BY RAISING THE STAKES

Negotiating in an environment where the stakes keep rising has all the tension of a high stakes poker game. A good bluff can make the other player drop out. But if your opponent has the cards you can lose your shirt.

A friend of mine was involved in a divorce action. The marriage had been a rocky affair for most of eight years. He and his wife had already settled a number of issues, including visitation rights, child support, sharing assets and purchasing a condominium for his wife. The major issue remaining was the amount of alimony and the length of time it would be paid. His wife insisted on $5,000 a month for eight years. My friend was willing to pay $3,500 a month for five years. Neither would budge from that position. Talks broke down.

At that point his wife decided to raise the stakes. She backed away from previous agreements and increased her demands in every area. She demanded a certified audit of all their assets. Her lawyer initiated actions to tie up major business assets so they could not be sold, transferred or borrowed against.

Suddenly my friend was faced with a difficult choice. If he continued to hold out for the $3,500 a month which he felt fair and affordable, he faced potentially disastrous consequences. His business would be tied up for years. Certified audits by accounting firms were expensive. Legal costs would soar. If the case went to a judge, there was even some chance that alimony payments might be more than $5,000 a month and continue permanently. The stakes were high. My friend settled for $4,700 a month for eight years.

Industrial or corporate buyers sometimes raise the stakes when dealing with distributors or service providers. One negotiation I recall involved an IT support provider who had serviced our Los Angeles division for four years. Because the economy was depressed, we were anxious to reduce costs. We decided to open bidding on our total California IT support requirement. This represented a dollar volume four times greater than the Los Angeles account. Low bidder take all. The stakes were high.

For the Los Angeles provider, this was a difficult choice. He could hold the price and risk losing his position in Los Angeles, or he could bid low and win the much larger contract covering California. That provider chose to bid low, but not low enough. Another provider reacted to the high stakes by dropping prices almost 20 percent.

High stakes intimidation sometimes occurs between tenants and landlords. I know a landlord who went to court to collect unpaid rent. The tenant countered by suing the landlord for a million dollars, claiming that inadequate security provisions in the garage led to his wife's breakdown. Off the record, he indicated he would pay back rent and drop the suit if the rent was reduced 25 percent. To make things worse, the tenant was a lawyer and did not need to hire an attorney.

The landlord was faced with allowing the reduction or defending against the large suit. My friend agreed to a 15 percent rent concession. He rationalized the large reduction by saying that it could have been worse.

THREAT AND ITS INTENDED AND UNINTENDED CONSEQUENCES

Threat is implicit in every negotiation, whether it is expressed openly or not. There is always the possibility of deadlock. Both parties are there for a reason, and if talks fail they can both expect to lose something.

The decision facing a threatened negotiator is whether he or she will gain or lose by believing the other party's threat. This is never an easy choice.

It reminds me of the story of an old farmer in Texas whose wagon was hit by a rich oilman driving a Cadillac. The farmer took his case to court to seek a settlement for his injuries. An attorney for the defense asked, "Did you tell the defendant immediately after the accident that you were hurt?"

"Well," said the farmer, "I'm not sure but I think he knew it."

'Answer the question," said the lawyer. "Did you or did you not say you were hurt?"

"Let me explain," said the farmer. "When that Cadillac hit my wagon, it threw me into a ditch. My horse was knocked hard and broke his leg, and my dog was hit by the falling wagon. Your client took a look at the writhing horse and the yelping dog and got out his gun. First he walked over and shot the horse. Then he walked over and shot the dog. Finally, with the gun smoking, he came to the ditch where I was lying and asked me whether I was hurt."

We don't know how the farmer came out in this lawsuit, but we do know that threat doesn't always work. We also know that threat creates hostility and may have unexpected consequences. Before using threats in a negotiation, I suggest you consider the following precautions:

First, threats have to be credible. The other party must believe that the threat will be carried out. The person who threatens but fails to follow through loses authority. President Clinton used to threaten a lot but looked weak when he didn't carry through. A threat is likely to be believed if the threatening party has made good on previous threats.

Second, threats have to be proportional to the problem at hand. If you want a small concession, don't make a big threat. Don't use an atom bomb to settle a local border dispute.

Third, before threatening, be sure you have the resources to follow through. Above all, be sure that your organization is willing to back you in taking the necessary action.

Fourth, threats may win momentary concessions, but they leave a residue of anger. Threatened sellers may get revenge later by overcharging on specification changes or by increasing prices when the balance of power favors them.

Fifth, threats can break up long term buyer-seller partnerships or create distrust between parties that have spent years building a relationship. The same often happens in manager-subordinate situations. I once worked for a supervisor who was trusted and respected by his subordinates for years. One day he jeopardized this hard-won trust by threatening to dismiss a long-term employee for missing a budget target. The other employees in that department never trusted him again.

Sixth, threats have a way of getting out of control. They have consequences that the threatener may not have intended. For example, in diplomacy a country that feels threatened may choose to make a preemptive strike. In business, a seller threatened with loss of future business may decide to deliver inferior merchandise, ship late, or stop servicing the buyer's account.

• • • • •

Despite the dangers associated with threats, all of us will be threatened at one time or another, either in business or in our personal lives. What should a negotiator do when threatened?

1. Find out whether the threat will, if executed, cause the threatener as much harm as it will cause you.

2. Stand by your position. If you are a seller, keep telling the buyer that your service offers added values not available elsewhere.

3. Look at past history. Some people do lots of threatening but seldom follow through. Their bark may be louder than their bite.

4. Superiors are not fond of threats made by subordinates. They may support you if you let them know you have been threatened.

5. Remind the threatener that threats often result in unintended consequences. Tell a story that makes this point.

Wise negotiators are careful about making explicit threats. They understand that restoring a relationship after a threat may be like putting Humpty Dumpty back together after his fall. At best, the relationship is hard to restore. At worst, it cannot be put back together at all.

STATUS INTIMIDATORS

The nineteenth century writer Balzac once described a negotiation between a French nobleman and a peasant. The peasant got the best of the deal for a strange reason. The high-born nobleman felt it was demeaning to bargain with a peasant who smelled so badly. The peasant, sensing the reluctance of the nobleman, asked for a high price and stood fast. With his head held high, the nobleman acted as if all this haggling about price was of little matter to him. With as much grace as he could muster, he gave in to the peasant's full asking price.

Social class can affect the outcome of negotiations. Even in the United States, people tend to be intimidated by those who are wellborn. In Europe this tendency is worse. Those in higher social classes are accustomed to deference, and it serves them well in business negotiations. Especially if, unlike the nobleman in Balzac's story, they go into talks well prepared and determined to bargain.

Americans are more responsive to social status than to class. While we do not have an aristocracy as they do in Europe, we do have a status system replete with its own symbols of power and prestige.

Men and women who have achieved power and prominence carry this strength to the bargaining table, as do those who are very rich or very successful. I am reminded of Tevye, the poor milkman in "Fiddler on the Roof," when he sings to his horse, "If I were a rich man, people would come to me asking questions that would cross a rabbi's eyes. It wouldn't matter if I got it right or wrong, because if you are rich, people think you know."

I am sure that people felt intimidated negotiating with legendary billionaires like John D. Rockefeller, J. Paul Getty or Malcom Forbes. Negotiating with today's rich and powerful would make even the most assertive and confident negotiator apprehensive.

Once I gave a series of negotiating seminars to bankers. I was surprised to learn that, though most of those attending were younger than thirty-five, many were vice presidents. "Why so many young vice presidents?" I asked the owner of the bank. "Good for business," he said. "Young loan officers are always dealing with older executives in the firms we lend money to. We have found that these older executives treat our loan officers more respectfully when they carry the authority of vice president."

In negotiation, a higher level executive – a CEO, President or Vice President – exerts more influence than those lower on the pyramid. Like status, educational level and wealth, a negotiator's place on the organizational chart plays a hidden role at the table.

If you are apprehensive about negotiating with people more powerful, higher on the organizational chart, more educated or wealthier than you, there is a good way to cope. Recognize that you will be intimidated and compensate for it by being as well prepared as you can be. The saving grace is that these "higher types" are less likely than you to be knowledgeable about the nitty-gritty of the issues in contention.

INTIMIDATION BY FINANCIAL HOSTAGES AND OTHER HOSTAGE TYPES

Hostages are collateral in negotiation. They can be traded for something else. The United States learned long ago in Iran and Lebanon that televised pictures of Americans held hostage by a foreign power, no matter how small or weak, have an enormous impact on our subsequent actions.

The hostage in business is rarely a person but something else of value. It may be money, goods, property, secrets or a company's reputation. In effect, the hostage holder says, "If you don't give me what I want, you won't get back what I'm holding."

Hostages in the world of business come in various shapes and styles. I once saw a movie in which a house was held hostage by a tenant who wouldn't leave and wouldn't pay the rent no matter what the landlord did. When the owner threatened legal action, the tenant threatened to tear up the place. In a similar but legal way, tax authorities tie up a citizen's bank account and then negotiate the merits of a tax delinquency case. All of us have heard of car mechanics who refused to release an automobile until the bill in dispute was paid by certified check. When the other side holds something we need, they limit our ability to deal freely. We are inhibited from taking actions we might normally pursue. The hostage taker gains the initiative.

As Presidents Carter and Reagan learned in dealing with Iran, it's never easy to bargain with hostage takers. But there are countermeasures we may employ which help us resist those who kidnap our assets and hold them for ransom.

We can raise the stakes by taking hostages in reprisal. We can forfeit the hostaged asset. Or we can place it in greater jeopardy by taking aggressive action that deprives the hostage takcr of things they need. We may go to court to settle the dispute, or resort to mediation or arbitration. Or we may do nothing and hope that holding the assets hostage may, in time, cost the holder more than they are worth.

Of course, the best way to deal with hostage problems is to anticipate them in advance. Introducing severe penalties into the initial contract will make it less profitable for the other side to hold your assets or property.

None of these defenses is easy or inexpensive. That's why hostages, or even the threat of hostage taking, is so intimidating.

PHYSICAL AND ENVIRONMENTAL INTIMIDATORS

Several years ago I read about a strange labor negotiation in the Los Angeles Times. Usually, when labor talks begin the opposing parties are cordial to one another. They don't want to complicate matters by starting out on a bad footing.

Not so this time. The negotiation opened with each party sitting opposite the other across a large table. After the management team leader had outlined his opening position, the labor representative, a big, tough-looking man, suddenly reached across the table, grabbed the management representative by the collar and yanked the shorter man out of his seat. The management negotiator turned pale. He was scared to death by the ferocity of the attack. Still shaking, he ran from the room and refused to go back.

Management promptly protested to the union. The union apologized but kept the tough looking man at the table. A new team leader was drafted by management to replace the first one. When the tough labor man was asked later why he did it, he said that he'd resented the guy since their last negotiation because he's acted so high and mighty with his big words.

The newspaper did not describe how the negotiation came out or what the relationship between the new negotiator and the labor man was. I would guess that it was like the old question, "How do you negotiate with an elephant?" Answer: "Very carefully." The replacement was probably on his toes in what he said and did. I doubt if he or his team were as assertive as they normally might have been.

I am not suggesting this as a viable negotiating approach. It isn't. Yet I believe it is harder to negotiate against people who look tough or against those who are considerably taller than you. I once read a study that found successful executives to be taller and heavier than their peers. I'm not surprised. There are brilliant negotiators and executives who are short, but the advantage generally lies in the other direction.

Fatigue and discomfort also influence results. Describing the signing of the "Declaration of Independence," Thomas Jefferson wrote, "treason was preferable to discomfort." It was July and Independence Hall was next to a stable. "The flies," said Jefferson, "bit through the delegates' silk stockings."

Jefferson may have been joking about treason being preferable to discomfort, but I have seen people reach an agreement simply because they were sick and tired of talking and not getting enough sleep. These inconveniences made it easier for them to accept the deal offered. A lot of automobile purchases are closed when the buyer gets tired of looking at new cars and dealing with different agencies.

Speaking of discomfort, there is one negotiation I'll never forget. It took place on a Saturday on the sixteenth floor of a glass-faced office building. After our team got there, we learned the air conditioning in the building had been routinely shut off for the weekend. None of the windows opened. The other party said they would have their building maintenance people turn on the air, but hours passed as we waited and sweated while we talked.

We dragged on through the day and part of the evening, but the air was never turned on. It was like negotiating for ten hours in a steam bath. Why didn't we walk out? Because we expected the air to be turned on any minute, even though it never was. Was the lack of air conditioning a deliberate tactic on their part? To this day I think so. They seemed to enjoy our discomfort but didn't make a show of it.

In retrospect, it's obvious what we should have done. Had we demanded better treatment, we probably would have gotten it. We should have moved talks to a hotel conference room and made them pay for it. Whenever you find yourself intimidated by physical or environmental factors, fight the tendency to go along. In business as in life you don't get what you deserve, you get what you negotiate. If you don't demand relief, you won't get it.

EMOTIONAL, NUISANCE AND EMBARRASSMENT INTIMIDATION

There are people who try to get what they want by becoming emotional, by embarrassing the other person or by becoming a nuisance. Most of us become defensive when we encounter such behavior. We are not prepared for people in business to display emotions or act in an embarrassmg way.

If an opponent starts to scream or speak loudly, we are inclined to believe he genuinely means what he says. This may or may not be so. A century ago, the British foreign service instructed their representatives in the colonies to speak louder if the natives did not do as they were told. The instruction book didn't say if it really worked, but they obviously thought it did.

A friend of mine manages a large hotel. He has seen his employees wilt in the face of loud protests by an irate customer. They will make almost any concession to avoid a scene, especially if the yelling and screaming takes place where other guests are waiting to check in.

He remembers one angry man with a grievance about a lost reservation who parked himself and his luggage in front of the registration desk. It was 6:00 PM, a time of heavy check-in traffic. The man refused to move from the head of the line. As the crowds grew longer, the desk clerk called the supervisor. The supervisor called the assistant manager. By that time the line was ten deep. Finally, the manager came to the front desk. The trouble was that he forgot his own advice. He gave the screaming customer the Presidential Suite at an ordinary room price just to get him out of the way.

I once saw a man cry during a contract negotiation. From that moment in the talks, I spoke softly and carried a small stick. He got much of what he wanted. I found his highly emotional behavior intimidating. Others who faced similar situations have told me they reacted as I did.

My friend the hotel manager claims that squeaky customer wheels get results. They get better rooms or extra service because they claim to know important executives in the newspaper or television business who could make life difficult for the hotel. Worse yet are politicians who get what they want because they sit on the health or police commissions. When they complain, everybody jumps. Nobody wants the kitchen inspected any more than necessary.

Is there a good way to cope with these kinds of intimidation? I believe there is.

The best approach to emotional, harassing, nuisance or embarrassing behavior is to play it cool. If you respond by becoming emotional yourself, the negotiations will degenerate into an argument. The person who can maintain composure under this type of stress will be respected even by those who start the uproar.

When the climate gets emotional, try to bring issues into focus by centering the discussion around facts rather than feelings. Rephrase the other person's comments to show that you fully understand their viewpoint. Angry people often have complaints that are general rather than specific. You can never respond properly to a general objection. Urge them to be specific about what is wrong and what they want. The more you stick to quiet diplomacy, the harder it will be for them to remain excited.

As for screamers and harassers, it's well to remember that some people communicate feelings they do not have. They do it because it has worked for them before. Be skeptical. Don't givein quickly. There are lots of good actors around.

CONCLUSION

Some of the intimidation tactics we have discussed are subtle, almost subliminal. Others are blatant attempts to put the other party on the defensive. None are easy to deal with.

The key to defending against them is to recognize these tactics for what they are – actions by others aimed at making you less assertive in supporting your position. Yet, as we have learned in this chapter, each tactic has its limitations. They can be offset by actions of your own and by knowing what you stand for and why.

THE INTIMIDATORS

---·---

#1 LEGAL INTIMIDATION AND HOW TO HANDLE IT

#2 INTIMIDATION BY EXPERTS

#3 INTIMIDATION BY RAISING THE STAKES

#4 THREAT AND ITS INTENDED AND UNINTENDED CONSEQUENCES

#5 STATUS INTIMIDATORS

#6 INTIMIDATION BY FINANCIAL HOSTAGES AND OTHER HOSTAGE TYPES

#7 PHYSICAL AND ENVIRONMENTAL INTIMIDATION

#8 EMOTIONAL, NUISANCE AND EMBARRASSMENT INTIMIDATORS

16

Ten Borderline and Dirty Tricks to Watch Out For

Most people in business live by their word. This is not to say anyone can afford to be naive. There are many who deceive others and take advantage of their trust. To use a baseball analogy, their philosophy is: "the way to hit a triple is to get close to the foul line."

The ten borderline and dirty tactics which follow are difficult to cope with. Sooner or later someone will use them against you. My purpose is to help negotiators recognize and defend against them.

1. ESCALATION – A CHEAP SHOT THAT WILL PROBABLY CATCH YOU UNAWARES SOONER OR LATER.

2. THE DEVIL IS IN THE DETAILS.

3. FAIT ACCOMPLI – THE DEED IS DONE.

4. FIGURE FINAGLERS.

5. WHITE HAT – BLACK HAT.

6. THE PHONY ACCEPTANCE STALL IN REAL ES-
   TATE NEGOTIATIONS.

7. THE SWITCH: WHERE ONE WORD MAKES A
   BIG DIFFERENCE.

8. "CHANGES ARE PROFITS IN ESCROW" – BUYER
   BEWARE.

9. THE FRIENDLY SERVICEMAN APPROACH.

10. HOW THE MOVIE STUDIOS BROKE THE AC-
    TORS' SEVEN-YEAR CONTRACTS.

ESCALATION – A CHEAP SHOT THAT WILL CATCH YOU UNAWARES SOONER OR LATER

Many years ago I was selling my 14-foot sailboat. What happened on this small deal happens to business people in multimillion dollar transactions. It also happens to diplomats on a grand scale when they negotiate international treaties.

Having purchased a new 20-foot sailboat, I placed an advertisement in the newspaper offering my old 14-foot sailboat for sale at $750. To get a rough picture of what $750 was worth in those days, multiply by ten. My asking price was somewhat below market because I wanted to move it. The amount at stake was small, but the lesson I learned was instructive.

For two weeks there was little response to the ad. Then, on a

Sunday afternoon in the middle of a good football game, a hot prospect called.

The caller asked to see the boat immediately. It was docked at the marina 15 miles away. I normally don't mind going to the marina, but I was comfortable and would rather have watched the game. In the end, however, my sense of responsibility won over. I agreed to meet him in an hour. I got there on time, but he didn't. Then, just as I began to feel he would never show up, he arrived with his wife. They asked to be taken for a short sail to get a feel for how the boat handled.

Frankly, I didn't want the hassle of putting up the sails and cruising the channel, but my sense of responsibility won out again. About 45 minutes later we returned to the dock a lot "clammier" than we started. But I was in luck because he offered $675, which, after a tiny bit of haggling, I accepted. Reluctantly, I took a $25 cash deposit on the boat because he said that was all he had. We agreed to close the sale on Wednesday night when he would bring a certified check for the remaining $650. I missed a good football game but felt it was worth it.

On Wednesday morning he called me at the office and told me his wife thought she had seen a tear in the sails. He wanted to check it out. That was no problem, I explained, because the sails, though used, were not torn. We met after work late in the afternoon. The weather was miserable. The man had me layout the sails on the wet dock while he minutely inspected every inch of them. I shivered in the cold until he was done, expecting the check afterward. No such luck. He explained that the check would have to wait until Saturday when his paycheck cleared at the bank. What choice had I but to agree?

On Saturday I once more met the couple at the dock. This time they brought up something new. "Did the little Sears outboard engine work?" they asked. The truth is I didn't know, not having used it for almost a year. They insisted that I put it on the boat and try it. After much hassle, and thirty pulls of the reluctant cord, it luckily kicked over.

Then they asked me to take them for a little motor cruise in the marina. I swore to myself as we rode around that I would either close the sale today or dump them both in the water. After we returned to the dock, I received another big surprise. He gave me a certified check for $600 instead of the $650 promised. I pointed out the mistake, but he replied that was all he could get.

Do you think I accepted it? Yes. After all that work, I think I might have taken $500 just to get that boat off my hands. I had been "escalated."

Escalation is an old trick in real estate. Someone agrees to purchase a residence for $300,000 and take possession in 30 days when escrow closes. The buyer makes the purchase contingent on obtaining sufficient loan financing and leaves a $5,000 deposit. The seller begins to make plans to move out, feeling secure that he has a real customer. A week before escrow closes, the seller rents a new apartment and begins to move some things out.

The surprise comes the day before closing, when the seller learns that the buyer is $10,000 short. The buyer says that his father won't lend him the money. He goes on to explain, "There is no way I can purchase the house unless you reduce the price to $290,000." What usually follows is an angry seller, a frustrated broker and a price reduction of close to ten thousand dollars.

Why, you ask, would the seller take a reduction in price? For the same reason I did on the boat. I was sick and tired of the whole thing and wanted to have the boat out of my hair. The seller of the house was in even worse shape than I was with the boat. He had already made deposits on a new apartment and had moved some furniture out before the buyer pulled the escalation trick.

Is there a good defense against escalation? There is, but neither the seller of the home nor I took the necessary action. The best way to handle an escalator is to call his or her bluff. The escalator is counting on you to give in as I did. What I should have done was to recognize that the escalator probably had as much work and emotional equity in closing the deal as I. They were testing my resolve to stand firm.

From now on, when in a negotiation anticipate the possibility of escalation. Protect yourself against it by practicing what you will say and do if the other side escalates. The probability of escalation can also be reduced by obtaining a big deposit or by writing a jointly signed memorandum of agreement. That's what I didn't do, and it turned out to be a mistake.

THE DEVIL IS IN THE DETAILS

Moe had been in business for 40 years. Usually a calm unflappable man, on this day he was angry. When I asked what the trouble was, he told me about a ploy that was driving him crazy. He was having trouble getting reimbursed for work his company had done because the fine print was doing him in.

Moe manufactures the custom plastic signs you see on large buildings. In the past he had made several small signs worth

$3000 each for Triton Construction and been paid promptly. When an order for an especially large and complex building display came in, Moe negotiated a $70,000 price. He tried to get an advanced payment but was persuaded to settle for payment in full thirty days after delivery. The sign was built to specification and an invoice for $70,000 was mailed to the customer's office in Los Angeles.

Forty-five days later, payment had not been received. Moe's bookkeeper called the Los Angeles office. She was told the invoice had never arrived. Another was mailed. Ten days later a follow-up call was made. Once more she was told it hadn't arrived, but this time it was suggested that perhaps it had been mailed to the wrong place. Moe's bookkeeper was told to look at the billing instructions on the purchase order. To her surprise, the fine print did indeed specify a post office box in Tucson where invoices were to be sent for payment. She promptly mailed two copies.

Sixty days had already elapsed by this time. Moe, who had followed the comedy of invoicing without apprehension, began to worry. He had laid out over $55,000 for labor and materials, and he was now sore-pressed for working capital. He needed the $70,000. Two weeks later, the $70,000 check had still not arrived.

This time Moe himself called the Accounts Payable Chief of Triton and asked why. He was told that Triton could not process payment until a "material certification" was received.

"Material certification? What material certification?" Moe asked as politely as he could.

"The one in Clause 9" said the other person.

That's when Moe discovered that he was obligated to provide three notarized copies of a "Certificate of Proper Materials" rendered on a specific form to be supplied by Triton. It took another week to receive the form and an additional week to fill it out because Moe went on vacation. Forty days later the $70,000 check finally came.

Moe later learned that it was all a well-thought-out plan designed to take advantage of suppliers who received orders in excess of $10,000. Triton knew that sellers did not read the administrative details of a contract carefully and rarely did what was specified. This gave the buyer a "legitimate" excuse for delaying payment, Moe's invoice was small compared to most. In all, Triton was working with about $5 million of supplier money by burying their invoices in a swamp of administrative detail. The Triton policy of paying small purchase orders promptly and large ones slowly provided them with a considerable quantity of interest free capital.

Moe's problem was minor compared to some I have seen in the aerospace industry. There, hidden in technical specifications, we often found requirements which, as sellers, would have cost millions to comply with. One I particularly recall required that Hughes warranty the performance of our space satellite for 100 years in orbit. This was hidden in a sentence on page 5 of a complex 30-page specification. Luckily one of our people caught it. Had she not recognized the error and if the satellite had failed, the company could have lost millions.

The ploy is always the same. Hidden in an obscure attachment, specification, or boilerplate document lies an administrative or technical nightmare. They are designed to be overlooked. Only after an agreement is signed and the contract moves toward completion do these costly requirements rise out of the shadows. The devil is in the details.

FAIT ACCOMPLI: THE DEED IS DONE

Action changes the balance of power. The strength of "fait accompli" is the fact that once a deed is done or an action taken it is difficult to undo. The Jesuit principle, "It is easier to obtain forgiveness than permission," is based on the same concept.

People employ "fait accompli" in their personal lives without realizing it. A man stops at a restaurant for a few drinks with fellow workers and comes home late. He should have phoned his wife earlier to advise her he would be late. This might have led to an undesired negotiation at the wrong time. Instead, he takes the action, comes home late, and negotiates forgiveness.

Fait accompli occurs in business more often than it should. One of the most daring faits accomplis I am aware of concerned a New York City apartment developer who built a twelve-story apartment house in an area zoned only for eleven. After it was done, he negotiated with the City, paid a nominal fine and enjoyed the extra income from the twelfth floor. One ploy of white collar criminals is to defraud investors in violation of security regulations. When caught, they consent to pay a relatively small fine and promise not to continue the questionable practice. But they have already made millions in the meantime.

Fait accompli also occurs close to home. A repairman takes your expensive $4,000, 60-inch flat screen television to his shop to find out what's wrong. Later, with the set taken apart, he calls to advise that fixing it will cost $800. The repairman knows that this is the best time to deal with the customer.

I have seen machine parts manufacturers deliberately ship slightly defective parts to their customers at the last minute, hoping that the customer would use the parts in their assembly rather than halt their production lines. Had the manufacturer tried to negotiate the use of these defective parts earlier, they would probably have been asked to accept a lower price. The fait accompli, shipping at the last minute, paid off for the manufacturer.

Irresponsible or devious contractors use the tactic when they receive advanced payments from a builder to buy materials. Once the job is underway, the contractor requests further funding because he has spent the money on something else. The builder, though angry, is usually coerced into providing some relief rather than start over again with a new contractor.

Buyers use fait accompli on sellers in a number of ways. I've seen buyers agree to purchase electronic components for 50 cents per unit but send a purchase order for 48 cents per unit. The seller often accepts the lower price rather than reopen the already closed sale. In another variation, buyers send a "paid-in-full" check for less than the seller's invoice by taking credits for advertising allowances or defective merchandise which may not have been incurred. The seller usually accepts the discounted check if the amount withheld is not too large. The seller shrugs it off as "goodwill." Buyers also use the technique to secure higher quality goods or materials at lower prices than they deserve. They have been known to order Grade B materials at bargain prices but then set so high a quality inspection standard that only Grade B + or Agets accepted.

In a clearly unethical variation of fait accompli, the buyer receives products or merchandise from a seller, sells them to someone else, collects the money, spends it and advises the seller that the company is close to bankruptcy and can only pay 20 cents on the dollar.

It's not easy to negotiate with parties who execute a "fait accompli." The best defense is to make the costs of the tactic so high that the other side will be forced to retreat. The defenses below make it less profitable for the other party to take an action against you and then negotiate.

1. Begin countermeasures promptly. Often a simple letter from an attorney is sufficient to cause the other party to back off. Don't allow the problem to get worse.

2. Take a "fait accompli" action of your own. Hold their property, then use it as trading collateral.

3. Protest at a high level to anyone who will listen.

4. Obtain the backing of a consumer action group, the Better Business Bureau or an influential mediator.

5. Involve a government agency like the City Licensing Department.

6. If you are a buyer, try to anticipate the fait accompli by negotiating a big performance guarantee or bond. Never pay in advance without good security.

7. If you are a seller, get a big deposit or advance. In business, as in life, the Jesuits had it right. They understood the premise and power inherent in the "fait accompli" approach.

FIGURE FINAGLERS

In negotiation, there are two assumptions that can safely be made about the numbers and figures which the other side is presenting to support their position:

1. The numbers and figures presented to you are always biased in their favor.

2. These numbers and figures are always open to challenge.

The adage, "Figures don't lie but liars figure," is true. It's not that negotiators are liars. Most are uncomfortable with lies. Nevertheless, they will choose to present numbers which support their arguments and leave out of their presentation those which favor the other side. While this is not always the case, I believe it to be true of most people you negotiate with. To assume otherwise would be naive.

We can get an insight into the murky relationship between reality and numbers from an old story. The owner of a relatively new business decides to hire a full-time controller-accountant. Not having employed such a person before, he asks his friend, "How do I go about picking the right man or woman?

"Just ask them," his friend replied, "How much is two and two?"

The owner interviewed three prospects for the job. The first answered, "Two and two is four." The second answered, "It depends on whether the first two are apples and the next two are oranges." The third prospect looked at the owner and replied,

"What do you want it to be?" You can decide for yourself which prospect the owner selected for the job.

Much of the data presented in negotiation falls in the category of "What do you want it to be?" In the aerospace industry, we required vendors to provide cost breakdowns with price proposals. They did so. The trouble was that the breakdowns were almost always unreliable. It was obvious that many contractors were making up figures to suit their purposes.

The problem was so bad that Congress was forced to pass a law called "Truth in Negotiation." It prescribed triple penalties for lying. Suppliers quickly became more careful with their proposal pricing. Supplier cost breakdowns were better supported and documented, but after a short time they once again became adept at presenting breakdowns which reflected what they preferred to show.

To prevent suppliers from playing with figures, a new profession arose, Cost and Price Analysis. Cost and Price Analysts are charged with determining the validity of cost breakdowns and estimating what the proper price should be. Their role is to challenge the assumptions and figures presented by the other side.

During my years as a corporate executive in contracts, sales and procurement, I cannot recall a single instance when we accepted the other party's numbers or they accepted ours. Each set of assumptions and numbers had flaws, although both sides had gone to great pains to make them look right.

Why can any set of numbers be challenged? Most numbers presented at the table are based on past history and estimates about the future. Even when a history is supported by certified audits, it can be wrong. Most of the savings and loan companies that failed during the late twentieth century were audited by big accounting firms. So were the financial records of Orange County in California, which failed in 1994. The accountants in both cases said that the assets audited were worth what management said they were. "All is well," they wrote after each audit. Well, all wasn't well. The reality was that many of these savings and loan companies went bankrupt, and Orange County lost billions.

The figures, even days before the end, continued to show what management wanted them to show. A similar scenario played out again with massive failures in the financial sector almost a decade into the twenty-first century. Here, too, banks and investment firms seemed fine on paper even days before they collapsed. Two plus two was not four. It was whatever someone in authority wanted it to be.

The numbers you run into in negotiation are usually accounting numbers based on company records. No accounting system is perfect. Cost accounts, overhead rates, labor figures, material numbers, expenses, profit margins and every other number based on history is subject to interpretation. Every one.

We can challenge how the data was collected, when it was collected,what should have been included and what should not have been included. We can challenge the accuracy, the timeliness, the people who put it together, the relevance and the system that collected the numbers. It's not hard.

Where numbers are used to estimate future costs or revenues, we can challenge not only the numbers themselves but the way they are used to make estimates of the future. Even when both parties are completely truthful, there will be honest differences in how each side views the future. There will be much to take exception to.

The Figure Finaglers, by Robert S. Riechard, discusses how people distort charts to favor their position, how percentages are manipulated, how sampling can create false results, how averages aren't average at all, how indexing can be made to create favorable or unfavorable numbers and how unavoidable errors creep into figures.

A negotiator has the responsibility to present his or her position in the most defensible way possible. When the other party provides figures or numbers, your job is to be skeptical. Challenge the figures when they are not to your liking.

As we have said, the numbers presented to you in the course of a negotiation are apt to be biased. However, the longer the parties work together, the more reliable the numbers provided by each side are likely to be. Even when they have worked together for a long time, they will still have differing viewpoints. There will be disagreements as to what the figures are, what they should mean and what kind of future they predict. Where numbers are concerned, there will always be plenty of room to negotiate your viewpoint.

THE "WHITE HAT-BLACK HAT", "SUGAR-VINEGAR" APPROACH

Some people call it the "Sugar-Vinegar" approach, some "Good Cop-Bad Cop" and others "White Hat-Black Hat," but they all work on the same principle. One partner of the team is so belligerent or extreme that the opposing side is driven to side with the "White Hat," whose positions now seem to embody moderation and reason.

The use of "Good Cop-Bad Cop" as a negotiating tactic is often seen in police dramas. The suspect under interrogation doesn't want to tell the police anything. Why should he? In order to break him, two cops work as a team. The bad cop insults him, puts a glaring light in his face, roughs him up and gives him no food, sleep or rest. Then the bad cop leaves and another policeofficer comes into the room. The good cop treats the suspect with dignity, allows him to rest a bit, brings food and cigarettes and is friendly. In response the suspect soon tells the good cop what both the good cop and bad cop want to know.

In negotiation, the White Hat-Black Hat technique is more subtle but functions the same way. I have been in talks where the "Black Hat" was not even at the table. He was my boss at the home office. I kept telling the other party that my boss would never sign off on their offer unless it was improved. My boss was, in this case, an invisible bad guy.

Other "Black Hats" who mayor may not put in an appearance are your lawyer, your accountant, your banker, your subordinates or peers, your spouse, your engineer, the union or some committee. They can all say "no" to the other side in an unreasonable, demanding way. You, on the other hand, can play the "White Hat" who appears reasonable in comparison to the invisible bad guy.

"Black Hats" are normally thought of as people, but some of the best "Black Hats" I've had to face were not human. They were computers. In one case I remember, the person I was dealing with insisted that she could not grant what I wanted because the computer said she couldn't. A "Black Hat" I often ran into in aerospace negotiations was government regulations. The person opposite me appeared quite reasonable compared to the regulation if he or she relieved me by bending the regulation just a little.

You will be facing "White Hat-Black Hat" tactics throughout your career. When dealing with this approach, there are actions you can take. If the "Black Hat" is a real person who insults or abuses you, you can choose to resist like water. Just listen and let them say what they wish. A negotiation is not settled by the person who is loud, angry or abusive. It is settled by the balance of power, by the reasonableness of arguments and by the creative both-win alternatives developed by working together.

When the "Black Hat" is not a person but a rule, regulation, procedure, policy or computer program, you can protest to higher authority, take your business elsewhere, appeal to common sense or use your own rules and regulations to legitimize your position rather than theirs.

The best defense to "White Hat-Black Hat" is to recognize that the "White Hat" and "Black Hat" both want to get as much as they can get. Like the good and bad cop, they are on the same side.

THE PHONY ACCEPTANCE STALL IN REAL ESTATE NEGOTIATIONS

The "phony acceptance" is an unethical selling tactic. It is most prevalent in real estate, but it also common in the sale of used equipment, antiques or other hard to find goods and services. Unscrupulous sellers use the phony acceptance this way.

A woman sees a house she likes. After considerable negotiating, she submits an offer of $240,000 against the original asking price of $270,000. The broker takes a deposit and agrees to present the offer. He implies that the offer has a good chance of acceptance but doesn't guarantee it.

A day later he calls to report that the seller is out of town but there is no need for concern. The only problem appears to be whether the chandeliers and fireplace screen are to be included at the price.

What follows afterward is the "big stall." Every day the broker says that he can't contact someone. One day he cannot contact the seller, the next day the buyer, the following day the bank or someone else. Before long, ten days pass. There is still no agreement, but neither is there disagreement. The broker continues to assure the buyer nothing is wrong.

A few days later the deposit is returned with a polite rejection note. The buyer subsequently sees a "SOLD" sign on the house. What has probably happened in this case is that the seller, having obtained a bona-fide offer of $240,000, used the offer as leverage in bargaining with another buyer. The "phony acceptance" can be handled in three ways. First, take things into your own hands as much as possible. Don't let third party intermediaries like brokers or middlemen handle the action. Insist on having your position heard by the principals involved. Find out who they are. Send a message or talk to them directly, regardless of what the middleman says.

Second, do the administrative and running around work yourself. It's amazing how quickly delays can be overcome if you have your secretary type the forms and then hand carry the papers yourself. In that way you won't hear that the mail was late or paperwork misplaced. Also be sure to tie the offer to a short term deadline. If penalties can be imposed after the deadline, all the better.

While these countermeasures do not always work, they do serve to reduce the likelihood that your acceptance will be used as a shill. The phony acceptance is a mean trick and you should do everything in your power to keep it from happening.

THE SWITCH – WHERE ONE WORD MADE A BIG DIFFERENCE

This happened to a close friend I advise from time to time. He is a prominent lecturer who was asked to make a video training film for a big studio. The studio offered him a generous 18 percent royalty based on gross revenue. I advised that he accept because, among other reasons, the usual royalty rate varies from 3 percent to 15 percent. Since there were no other serious differences in their positions my friend agreed to the settlement.

Two weeks later a neatly typed five-page contract arrived from the studio. It was exactly as agreed except for one word well hidden in the contract text. Instead of reading, "18 percent of gross revenue," it read, "18 percent of net revenue." Luckily, my friend caught it. Had the contract been signed, he would never have received a dime.

In the movie business, the name of the accounting game is never to show a net profit unless they absolutely have to. After he found the error, negotiations started over again. In the end they settled at 14 percent of gross revenue, which the studio did pay as agreed. Earlier in this book I said, "Never trust your assumptions."

One of the most dangerous assumptions we make is that the agreement we shake hands on is the one that will be written into the contract. I don't want to be cynical, but a safer hypothesis would be that the contract you are asked to sign is NOT the agreement you made. If it was written by the other party, it will probably favor them in some way. Rarely, if ever, will it favor you.

Some people will deliberately test whether you are alert. They will switch a word, a phrase or a number in their favor. If you catch the switch they will claim a typist made the mistake.

From now on, remember my friend when reviewing a contract. Had he not caught the switch of a single word he would have earned nothing for his hard work.

"CHANGES ARE PROFITS IN ESCROW" – BUYER BEWARE

In my opinion, few things are as difficult for buyers as the negotiation of changes to an existing contract. In this section we will cover some of the pitfalls facing a buyer when negotiating a contract in which changes are likely to occur. "Changes are profits in escrow." That's what the vicepresident of a large software firm once told me. He started his company underbidding competitors by wide margins. After winning the contract, he made his money back on changes in the contract. "Changes are profits in escrow," he said with a knowing smile. "You'd be surprised," he continued. "A clever project manager or engineer can earn his salary many times over by encouraging a customer to make changes. That's where the real money is."

Not long ago a headline in the Los Angeles Times read, "Subway Builder's Tenacity Pays Off in Cost Disputes." The sub-headline read, 'Auditors say Tutor-Saliba has inflated expenses, but firm's leader insists he merely demands what's fair." Tutor's company had won more competitively bid contracts ($220 million worth) than any other subway builder on the first segment of the huge Los Angeles subway project. After the contract was awarded, they won $76 million more in contract changes.

The article went on to say that the Mayor labeled Tutor, "the greatest change order artist, someone who bids low to win contracts and then makes his profits on contract amendments." Tutor told the Times that the label is undeserved because other contractors have gained in the same proportion.

While I am in no position to personally judge whether the Tutor-Saliba change order claims were fair, correct or reasonable, I can say that such changes are always difficult for the customer to cope with. In the face of changes, the balance of power shifts rapidly in favor of the seller, no matter how competitive the original bidding was.

A seller's ability to exploit the situation increases when a buyer is unclear about the specifications they wish to meet or the scope of work that must be done. The more fuzzy their thinking along these lines, the more they will pay as things change. And change they will.

When it comes to changes, it is often the customer's own management that is at fault. To meet budget constraints, management makes optimistic estimates about project schedules and costs. Later, they are forced to admit that changes are necessary. Had they faced reality sooner, contractor bids would have been more accurate and the work completed at less cost.

To understand how to cope with changes, we will look at a situation that frequently arises in painting a house or apartment. What follows is applicable to any contracting or consulting agreement. These are the precautions you can take to protect against exploitative "change artists":

1. Recognize that even in something as simple as painting an apartment, changes to the contract will occur.

2. Make a list of potential changes in your requirements before you place the job with any contractor.

   a. For example, before painting begins, you may not want to paint the closets or hallways because they look good enough. Later when the other rooms are painted you are likely to feel that the unpainted halls and closets must be spruced up to match the newly painted ones.
   b. Other changes which may occur are changes from one coat to two, from one color to another, from paint to wallpaper, from more rooms to less rooms, from a better paint to a less expensive one or vice versa.
   c. Carpentry work may be added because the existing wood may not take paint well or bad spots may require reconstruction. Also tile work may be needed to support or enhance the paint job.

3. Get a price from the preferred paint contractor for each of the above changes and addons before you award the contract. Then, when changes actually occur you'll have a basis for fair pricing.

4. Talk to each contractor about these potential changes. They are likely to provide good advice as to how best to

manage the changed requirements and how they will alter the work schedule.

5. Try to include as many probable changes into the original competitive bidding as you can. Get pricing breakdowns on a room by room basis and an item by item basis. The better the cost breakdown you get, the easier it will be to negotiate changes later. You'll pay less.

6. Recognize that the paint contractor will raise the price of every change as much as he can. Negotiate hard.

The ideas for anticipating changes and dealing with them apply as well to complex contracts as to simple ones. On complex contracts, like the subway system, expensive changes are sure to occur. A good change control system and procedure is essential. Close supervision by management and prompt negotiation of every change keep costs and aggravations down. Alert buyers who are aggressive in protecting their position can reduce the financial impact of changes.

THE FRIENDLY SERVICEMAN APPROACH

The Friendly Serviceman Approach is a borderline tactic. It is employed by some contractors, consultants, lawyers, and other providers of labor services. On a personal level, there are car mechanics, repairmen and even dentists who take advantage of their customers using the same approach. The example which follows will show how it works and what to do to keep from being exploited.

Assume for a moment that you need a small plumbing repair in your home. You search the internet and find a plumber with good online reviews. He does the job and gives you a surprisingly small bill. "Hooray," you think, "I've done the impossible. I've found a good plumber at a fair price."

The next time something goes wrong you call the same plumber, Again a small bill. Incredible. Over a period of time you build trust in the plumber based on his reasonable prices and high quality work.

Suddenly, one Saturday night, a pipe in the attic bursts. Your friend the plumber (now he is more than just a plumber, he is a friend as well) comes right over. He stops the leak with a temporary clamp, chats a while and then suggests that he had better finish the job on Monday. You ask him how bad it looks and he says, "Not too bad, but it's pretty dark up there. We'll see more on Monday."

On Monday he arrives with two men and starts work just as you and your wife leave. You ask him to call and give you an idea of the cost. He nods. At noon he calls. "This is what it looks like," he says, "your pipes are 25 years old and rusted through in several places. We've taken out the one part that leaked, but if I were you I'd change all the pipes up there. As long as we're here, it's probably better to do it right now."

You ask, 'About how much will it run?"

He answers, "Not too much. We'll charge our normal rate and will be out of here fairly soon. If something else comes up, I'll call you. Should we go ahead?"

"Sure, go ahead Charlie," you reply. "You're the Doctor. Do what has to be done."

You come home at five and the plumbing truck is still there. He tells you that the job was a little larger than expected because they had to rip out and restore a walled area. They promise to return for a short time tomorrow morning to finish.

Sure enough, the crew arrives early to complete the work. By time you come home that evening they are gone. The job looks OK. The workers cleaned up after themselves. You expect that the plumbing bill, when it comes, won't be small because quite a lot of work was done. However, you are sure it will be reasonable. A week later an invoice for $4020 arrives in the mail.

You can't believe it. That is more than twice what you expected. There must be a mistake. You call Charlie. Charlie tells you that he will go over the job sheet and call you back. An hour later he calls you back and tells you the bill is correct. It consists mainly of labor and materials: three men for 15 hours each at $70 an hour ($3150) and $700 for materials. The rest is travel time and miscellaneous small charges. That's when you learn for the first time about the $70 per hour rate, travel time and the high price of copper pipe.

Charlie the plumber has abused your trust. It was part of his pricing strategy. He made a marketing decision years ago that the big money in plumbing was not in small jobs but in big ones. The small ones were like "loss leaders" in merchandising. They were designed to lull the customer to sleep. Once a rapport was established, Charlie knew he would someday get the big job without having to bid for it.

There is hardly a person I know who has not been caught by Charlie's approach at one time or another. It's easy to understand   how relatively inexperienced consumers are fooled.

But how about the professional purchasing people? Do they get caught by the "Friendly Serviceman Approach"? The answer is "Yes." The only difference is that when they are caught the dollar amounts are much larger.

What can you do about countering this tactic? Always get an up front price. Learn to say over and over again, "How much will it cost?" Get the seller to put it in writing. Have them put down what the price includes. If they hesitate to give you a firm price, have them give you a "not to exceed" figure. Make sure they do no work without pricing it and telling you in advance. Be ready to ask, "How much?" before the work starts and every time the scope of work changes. Above all, get three or four bids. You'll be surprised at the large differences in their prices. These precautions are worth taking, even if you have dealt with the other party many times before.

HOW THE MOVIE STUDIOS BROKE THE ACTORS' SEVEN-YEAR CONTRACTS

If there was ever an industry that could serve as a model for borderline tricks, it's the movie industry. During the heyday of the 1930s, attractive men and women were signed to seven-year contracts by the studios. The great depression was at its height, and those earning $500 or $1,000 a week were considered incredibly wealthy by those who read movie magazines. Imagine earning all that money while learning a craft and being groomed for stardom. What people didn't read about was how the studio heads treated the vast majority of actors and actresses who never made it big.

Once the studio decided to get rid of them, their contracts weren't worth the paper they were written on. The studios employed large staffs of lawyers who had connections in the political and judicial world of Los Angeles. They had the money to fight lengthy legal battles and the power to blackball all but the most prominent stars. When the studio wanted to break a seven-year contract, they did it with impunity.

First the lawyers would go through the contract line by line. Every contract has flaws. In these contracts, the studio made a science out of deliberately building in language that was full of loopholes. If the actor was lucky enough to have a first-rate lawyer, some of the flagrant loopholes and ambiguities were negotiated away. But even that didn't help the hapless actor on his way out.

If the loopholes weren't big enough, the studio broke the contract by making the actor's life so miserable that he begged to be free. Books about Hollywood are full of stories about actors who were never given a role. Worse yet, they were forced to report to the studio at 8:00 AM and stay until 6:00 PM with absolutely nothing to do, day after day, year after year. Many of those who were stubborn enough to stick it out became alcoholics. Actors who sued soon found their weekly checks tied up and their careers stymied because they were labeled as troublemakers. By the time the legal process with its trials, appeals and countersuits was over, the actor's professional and personal life was likely to be in shambles.

What the actors often forgot was that a contract is only as good as the parties that make it. Integrity and commitment to mutual satisfaction is essential. The best advice for those who must deal with people whom they have reason to doubt is to do as J.P. Morgan used to say: "Put the facts and figures into law-proof shape."

Or do as Isaac Singer of sewing machine fame did in 1853. He gave a substantial block of stock in the then small Singer Sewing Machine Company to the best law firm in New York. In exchange, they offered to protect his patents against all who might contest them. Although the Singer patents themselves were not strong, Singer was able to defend himself successfully against a myriad of infringement suits for the next thirty years.

Had Singer, a man with no financial resources in his early years, not made the unusual arrangement of giving considerable equity to the law firm, he would probably have lost everything. Instead he became one of the wealthiest businessmen of the nineteenth century.

What happened to the movie actors can happen to you in any negotiation. Things change over time. The legitimate heirs to an honorable agreement may not like it, even if the original negotiators still do. In a free enterprise society like ours, you can expect the opposing negotiator to change jobs and new people to take control. You can expect the balance of power to change as whole companies are bought and sold. Old loyalties fade away. Business strategies change, making old agreements better or worse in relation to new objectives. That's the story of our times. Most businesses today are like the movie business of yesteryear – they exist in a world of rapid economic change.

The best way to reduce the risk that the other party will change their mind about a contract is to have it reviewed by a competent lawyer before signing. As many movie actors learned to their regret, you pay for a good lawyer one way or the other – either before you sign or later when things go wrong. Before is less expensive.

MORE ABOUT BORDERLINE AND DIRTY TRICKS

A whole book could be written about dirty tricks in negotiation. You may wish to read more about these difficult tactics in my book, Give and Take. Included are such borderline and dirty trick tactics as "low balling," "deliberate errors," "deliberate default," "scrambled eggs," "shill," "shyster" and "spying and bugging."

There is no sure way to protect yourself against every dirty trick, but the tips which follow can save you lots of grief:

1. In business, it doesn't pay to overlook small lies and early delays in performance. Look at these lapses as early warning signals. The worst is yet to come.

2. People who use dirty tricks are like bullies. They are looking for an easy mark. If you call their bluff, most are likely to retreat or compromise.

3. Know the people you deal with. Those with a record of integrity are unlikely to deviate from it. At the risk of being overly cynical, there is a Russian saying, "Once a thief, always a thief." If their record is bad, don't hope for the best.

4. Get things in writing. The more detail the better. The more witnesses the better. The more signatures the better.

5. When you reach agreement and write a contract, have a good lawyer check your vulnerability. Then make up your own mind whether to proceed or not. A lawyer is not a substitute for good business judgment.

I have learned from bitter experience that it is far better to face unpleasant problems at the bargaining table than to suffer later aggravation and expense. The way to avoid or reduce future hassles is to look at each paragraph of an agreement and ask this question: "What am I trying to accomplish and what can go wrong?" Only when satisfied that you have negotiated a level of protection consistent with the stakes involved should the agreement be signed.

As for those considering the use of such tactics, think about the Talmud. "Bad deeds," says the Talmud, "are like an open pillow case; you never know where the feathers will land."

BORDERLINE AND DIRTY TRICKS TO LOOK OUT FOR

•

#1   Escalation - a Cheap Shot That Will Probably Catch You

#2   The Devil Is in the Details

#3   Fait Accompli - the Deed Is Done

#4   Figure Finaglers

#5   White Hat - Black Hat

#6   The Phony Acceptance Stall in Real Estate Negotiations

#7   The Switch: Where One Word Makes a Big Difference

#8   "Changes Are Profits in Escrow" - Buyer Beware

#9   The Friendly Serviceman Approach

#10   How the Movie Studios Broke the Actors' Seven-Year Contracts

17 | Fourteen Ways to Bridge the Settlement Gap When Talks Break Down

FOURTEEN WAYS TO BRIDGE THE SETTLEMENT GAP WHEN TALKS BREAK DOWN

Too many negotiations end in deadlock, even when the parties are anxious to agree. People go into negotiation to make a deal, not to waste time on tasks that end without results. In this chapter we will cover fourteen time-tested ways to keep the talks going when they break down or appear to be falling apart.

The Jules Feiffer cartoon on the following page captures the essence of this important idea. Feiffer focuses on the negotiating process and how people react to deadlock. He shows their longing to get together, their joy in building bridges toward agreement and the last minute hitches and ego barriers that lead to deadlock rather than the agreement they both urgently want.

Jules Feiffer, in his ability to get to the heart of the psychological conflicts facing people in their social, political and business lives, is one of our most brilliant cartoonists. The more you study the faces and gestures of the protagonists in each section of the cartoon, the better you understand the ebb and flow of emotions associated with deadlock in any negotiation situation.

Jules Feiffer, in his ability to get to the heart of the psychological conflicts facing people in their social, political and business lives, is one of our most brilliant cartoonists. The more you study the faces and gestures of the protagonists in each section of the cartoon, the better you understand the ebb and flow of emotions associated with deadlock in any negotiation situation.

FEIFFER®

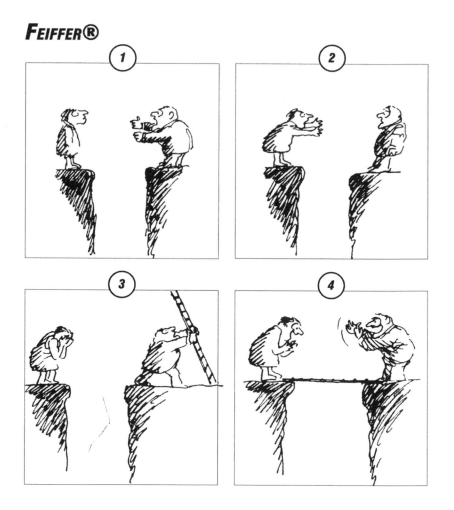

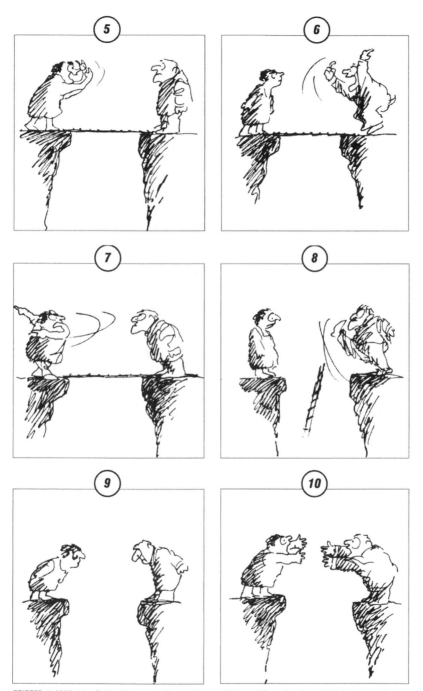

FOURTEEN WAYS TO AVERT OR
BREAK A DEADLOCK OR IMPASSES

The fourteen "icebreakers" which follow will help you walk away and reopen talks in a graceful way. They will allow you to do so without loss of bargaining power or "face." They are effective because they re-involve the self-interest of both parties. Each technique paves the way for negotiators to discuss new ideas and solutions ideas neither thought possible before talks broke down. These approaches lead to win-win agreements and help build long term The relationships.

1. THE GRADUAL APPROACH.

2. THE "BOOKKEEPING" APPROACH.

3. MOVE FROM THE WHOLE TO THE PART OR FROM THE PART TO THE WHOLE.

4. HOW JOINT COMMITTEES HELP BREAK DEADLOCKS.

5. BRING OUT A FIFTH.

6. MOVE FROM THE STICKY ISSUE TO ANOTHER ISSUE.

7. CHANGE THE TIME SHAPE OF PERFORMANCE.

8. CHANGE THE TIME SHAPE OF MONEY.

9. USE A MEDIATOR.

10. CHANGE THE SHAPE OF SATISFACTION AND DISSATISFACTION.

11. CHANGE THE NEGOTIATOR.

12. GET YOUR MESSAGE DEEPER INTO THE OTHER PARTIES ORGANIZATION.

13. THE UNITED NATIONS COALITION.

14. THE ENTREPRENEUR'S APPROACH: NEGOTIATE A WIN-WIN DEAL

FIRST: THE GRADUAL APPROACH

When the differences between two parties are large and talks begin to fail, one way to bridge the gap is to do it a little at a time rather than in one large compromise. I call this technique for breaking an impasse "the gradual approach."

For example, assume you are buying a million portable DVD players a year from a Chinese manufacturer. They want to raise the price from $20 to $24 a unit, an increase of $4 million. Deadlock is close. The Chinese feel their $24 price is fair. As the buyer for your company, you have a budget to meet and cannot pay their price.

One of the best ways to overcome such a gap is the gradual approach. The large price increase between $20 and $24 may be bridged by agreeing to accept the increase in increments over a period of time rather than immediately. For example, the price could be $21 for three months, $22 for the next three months, $23 for the next three and $24 for the 250,000 portable DVD players shipped during the final quarter of the year.

Stretching out the increase rather than incorporating it all at once has several advantages. Buyer and seller have time to pursue a win-win strategy. They can find creative ways to reduce production costs and thereby make future price increases smaller. With the extra time, the buyer's marketing people can explore raising portable DVD prices to preserve their profit margins. Change by slow degree allows both parties time to accept and adjust to the situation.

Virtually all legislation passed by Congress is a product of negotiation. Gradualism plays an important part in reaching these compromises. One of the most fiercely fought Congressional battles some years ago concerned the deregulation of natural gas prices. One side favored complete regulation of prices, while the other believed in immediate deregulation. The gap was large. Deadlock was avoided by putting gradualism to work.

Both sides found it easy to agree on one thing. They wanted a law which would increase gas production without damaging gas users. Those against deregulation were afraid that prices would rise threefold if controls were removed. This would injure industries dependent on natural gas for energy. The problem was resolved by deregulating gas over a period of many years. In that way, economic dislocations were minimized. Gradualism permitted changes in price and consumer demand to occur at an acceptable rate.

SECOND: THE "BOOKKEEPING" TECHNIQUE

Ronald Reagan was purported in some political circles to be a wily negotiator. Perhaps it came from his dealings with movie moguls during the 1950s. As governor of California, he was once called upon to help break a deadlock between the City of Los Angeles and its bus drivers. The strike threatened to cripple the city.

Reagan, then aiming for the presidency, found the publicity useful. He flew to Los Angeles with great fanfare, but what he did was simple. The Los Angeles Times reported that Reagan began by using the bookkeeping approach. The status of the deadlocked talks was tabulated in three steps on a blackboard:

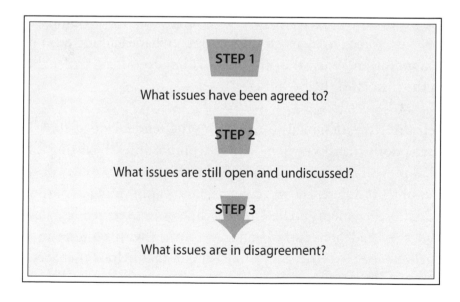

STEP 1

What issues have been agreed to?

STEP 2

What issues are still open and undiscussed?

STEP 3

What issues are in disagreement?

By using the "bookkeeping" technique, Reagan sought to bring clarity to a complicated situation. Writing down the score of settled and unsettled issues may seem simple-minded, but it serves to focus attention on what has been accomplished rather than on points of disagreement. It thus reduces the level of tension felt by both parties.

There are usually many points that deadlocked parties, however far apart, find easy to agree on. It is well to focus attention on these successes because they breed confidence. In the heat of conflict, the natural tendency is to be more aware of differences than similarities. The first "bookkeeping" step was to refocus thinking in a positive direction. Reagan, ever an amiable man, was well suited to this role.

The second step was not difficult or inflammatory. Those issues not yet discussed were listed, with the easiest to settle first and the hardest last.

The third step was to list the areas of disagreement. By doing this, they were forced to focus on the present – what each side was now demanding and what the other was willing to offer – rather than on the history of their conflict.

Step three was designed to overcome the tendency of people to listen poorly to others when their viewpoints differ. By listing each side's present position in a less threatening setting, much of the heat of their differences was channeled toward finding a solution. Many disagreements melted away, while others seemed less sharp than they had previously been. By starting with disagreements that were easy to settle, they built bridges that helped them settle the more difficult issues.

The benefit of "Step 1, 2, 3 Bookkeeping" is that it forces the parties to communicate. It becomes easier to see what concessions each party has made. Positives are accentuated, negatives defused, and it becomes easier to find areas where broad trade-offs are possible.

As for the strike, it did not end quickly as a result of Reagan's effort. I am certain, however, that his negotiating strategy reduced tensions and paved the way for a settlement several weeks later.

THIRD: MOVE FROM THE WHOLE TO THE PART OR FROM THE PART TO THE WHOLE

Another technique to avoid an impasse is to change how you negotiate the issues. As we have said before, most Americans prefer to bargain on an issue by issue basis. They develop positions and goals for each matter and settle them one by one. The theory is that the sum of the settled parts will lead to settlement of the whole. The French and Chinese prefer to hammer out agreement on a broad basis and then settle individual issues. They believe that once settlement is reached on the whole, the parts will fall into place.

I recall a negotiation that took place several years ago in which both sides tried to hammer out an issue-by-issue agreement. We tried to settle problems related to scope of work and specification, but we could not reach an accord. Then we attempted to agree on man-hours, but to no avail. Seeing that things were going nowhere, we tackled labor rates, a relatively easy matter we thought. Still no agreement. The talks were almost at a standstill. Deadlock appeared inevitable.

Frustrated by the impending impasse, we changed our approach. We moved discussion to settlement on a lump sum basis.

Management offered $20 million to do the entire job. Both parties found it easier to agree on the funds available for the overall package than to decide on individual expenditures. Once the broader agreements on spending were reached, it became possible for our staffs to settle detailed issues, such as what could reasonably be spent on different phases of the project.

The rule is: if you encounter strong resistance on the issues, move the discussion to the whole. Conversely, if you cannot reach an overall settlement, focus on each issue one by one. Either road provides a face-saving way for the parties to say "yes" – no matter how many times they've said "no" before.

FOURTH: HOW JOINT COMMITTEES HELP BREAK DEADLOCKS

We said earlier that the key to avoiding a breakdown lies in re-involving members of the other party's organization in pursuit of their self-interest. When talks break down, joint committees are useful in bringing the discussion back on track.

Joint committees have a dynamic of their own. There is nothing like a committee to generate talk and ideas. The more those on the committee work together, the more they will want the parties at the table to reach agreement. Given time, they are certain to come up with new ideas and choices not previously discussed.

For example, a joint finance committee will discover possibilities for making mutually beneficial financial arrangements. An engineering committee will find better ways to improve product specification or quality control. These ideas will find their way to the table and keep the talks moving.

These committees have a special role when talks break down entirely. They provide the opposing parties with "face-saving" reasons to meet again – usually on a less formal basis than before. This is important because negotiators are generally quite anxious when deadlock occurs. They are like the man and woman in the last two panels of the Feiffer cartoon on page 407. The value of a joint committee is that the ideas they generate allow both negotiators at the table to resume discussions without loss of face. Both welcome the chance to get together.

FIFTH: BRING OUT A FIFTH

It is amazing how many important deals are made in restaurants or on the golf course. When things bog down in the conference room, learn to forget business for a while. Do as the Japanese do. Take the other person out for a good time, Break bread together. Let the subtle chemistry of goodwill, trust, and a fifth of good Scotch become a catalyst in moving toward agreement.

SIXTH: MOVE FROM THE STICKY ISSUE TO ANOTHER ISSUE

One of the most skilled negotiators I know is the owner of several office buildings. When a negotiation with a prospective tenant appears to be failing, he shifts talks from the sticky issue to another issue. For example, if the tenant wants an option to renew for ten years and the owner doesn't want to grant it, he quickly moves on to the matter of sub-lease privileges. If that issue becomes sticky, he brings up maintenance or something else.

The point of shifting issues is that he wants to avoid a hardening of position and "no" answers. He knows the issues in contention and how far he is willing to bend on each. He is also aware that every negotiation has a momentum of its own. The more points the parties agree on, the greater will be the impetus toward settlement. Movement from sticky issues to ones easier to agree on helps my friend maintain the momentum toward agreement.

SEVENTH: CHANGE THE TIME SHAPE OF PERFORMANCE

When and how a job gets done is subject to many variations. It can be done all at once or over a period of time, It can be spread out in equal portions or bunched up early or late in the time schedule. Every revision in the proposed performance plan has an effect on the risks and rewards for both parties. The moment one party offers a different production plan or schedule, somebody in the other organization has something to gain or lose, so they listen.

Many a deadlock has been broken merely by offering to change the time shape of performance. To start sooner or later, or to do some things before others, can be of great value to one or the other party. The potential for mutual gain or cost saving exists because there is always a better way to fit the buyer's need to the seller's capacity to produce.

EIGHTH: CHANGE THE TIME SHAPE OF MONEY

There is a song whose words go like this: "It ain't what you do, it's the way you do it." When it comes to breaking an impasse a good approach is: "It ain't what you pay, it's the way you pay it."

Probably the most common cause of deadlock is price. A buyer is willing to pay $1,000, but the seller wants $1,200. One way out of the dilemma is to change the time shape of money.

Money may be paid in a variety of ways, or payments may be delayed. One party may prefer a large advance and another none. The payment period can be made long or short. Monthly obligations may be designed to suit the parties' changing needs. Some prefer variable payments, others want fixed monthly payments. In some cases people may not want payment to be made to them but sent instead to others for tax reasons.

The key point is that people have differing preferences for cash. Even the wealthiest may find themselves short of working capital. They may be desperate to get paid quickly in order to meet their own capital needs. The negotiator who is wise enough to explore the time shape of money can make a better deal on the price itself.

NINTH: USE A MEDIATOR

History has been kind to President Carter. While he continued to perform a variety of public services after he left office, his most valued role has been as a mediator of difficult international disputes. This should come as no surprise. While in office, Carter mediated one of the most difficult conflicts in history.

Carter accomplished something that no statesman before him had done. The Israelis and the Egyptians had been at each others' throats since Israel won independence in 1948. The President invited the heads of state from both countries to Camp David for face-to-face talks. They isolated themselves completely from world publicity for twelve days. When they emerged, they had an agreement in principle. Without President Carter's role as mediator, these ancient antagonists would probably not have gotten together for many years.

In Japan, mediators playa large role in buy-sell negotiations. Mediators, usually old friends of both, introduce buyer and seller. When the seller is ready to make a proposal, the mediator assures that the seller's price, terms, specification and scope of work for the product or service to be rendered are in line with the buyer's needs. There are few surprises for either party when these mediators do their job well.

During the performance phase, it is the mediator who helps settle disputes. If prices must be changed because the seller is losing money, or if the buyer has reason to need a lower price, it is the mediator who harmonizes the divergent viewpoints. Disputes between buyer and seller about property rights, sharing of production improvements, quality standards or layoffs of employees are resolved with the mediator's help rather than by law.

Such disagreements rarely go to court in Japan, which has far fewer lawyers than the United States. Mediators are the catalysts who maintain the state of harmony between Japanese suppliers and their customers. They facilitate agreement in several ways:

- They can sell new ideas to each side more easily than if the same ideas were proposed by either party alone.
- They can cause both buyer and seller to ask themselves: "What decision do I want the other side to make and what must I do to help them make that decision?"
- They can suggest realistic expectations.
- They can invite both parties to talk once more after they

walk out.

- They can listen privately as each side expresses controversial ideas without angering the other.
- They can stimulate mutually beneficial win-win creative thinking.
- They can listen in private to one side expressing distaste or distrust of the other without angering the other side.
- They can suggest compromise positions that either party alone would be afraid to propose for fear of weakening its bargaining position or power.

The best mediators come from outside the buying and selling organizations, though there are occasions when a member of one or the other organization is satisfactory. A well-regarded engineer, accountant or executive could act as mediator for both sides. The important thing is that they possess the social skill, knowledge, integrity and charisma to win respect as peacemakers, and that both sides view them as trusted friends.

Mediators are not used often enough in buy-sell relationships in the United States. They should be. The next time you experience a stalemate or see one corning, try bringing a third party into the talks. If that person acts judiciously, both sides will discover a face-saving way to resolve their differences.

TENTH: CHANGE THE SHAPE OF SATISFACTION AND DISSATISFACTION

A negotiation is like an investment, When people deadlock, they are saying, in effect, the return on doing business with one another isn't worth the trouble. No deal is better than a deal.

A person who invests in a $1,000 bond weighs the flow of satisfaction against the flow of dissatisfaction over the life of the bond. If the bond pays $100 a year for ten years and then returns the full $1,000, the holder has achieved a positive flow of satisfaction. On the other hand, if inflation is 10 percent per year, the $1,000 will buy very little after ten years. This will be a source of dissatisfaction.

What the investor tries to do is balance the probable flow of satisfactions and dissatisfactions in his or her favor before saying "yes" to buying the bond. Essentially, a negotiator thinks the same way before making a decision to agree.

An efficient technique for moving a stalled negotiation back on track is to change the other party's stream of satisfaction and dissatisfaction. A buyer can enhance the seller's flow of satisfaction by offering a long-term contract or by purchasing additional products. He or she can reduce the seller's stream of future dissatisfaction by guaranteeing payment or by a willingness to be open minded if slight problems of delivery or quality arise. Whenever the flow of pleasure or pain is altered, a new negotiating relationship is possible.

A good example of changing the balance of satisfaction and dissatisfaction comes from the world of merchandising. One of the most aggravating sources of dissatisfaction for consumers is paying good money for shoddy products. Over one hundred years ago, Sears changed merchandising forever. They broke the deadlock between themselves and American farmers, who liked the goods pictured in the catalog but were afraid to buy. Sears pioneered "Satisfaction guaranteed or your money back," and the farmer felt secure enough to open his purse. Sears changed the shape of future satisfaction and dissatisfaction for the farmer and thereby closed the sale. You can do the same to avoid or break a deadlock in any negotiation.

ELEVENTH: CHANGE THE NEGOTIATOR

Breakdowns are not always caused by world-shattering issues or great matters of economics. Sometimes opposing negotiators simply dislike one another for reasons that make no economic sense.

I have participated in negotiations in which deadlock occurred because our team leader was unwilling to face the fact that his line of reasoning was wrong. He didn't want to admit error to the opposing leader by saying "yes" to the other party's logic. To save face and protect his ego, he preferred to deadlock rather than settle. When we changed negotiators, the tension disappeared and we were able to reach a satisfactory agreement.

Many deadlocks are the result of personality differences, fear of losing face, organizational infighting, a poor working relationship with the boss or the inability to make decisions. Any consideration of how to break an impasse must take into account the human factor.

Personality clashes between opponents is not the only reason for changing negotiators. Often stalled talks can be recharged by raising (or lowering) the authority level of the bargainers. Sometimes one can get things going again by having one participant drop out and replacing her with an associate, friend or spouse. A salesperson can forestall an impasse by bringing in an engineer or pricing specialist to support the seller's position.

Changing the negotiator or the team can bring new perspectives to the table and change the direction of the talks. It can serve to soften the impact of prior disagreements.

TWELFTH: GET YOUR MESSAGE DEEPER INTO THE OTHER ORGANIZATION

Negotiators bargain for others in their organization as well as for themselves, Understanding how a negotiator deals with those she negotiates for is important because it provides a key to unlocking a deadlock when it arises.

Every person in an organization has her own set of needs and expectations as well as a highly individual viewpoint about which issues are important to her and which are not. All these people, whether at the table or not, have goals. At best, these goals may be shared; at worst they may be in conflict with the goals of others in their organization.

These individual differences in viewpoint and priority arise from many factors. Some people will have to do more work if agreement is reached, others less. Some will benefit more from the deal, others may be worse off. Some will rise in the organization, others fall. Each person involved represents a different level of power, status, functional responsibility, expectation and ambition. More likely than not, there will be some degree of conflict between them.

Conflict in the organization also results from different facts, methods and values. These variations cause group members to look at issues in a personal way and to search for group solutions that provide them as much safety and satisfaction as possible. It is obvious that negotiators are faced with the uncomfortable task of reconciling a bewildering number of organizational demands besides their own.

The negotiator's dilemma may be intense. If she is passive about the excessively high group goals and expectations in her own organization, she may encounter a difficult situation at the table. On the other hand, if she persuades her own members to lower their expectations, she may be accused of not believing in her organization's goals or values. The negotiator's boundary role between her organization and that of the other party requires balancing the needs of the factions at the table with the needs of those who are not there.

When there is a deadlock, it is often because the negotiators cannot say "yes" to the other party while others in their organization are saying "no." As the opposing negotiator, your role is a strange one – to help your opponent get a "yes" answer from his or her own people. You can accomplish this in a number of ways, all of which require a degree of tact and good business judgement. The suggestions below are designed to make it possible for you to gain support in the opposing party's organization for your position and arguments.

ONE: Consider function-to-function contacts such as engineer-to-engineer, service giver-to-service giver or consultant-to-affected manager. Be sure they understand how your position benefits them.

TWO: Consider a summit meeting between high level executives of both parties.

THREE: Consider whether it is wise to bypass the opposing negotiator's authority level. You will often find the other side's boss easier to deal with than the person opposite you at the table.

FOUR: Consider the appropriateness of distributing information directly to members of the other organization if you think that your message is not reaching them.

FIVE: Consider going off the record. A private meal with the team leader of the other side can do much to break barriers.

SIX: Send a message through third parties. That's what the Japanese do.

The negotiator on the other side can rarely agree to settle if those she represents do not want an agreement. Your job is to help the opposing negotiator win their approval so that she can safely say "yes" to you.

THIRTEENTH: THE UNITED NATIONS COALITION

Another widely used technique for bringing parties toward settlement is what I call the "United Nations Coalition." This approach brings into play the interests of diverse outside groups in reaching a solution. Sometimes a coalition that includes the government, local politicians, unions and bankers can push the buyer and seller into agreement, even when the gap between them is wide.

In Japan you can hardly close a complex transaction without considering the needs of institutional forces far from the table. Balancing the interests of everyone involved in a multifaceted transaction is essentially a political decision. It is best resolved and settled by a high level coalition.

FOURTEENTH: ENTREPRENEUR'S APPROACH: NEGOTIATE A WIN-WIN DEAL

In Chapter 3, we discussed the most powerful strategy a negotiator can pursue – the win-win strategy. We saw how satisfaction for both parties can be increased at little or no cost to either party. When people deal with each other on a win-win basis they succeed. Together they make 2 + 2 become not 4 but 5 or more. They create value, and bargaining becomes easier since there is more for both parties to share.

I have personally used this approach many times and can assure you that it works remarkably well. The magic of the "both-win" is that it captures the attention of the other party instantaneously. Who among us is so stubborn as to refuse to listen to an opportunity for gain? Both-win strategies broaden the scope of negotiation by enlarging the sphere of mutual interests. Suddenly buyer and seller see the potential for further profit; the pie gets bigger and better for both.

The next time you are in a negotiation that appears to be going nowhere, try saying, "Let's find a better way to benefit both of us." You'll be amazed at how quickly the discussion moves to a cooperative track. The threat of deadlock withers away.

Win-win is, beyond a doubt, the most powerful payoff strategy in negotiation.

CONCLUSION

Deadlock is a normal risk of bargaining. People from other cultures handle it better than Americans. For them, walking away from a deal is a matter of habit. They've done it in their daily lives since childhood. Walking away is just another way to tell the other side that the offer is not yet good enough. For Americans deadlock is usually more of a trauma – a psychological battle involving two parties whose egos are at stake.

Deadlock is a legitimate test of the balance of power and resolve of opposing parties. It need not be feared or shunned as a tactic. It mayor may not mean "dead." In most cases, if properly handled, it is merely one more stage of the bargaining process. If the parties are convinced they have something to gain by continuing to talk, they will talk.

Each of the impasse-breaking approaches discussed in this chapter has the power to build bridges that re-involve the self-interest of the opposing parties. They can lead to sound long-term agreements rather than the emptiness of deadlock.

FOURTEEN WAYS TO AVERT
OR BREAK A DEADLOCK

———— • ————

#1 The Memorandum of Agreement

#2 Last Minute Hitches

#3 Get Elvis Presley's Ashtray

#4 How Haste Makes Waste in Closing

#5 Physical Actions that Lead to Closure

#6 The Sunk Cost Principle

#7 Try an Off-The-Record Closure

#8 Why it's Crucial to Agree on How Performance Will Be Measured

#9 Psychological Approaches That Lead to Closure

#10 The Nibbler

#11 Deal Killers

#12 Delight Factors

#13 One Big Reason You Really Won't Get What You Bargained For

#14 The Law of "Unintended Consequences"

18 | Closing Strategies and Tactics

The purpose of this chapter is to cover strategies which help negotiators close better deals and reduce the likelihood of dissatisfaction after agreement is reached. People have a great deal of trouble at this late stage. Not only are they under severe pressure to make difficult decisions, but they are forced to handle more information than they are normally accustomed to. Mistakes are made, omissions go undetected, and misunderstandings arise at this late stage of bargaining.

Settlement generally occurs when each party believes that the agreement close at hand offers greater satisfaction than no agreement. The agreement is perceived as better than other available alternatives, and each side believes that the other has conceded most of what it will. Both believe that further effort spent negotiating is not worthwhile.

The question of what causes the talks to conclude and when that will occur is important because, as negotiators, we have a major role in changing the other party's perceptions, expectations, and satisfaction level. We can say or do things which cause them to search for alternative sources of satisfaction, or we can lead them to settle with us. By the manner in which we make concessions or show our strength, we can encourage the other side to either settle or try to win further gains. Our action or inaction affects their decision to close.

When people negotiate with one another, they are exchanging satisfaction. Much of the satisfaction typically exchanged in the negotiating process consists of goods, services, and money. As we saw in Chapter 4, these issues comprise the tip of the motivational iceberg. Other parts of the exchange are hidden from view. It is these normally unspoken, personal needs that lead negotiators to finally say "yes."

Successful closing is an art, not a science. Many psychological factors come into play as settlement approaches. The fourteen closing strategies which follow are designed to help both sides reach more intelligent, long-lasting agreements – agreements that will lead to greater mutual satisfaction on both a personal and organizational level.

FOURTEEN CLOSING STRATEGIES

---

1. THE MEMORANDUM OF AGREEMENT.
2. LAST MINUTE HITCHES.
3. GET ELVIS PRESLEY'S ASHTRAY.
4. HOW HASTE MAKES WASTE IN CLOSING.
5. PHYSICAL ACTIONS THAT LEAD TO CLOSURE.

6. THE SUNK COST PRINCIPLE.

7. TRY AN OFF-THE-RECORD CLOSURE.

8. WHY IT IS CRUCIAL TO AGREE ON HOW PERFORMANCE WILL BE MEASURED.

9. PSYCHOLOGICAL APPROACHES THAT LEAD TO CLOSURE.

10. THE NIBBLER.

11. DEAL KILLERS.

12. DELIGHT FACTORS.

13. ONE BIG REASON YOU DON'T GET WHAT YOU BARGAINED FOR.

14. THE LAW OF "UNINTENDED" CONSEQUENCES.

THE MEMORANDUM OF AGREEMENT

Many negotiations are aborted soon after the parties reach agreement. After spending hours or days together discussing issues such as price, terms, and specifications, settlement is finally achieved. Both sides breathe a sigh of relief. All that remains to be done is to write a contract reflecting the agreement. No big problem – or is it?

The trouble is that the contract and other binding documents often take days or weeks to be written and signed. In the movie business, for example, it's even worse: the contract between producer and movie star can take more than a year to formalize. This is what makes a memorandum of agreement so crucial; it represents the agreement as both parties thought they understood it when talks ended.

Notice that I just said, "as both parties thought they understood it when the talks ended." I didn't say, "as both parties agreed when the talks ended." There is a big difference, and this difference can be quite important.

The reason there is a difference between what they "thought they agreed to" and what they "actually agreed to" is this: It is virtually impossible to remember all that has gone on during the course of negotiations. Some parts of the settlement take place early in the talks, others take place off the record, and still others take place at closure. Too much is talked about to recall every issue and detail agreed to, even important ones. That is why it is wise to take good notes as you go along, and why a prompt memorandum reflecting the major terms of settlement is essential.

Every negotiation of any significance should end with a written memorandum signed by both parties. Experience shows that a few minutes spent writing down the highlights of an agreement reduces aggravation later. A good memorandum of agreement will, of course, reflect settlement in such areas as final price, terms, delivery, and products or services to be provided. It will also include references to key documents, specifications, and procedures. This helps those writing the final contract to understand the intent of the parties at the table. Simple everyday phrases are preferable to legal terminology. A well written memo of agreement establishes the legitimacy of an oral agreement. It makes it harder for either side to retreat from agreement.

I believe that the person writing the memorandum is in a better position than the one who does not. The writer can use language that best reflects his or her interpretation of what occurred at the table. Too much goes on as talks close to be remembered accurately by anyone. To my amazement, I have seen people forget even the price they agreed to in the heat of closing.

I recall one situation where the buyer thought he settled for more and the seller thought he had settled for less. Their concessions had passed each other without being heard by either. They sheepishly agreed to split the difference when the mistake was recognized.

I am not suggesting that the party writing the memo take advantage of the other side when penning the agreement. They should write it as they honestly believe it to have been settled. Yet there is no question that subtle factors can cause memory to be less than perfect when tensions are high. The rapid flow of last minute give and take distorts perception. The person writing the memo should write it as she believes it to be. The person reviewing it has the duty to see that the final memo represents his interpretation of the settlement.

Before presenting your written memo to the other party, your people should review it. They are likely to find errors and omissions you overlooked. Then, give the other party all the time they need to read the document and amend what they believe in error. Differences in interpretation are sure to arise and require further negotiation.

It takes good business judgment to pen a well-written memorandum. On the one hand, it is important to cover the important issues and terms agreed to. On the other hand, it may be well to leave some minor details unresolved if they delay the already achieved settlement. Some differences simply fade away at contract signing time or during the performance phase.

There are times when a negotiator may want the other side to write the memorandum of agreement. In that case, the best defense is not to be naive. Be sure to review the memo carefully; it will favor the writer. If you don't understand something, get it clarified and insist on better wording. Get others to review it with you. Above all, don't read or sign the agreement if you are tired. That's hoping for the best.

A jointly signed memorandum of agreement is a powerful document; it can't completely prevent the parties from changing their minds later on, but it can put a brake on such problems. Having signed, they are apt to feel committed. Later, when the final contract is written, check it against the memo of agreement; differences between the two do arise. I have seen "final contracts" that altered essential terms of agreement, left other terms out, or deliberately added requirements that were never even discussed, let alone agreed to. The negotiator who reads the final contract and has the courage to face differences promptly and assertively wins better performance and avoids later aggravation.

LAST MINUTE HITCHES

If there is one thing you can count on in negotiation it is that there will be last minute hitches. As settlement approaches, problems not previously visible become apparent. Immediately after the parties shake hands, or later when they write the final contract or purchase order, they will suddenly recognize troublesome oversights, risks, and vague understandings not covered at the bargaining table. Both sides will become apprehensive about things they should have discussed but didn't.

Why does this happen? Because, as final agreement comes closer and words are put on paper, the parties find themselves engaged in the specifics of procedure, measurement, and definitions. Words take on different meanings when written rather than spoken. Potential problems become visible. Issues that appeared to be nailed down are opened to semantic debate. Dates, discounts, and dollar agreements become subject to "what if" and "who is responsible for" arguments.

Most agreements made at the table require the approval of others. Everyone in both organizations who has any part in approving the settlement can provide inputs as to how it can be improved. Engineers suddenly want to tighten the specification, quality control people want to reduce tolerances, lawyers want terms clarified, production people want more time to deliver, and sales management wonders if the lower discount offered was warranted. Second guessers and "Monday Morning Quarterbacks" abound.

These inputs inundate the negotiators on both sides with problems they must resolve. The immediate effect is to place the agreement in jeopardy. Both negotiators find themselves under severe pressure to deal not only with each other, but with those in their own company, to resolve these last minute hitches.

Last minute hitches occur in diplomatic affairs as well as business. Hardly a day goes by in international negotiations when the press does not report that an agreement between this nation and that is imminent. The next day chaos seems to break loose. The treaty or trade agreement is reported to be falling apart for what appears to us as minor reasons. Then, a few days or weeks later, the negotiators meet again, shake hands, and announce that a settlement has been reached. In diplomacy, as in business, the Monday Morning Quarterbacks are at work criticizing the agreement and trying to improve it.

History is replete with such last minute melodramas. When President Reagan met with President Gorbachev in Iceland, the meeting seemed to fall apart, but significant agreements were later reached. The Palestine-Israel negotiations ground to a halt a dozen times on seemingly minor details before the two sides finally reached a tentative agreement. Trade negotiations with the Japanese rise, fall, and rise again as last minute hitches, important to each country, require resolution. The more complex the negotiation, the more certain the hitches.

Negotiators do not, as a rule, welcome last minute hitches. However, they should be expected by both sides as a normal, and to some extent, a positive part of the bargaining process.

GET ELVIS PRESLEY'S ASHTRAY

Colonel Parker was Elvis Presley's business manager. He was reported to be the toughest agent in the entertainment world.

Colonel Parker was a hard negotiator. When he made a deal for Elvis, he made sure it would be enforced. The logistics of a successful concert performance are mind-boggling. Most producers are honest, some are flaky, still others do not have enough money, and some are just con men. Entertainment producers too often have dreams of fantastically high show revenues that don't live up to expectations. It was up to Colonel Parker to protect Elvis and the high price he commanded. It was his responsibility to see that everything necessary for a great performance was ready as promised.

Contract negotiations were hard fought. The Colonel was a

painstaking man who read every clause, dotted every "i" and crossed every "t." The terms and conditions left little room for producers to do other than they agreed to do.

But Colonel Parker threw one clause in his contracts that mystified the producers. He handed them a specially designed Elvis Presley ashtray. In the contract he specified that this ashtray, along with the balance of payment for Elvis' performance, be sent to Colonel Parker's office three days before Elvis would appear. No ashtray – no Elvis. No money – no Elvis. They laughed, signed the contract, and in most cases delivered the money on time, but not the ashtray.

That's when the Colonel went to work and the producers stopped laughing. Colonel Parker made it clear that if any term in the contract was not fulfilled Elvis would not sing. No exceptions. The producers went back and read the contract. The ashtray was soon delivered by courier. As for the producers, they learned to do exactly what was written in the contract. They performed 100 percent; Elvis performed 100 percent.

We can learn something from Colonel Parker and his ashtray. One of the biggest mistakes a negotiator can make is to include a stipulation or requirement and fail to execute it. If you put an ashtray into the contract, make sure you get it. If you don't enforce the terms agreed on, you may find other, more critical areas of performance eroded beyond repair. Be sure to get the ashtray every time.

HOW HASTE MAKES WASTE IN CLOSING

Henry Kissinger, our former Secretary of State, was widely recognized as a careful negotiator. But even he made some serious mistakes. One of his worst occurred when he wanted to close an agreement with the North Vietnamese four weeks before the 1972 presidential election. Kissinger wanted the deal, wanted it badly, and wanted it then and there. Marvin and Bernard Kalb in the their book, Kissinger, described the closing this way:

"In a grand rush toward the finale, there was simply not enough time to scrutinize the fine print and the numerous appendices of the draft agreement. The Americans were careless and permitted ambiguities to slip into the draft. If Kissinger had been negotiating with the Russians or the Chinese, he no doubt would have been meticulous about every syllable; but with the North Vietnamese, after more than three years of painful negotiations, he seemed more concerned about nailing down the deal than about making sure that every detail was correct – an attitude that played right into the North Vietnamese hands."

The United States paid dearly for Kissinger's rush to closure. The North Vietnamese took advantage of every ambiguity to the great distress of our allies in the South. Several years later we were ignominiously driven from Vietnam without a shred of honor.

If Kissinger can make a mistake like that, so can you or I. Whether you want the deal badly or not, take the time to cross the "t's" and dot the "i's". Don't just hope for the best as Kissinger did.

PHYSICAL ACTIONS THAT LEAD TO CLOSURE

At the moment of closure, a negotiator is not in an enviable position. He or she is torn between the choice of accepting "the bird in hand or the two that may be in the bush." You can, however, take physical actions that will push the other side to accept the bird in hand.

I have seen salespeople move a hesitant buyer into placing the order by starting to write the sales order. Some buyers get a seller to accept a lower price by acting as though the seller has already accepted it. The buyer gives the seller a purchase order number, stands up, shakes hands, and escorts the salesperson out the door with a big smile and a word of congratulation.

Taking out the champagne and pouring drinks can help close a deal that isn't quite there. So can making reservations at a good restaurant to celebrate the closure of the deal. Many negotiators end the final give and take by simply writing up the memo of agreement on their lap-top computer. They may even bring the computer to the restaurant to maintain closing momentum.

One of the most graceful closure actions I've seen occurred when I bought a car. I wasn't sure whether I wanted to settle or not. The car salesman, sensing my indecision, asked to borrow my pen. I gave it to him. He proceeded to write the order. I watched. Then I signed and returned the pen to him. I never saw that pen again.

THE SUNK COST PRINCIPLE

There are two principles of human behavior which I have found useful in closing:

The principle of "sunk cost."
The principle of "hard to get."

The "sunk cost" principle is this: The more effort a party puts into reaching agreement, the more they will want to close. In a buyer-seller transaction, the buyer who invests considerable time and energy in selecting several sources of supply, speaking to each of them, and negotiating with the preferred vendor, wants the investment to end in agreement. The seller has also invested a lot of time and money in making the sale and negotiating with the buyer. Sunk costs propel both buyer and seller toward closure. They do not want to lose their investment; they want a return on it.

The second principle – "hard to get" – relates to closing in this way: People have a greater appreciation for things that are hard to get. Negotiators who work hard to achieve their objectives are more willing to settle. They prefer the deal at hand to the one they might get if they started all over again with someone else.

The "hard to get" principle is a good one, and it works well with "sunk cost." Make the other party work hard and long for everything they get at the table. Give in slowly and reluctantly. Talk, talk, talk. Let the dual principles of "sunk cost" and "hard to get" do their work. It will raise the other party's level of satisfaction and thereby lead to earlier closure.

TRY AN OFF-THE-RECORD CLOSURE

Some things are not settled in the light of publicity or under the scrutiny of others at the table. Much of what is said at the table is said not to reach agreement, but to prove to others in the negotiators' organization that their views are being expressed and fought for. Off-the-record talks permit each party to tell the other what the real impediments to agreement are and why some issues are more important than others.

Off-the-record discussions also set the stage for later accommodation at the table. In her ten-year research study of labor negotiations, Ann Douglas found that private talks between principal negotiators frequently preceded settlement. I had the same experience in customer-supplier negotiations. What we learned from each other during private meetings could not have been said before others. Yet it was what we learned off the record that closed the deal.

Off-the-record talks foster movement toward settlement because the opposing negotiators can talk about their personal feelings as well as their organizational constraints on a person-to-person basis. They can privately indicate a willingness to compromise or to exchange one issue for another. These informal moves toward reconciliation might be politically unwise if discussed at the table.

There is a downside, however, to off-the-record talks. Good negotiators know that not everything can or should be said off the record. They also know that some people, especially those with a strong need to be liked, talk too much in the privacy of a comfortable restaurant or under the gentle influence of good wine. Therein lies the danger inherent in off-the-record talks.

WHY IT IS CRUCIAL TO AGREE ON HOW PERFORMANCE WILL BE MEASURED

It is not enough for a buyer and seller to reach agreement on what is to be done and what is to be paid for it. There is another problem, a difficult one, that often rears its head at the very end: "How is performance really going to be measured and when is 'done' done?" Most people do not give this matter enough thought, and they often suffer serious consequences later. That's why the ideas in this section are important. They apply whether you call a plumber to work at your home or contract with the largest manufacturing companies on a multimillion dollar deal.

Let's say, for example, that you hire a contractor to design and install a rooftop solar panel system. The contract calls for solar panels, a specialized mounting, a grid tie-in system and upgraded electrical equipment. Materials and labor are given a one-year warranty. That's good, but there is more to it.

Do the warranties on materials start one year from when the manufacturer shipped the solar panels and mounting, or one year after the panels were installed, or one year after the new solar panel system is working satisfactorily? In fact, when is the solar panel project really done? When you can begin to produce electricity, or when the contractor says it's done? Is it done if the site has debris around it or the rooftop mounting needs to be refit and the grid tie-in isn't working efficiently enough? When "done is done" is the forgotten issue in too many negotiations.

The measurement of services is more difficult than the

measurement of product. Once my department was responsible for the acquisition of consulting services for an advanced research facility. All kinds of measurement problems arose. We agreed rather easily on a rate per hour. What we had trouble with was how to measure an hour. When did it start or stop? Was flying time chargeable? How many hours in a day? Who kept the records? How were they to be kept? When was the job done? Was the final report the point at which work ended? What if we found it incorrect or otherwise wanting? What action constituted acceptance and by whom? Who did the measuring? Who checked the measurer and how? Both the quality and quantity of services are hard to measure and control.

The absence of reliable measurement standards and procedures leads to inadequate compliance as well as certain aggravation later on. Before closing your next negotiation, ask yourself, "Have I defined the work or service to be done well enough, and have I set up good procedures to measure whether it is done as agreed?" You'll be glad you did.

PSYCHOLOGICAL APPROACHES THAT LEAD TO CLOSURE

Negotiators settle when each party believes the other has conceded most of what it will and further efforts are not likely to be very productive. At this point, the desire to close starts to outweigh the desire for more concessions, and the parties move toward closure. To reach this point is in part a psychological process.

Psychological approaches like those suggested below can help lead to settlement:

ONE: Assure the other person that she is wise to reach agreement. Give her good reason to support a closing decision now. Good references from pleased customers help. Tell her why she will be pleased and satisfied.

TWO: Act as though agreement has been reached on the main issues and price. Start talking about details like where and when delivery should take place, the wording of a clause, or whether payment will be made by check, credit card or cash.

THREE: Make repeated requests for agreement and closure. Don't be afraid to say, "We know everything we need to know to agree, don't we." Say it again and again as you go along.

FOUR: If you get a "no" answer to the above, ask why. The other party will probably tell you. You will then have something specific to overcome or improve on. Do it again if closure doesn't follow.

FIVE: If you are a buyer dealing with a seller, get the seller as close to the money as you can. Show him the purchase order or the cash. Let him hold your credit card or your signed check. Make the sale real and immediately accessible to him.

If you are the seller dealing with a hesitant buyer, it's wise to connect the buyer with the joys of the product or service. Put her in the car. Sit her down with the laptop. Let her print out some color photos of his kids. Give her a chance to play with the special features on the digital camera. Let him push the buttons. Get him to try on the new suit, shirt, and tie. Have him handle the product or get a hands-on feel for the service.

SIX: There are people who coerce themselves into agreement because they feel guilty about wasting the time of the person they are dealing with. Rug merchants in Turkey know that Americans tend to buy if the merchant spends a lot of time with them.

SEVEN: Fear of loss can be as strong a motivator as the desire for gain. Many people are more strongly motivated by the desire to avoid loss than the pleasure of making gains.

A seller may urge closure on the buyer because without it they may have to sell their total capacity to someone else. This could be a disaster for a buyer's organization, which has counted on the seller's production capacity and technology. A large computer chip company did just that and thereby captured a huge order from a prime computer customer. The computer manufacturer could not risk losing the seller's production capacity on its newly developed chip, so it decided to take no chances. It tied them up completely.

Likewise, a buyer can tell the salesperson that if the seller does not accept the offer now the money will not be available later. This is often done when budgets expire on specific dates and cannot be extended without government or higher executive approval.

EIGHT: Offer the other party a choice between acceptable choice A and acceptable choice B. It shifts the other party's decision from choosing to agree or not to choosing between two choices which are both satisfactory.

NINE: Offer the other party a "multiple choice with a negative": X, or Y, or Q, where Q is sure to be rejected as undesirable. The decision is then likely to focus on acceptable choices X and Y.

TEN: Make the final deal a little sweeter than the other party thought it would be. An unexpected bargain or treat carries special value.

ELEVEN: Provide a special benefit that cannot be offered later. This can be a price bonus, a special value-added service, a better discount, a stronger warranty, or better financial terms. Make the reason why it cannot be offered later as credible as possible or it will not influence the closure decision.

TWELVE: People love a bargain. See Chapter 11 for many psychological ways to create a bargain without giving much away.

THIRTEEN: Tell a story which supports closing the deal right now. I know a real estate broker in California who closed many sales in the boom period of the early 2000s by telling prospective clients about people who had passed up big profits by hesitating to buy. His stories were all the more credible because such big profits were reported in the press every day. *An appropriate story can make your drive toward closure more persuasive than a wealth of rational arguments.*

People act in their self-interest. Most of the psychological approaches suggested here lead the other side toward closure because they take into account people's needs and help relieve the ambiguity inherent in making the decision to close.

THE NIBBLER – "IF YOU CAN'T GET A DINNER GET A SANDWICH"

I have a brother-in-law who is a nibbler. Whenever he buys anything he tries to get the merchant to throw something else into the deal for nothing or at dealer's cost. He almost always succeeds. If his wife is with him when he nibbles at the store, she tries to hide. She is not a nibbler and is embarrassed to be with one.

Nibbling is effective. After my brother-in-law has negotiated with the car dealer and settled on a price for the Audi, he waits until the seller is writing up the sales ticket. Then he asks for things like a full tank of gas, floor mats, upgraded hub caps, a lower interest rate, and a free loaner if the car requires repair during the next month.

He rarely gets all these at no cost, but he usually succeeds in winning lots of them. Some he has to pay for, but at the dealer's invoice cost, not at retail like most of us. Why? Because the car dealer does not want to risk losing the sale for these small items. My brother-in-law looks and acts like he might walk out. The dealer responds by giving something.

Buyers nibble on sellers and sellers on buyers. That's the way the world works. There is nothing unethical about it. Some nibbles are worth the time, effort, and aggravation it costs the nibbler. Others are too small to be worthwhile.

Those willing to try should understand that the nibbler gets results because the other party may be driven to close the deal quickly or they want to be liked. The other party may also give in because they want your future business, or they simply want to show how fair they are. Nibbling should be considered an optional part of a every negotiator's arsenal of behaviors.

Do professional buyers and sellers from large companies nibble? You bet they do, especially after agreement is reached and the performance phase starts.

Buyers nibble by paying bills late, by taking discounts for cooperative advertisements they never earned, by insisting on earlier delivery dates or by demanding higher quality levels than were agreed to. They are not the least ashamed to nibble for extra samples, free work and more training than the contract calls for. These can be very costly to the seller who hasn't built the nibbles into her price.

Sellers, of course, do lots of nibbling on buyers. They supply some Grade B product when the contract calls for 100 percent Grade A. They don't provide all the promised services. They deliver late, bill early, and add special charges where none were expected by the buyer. Such nibbles can raise the total cost for the buyer in a significant way if she is not strong or alert enough to stop them.

Sellers and buyers can handle the nibble successfully if they recognize that it is going on and have a firm policy to stop it. While sellers may permit some nibbles to build goodwill, past a certain point, they are best stopped with a firm sales policy that puts limits on what can be "thrown in." Sellers can also reduce nibbles by putting a price on those things the nibbler is likely to ask for. Sometimes even a small price placed on a nibble can stop it because it may require the nibbler to write a purchase order just for a small item.

Nibbling is a common practice in most cultures, but it is less common in the United States and Canada, where we tend to feel uncomfortable with it. It is better that we approach nibbling in a mature way. There is nothing wrong with it. Whether to nibble or not is a question of business choice. It depends on your willingness to invest the time and effort it takes to succeed. The rallying cry of those who negotiate should be, "If you can't get a dinner get a sandwich."

DEAL KILLERS

In the world of negotiation, there are essentially two types of people – deal makers and deal killers. Both have an important role.

This book is designed to help deal-makers negotiate – to make better agreements for themselves and for the other side at the same time. Deal killers are not against making deals; at least that is what they say. However, what seems to happen in most negotiations, whether simple or complex, is that the deal killers come out of the woodwork at the last moment to tell those at the table not to settle "unless ... " They view their job as protectors of the negotiators' best interest, not as "nay-sayers." Yet what they say and do makes it much harder to close.

I've learned never to be surprised by the deal-killers. I expect them before the final agreement is signed. I have even learned to reluctantly welcome them and their comments because they have occasionally kept me from making mistakes I might otherwise have overlooked.

In personal negotiations, some of my closest relatives are deal killers. They do not hesitate to tell me what a poor agreement I am making. They warn me not to trust the other party, even a little. They remind me of every disaster and performance problem the future can possibly hold. "Cover yourself," they say. "Get the warranty or get the money in advance or else you'll suffer." The trouble is that the other party is rarely willing to grant me all the concessions necessary to cover every risk uncovered by the deal-killers. In the end, I have to make my own business decisions despite their suggestions. They tell me what to watch out for; I make the judgments necessary to reach agreement. The deal-killers do their job; I do mine.

Lawyers are great deal killers. They tell you everything that can go wrong and more. If you tried to bargain away every danger the lawyers foresaw, the negotiation would never end. It would become so complicated that neither party would trust the other. In most cases the result would be deadlock.

Despite the fact that complex negotiations always require legal sign-off, we rarely permitted the lawyers to attend bargaining sessions when I was a professional negotiator. When the lawyers came, things slowed down to zero. You could sense the walls of distrust rising as they commented on different issues from a legal viewpoint. We learned to leave them home and things went more smoothly.

Lawyers, nevertheless, had an important function in reviewing the final contract. They found areas in which our company vulnerability was too high for comfort. They left us to decide whether we could live with the potential danger or if we needed greater protection. Our decision was made on the basis of the other side's track record as a reliable seller and their willingness to relieve our vulnerability by granting necessary warranties.

Our job was to look at the preferred agreement and then use our business sense to choose the best deal possible. While I cannot say we loved the lawyers for their comments, I can say that we were open to their suggestions and did what we could to reduce the risks they discovered.

Other deal-killers on the selling side are pricing people. It is they who often stymie closings by telling sales management that they should insist on higher prices or smaller discounts.

Credit people also play the role of deal-killers. They advise sales that "The customer's credit is not good enough." or "Get him to pay net in 30 days rather than 60 days because they are always 30 to 60 days late."

The trouble with these deal-killers is that they are far removed from the real marketplace, while the salesperson is on the front line with buyers every day.

An effective negotiator is one who can also negotiate in his or her own organization. Good negotiators are sensitive to the deal-killer's functional responsibilities and expertise. The negotiator's role in working with the deal-killers is to persuade them that the agreement, while imperfect, does indeed protect the company as well as it can considering the needs and expectations of the opposing party. No agreement is likely to offer complete safety. Even the deal-killers know that.

DELIGHT FACTORS

Few concessions give as much satisfaction as a surprise treat provided at or near closing with no strings attached. The Japanese call these bonuses "delight factors." Experienced car dealers know that customers are pleasantly surprised when they throw in free floor mats or car washes without being asked to. The car buyer will remember this years later, long after they have forgotten the price of the car.

In my book The Negotiating Game, I described how much goodwill an arctic fur trader gained when he gratuitously gave an Eskimo hunter returning to the cold north some sweets and goodies for his family. The delight factor made later negotiations between the trader and the Eskimo easier.

From now on, save a few items to give away as "delight factors". They will raise the satisfaction of the other party far more than their cost to you.

ONE BIG REASON YOU DON'T GET WHAT YOU BARGAINED FOR

Auditing is the neglected stepchild of negotiation. People do not do a good job of checking to make sure they got what they bargained for, especially if the purchase is complex. Too often, they hope for the best and it doesn't happen.

The point is illustrated by a Hungarian folk tale about Moritzka, a simple but well liked peasant in a small village. One warm evening, the villagers are on their way to Mass and they see Moritzka on his hands and knees looking for something under a lamp post. They ask him what he is looking for. Moritzka replies, "I'm looking for my crucifix. I dropped it."

The villagers, eager to help the simple man, ask him where he lost it. Moritzka points in the direction of the river about 100 feet away and says, "I lost it there by the river."

Surprised, the villagers ask, "Moritzka, why are you looking here, if you lost it there?" Moritzka replied, "Because it's dark there; the light is better over here."

Humorist Art Buchwald put it another way in a piece I read in the Times. It was a funny but true story about a 28-year-old investment banker who bet a billion dollars of his bank's money on derivative bonds and lost it all. The 230-year-old British institution went bankrupt.

Buchwald asked jokingly, "How can anyone lose a billion dollars in a vault without someone knowing about it?" His answer: "As I understand it, the bank was watching the man's lunch expense account closely, and it overlooked what he was doing with its funds. This happens all the time. We focus on the petty cash but ignore anything with more than three zeros attached to it."

Negotiators tend to assume that what they bargain for and agree to will be done. Then they leave the job of checking to others. The trouble is that nobody ends up checking performance very well. The reason is that we are all a lot like Moritzka; we check for discrepancies or problems under the lamp post, where the light is good. Where it is dark and hard to see, we don't look. That is why we, all too often, do not get the performance we bargained for.

THE LAW OF "UNINTENDED CONSEQUENCES"

The law of "unintended consequences" works in strange ways. Not too long ago, the Los Angeles Times reported that the dean of a California college discovered that a large number of students were signing up for evening classes and dropping them shortly after. Wondering why, he mailed questionnaires to their homes asking what their reasons were. The dropouts were asked if the problem was the class instructor, class time, personal matters or class content.

The article went on: "Before long he started to receive telephone calls from very puzzled husbands and wives. They didn't understand where he had gotten the idea that their spouses had dropped their classes. Several remarked that their spouses had perfect attendance." The dean promptly dropped the idea. That's how the law of "unintended consequences" does its mischievous work in life or business.

The same thing often happens in politics. Every law passed by the Congress and signed by the President is the product of a negotiation. Our representatives present their viewpoints to one another, decide what they want to accomplish, compromise and write a bill which reflects, to the extent it can, their diverse objectives. The bill is then signed, funds are set aside, organizations created, audit oversight functions implemented and the law or regulation administered. Every part of the legislative process is negotiated.

The trouble is, as in the dean's well-intentioned questionnaire, that once again we find the law of "unintended consequences" at work. Things happen that nobody anticipated. Often, the "unintended consequences" are worse than the problems the law was intended to solve.

The implementation of Medicare is a good example. Medicare was designed to meet a pressing national need. Older people could not afford the care they needed. The "unintended consequence," however, was that medical usage by seniors soared. In addition, doctors, lawyers and hospitals learned to use the system to their advantage. Medical expenses increased at rates never dreamed of by the bill's advocates. Medical purveyors such as doctors, hospitals and therapists proliferated and formed strong lobbies to defend their position. In 1965, when Medicare began, anticipated costs for 1995 were estimated at $6 billion a year. A slight mistake. By 1995 they were about $100 billion a year. Something had gone wrong in the great scheme of things.

Does this happen in negotiation? Yes. Some years ago I had a friend who used the "reverse auction" to contract for his swimming pool. He put one contractor after another through the auction. Each knew that others were in the running. Each bad-mouthed the competition and offered more quality, equipment, and service than the others. My friend gave the job to the pool contractor who offered the most for the least money.

The only issue the winning contractor held firm on was getting payments as he purchased materials and as the work progressed. My friend conceded on these issues. A progress payment schedule was negotiated based on certain specific events occurring. It seemed simple enough.

Unfortunately, the contractor knew more about building a pool than my friend. They agreed on 25 percent payment at what the builder insisted was the 25 percent construction point, 50 percent payment at the 50 percent construction point, 75 percent at the 75 percent point and total payment at completion.

Things appeared to go on schedule. Trouble began after the builder received the 75 percent point payment. At that point, the contractor started submitting heavy charges for every change along the way. The builder refused to continue unless the total price was increased by 35 percent. That's when my friend went out for other bids to finish the pool. Most pool contractors did not want to touch the mess. Others bid astronomical prices. They pointed out that the pool was not 75 percent complete but only 40 percent complete by their calculations.

My friend ended up paying the original contractor what he wanted. He was a victim of the law of "unintended consequences." The reverse auction did win him a low price and a promise of superior performance. The "unintended consequence" was a shady contractor who from the beginning set the stage for extra costs through changes in requirements and progress payments that were in effect advance payments. The builder knew that power would change in his favor over time. My friend thought about suing the contractor but learned that legal costs would likely be greater than accepting the contractor's demands.

I have seen many situations involving unintended consequences in the world of buying and selling, often after generous incentive contracts were given to manufacturers to get a job done quickly. The "unintended consequence" of such an incentive was a seller who did shoddy work in rushing to earn the handsome bonus.

I have met sales managers who paid their people higher commissions to motivate them to sell more. The "unintended consequence" was that it only worked with the best salespeople. They worked harder and produced more sales. Most others were happy working shorter hours. They valued recreation time more than earning more money.

Once when I worked in the plastics industry, we were surprised by a seller of combs. Our buyer had negotiated a very low price. One day somebody in receiving with nothing to do decided to count a large carton of plastic combs. It turned out that the price was low because the seller had decided long ago to ship 940 combs per carton but charge for 1,000. Nobody ever got around to checking earlier because it was too much trouble to count all those different sized combs lying helter skelter in a carton.

Beware the law of "unintended consequences." Ask yourself before signing the contract, "What could turn out differently than I expect or want?" That's the only way to minimize the impact of "unintended consequences," even in a good relationship.

FOURTEEN CLOSING STRATEGIES

—————————— • ——————————

#1   The Memorandum of Agreement

#2   Last Minute Hitches

#3   Get Elvis Presley's Ashtray

#4   How Haste Makes Waste in Closing

#5   Physical Actions that Lead to Closure

#6   The Sunk Cost Principle

#7   Try an Off-The-Record Closure

#8   Why it's Crucial to Agree on How Performance Will Be Measured

#9   Psychological Approaches That Lead to Closure

#10   The Nibbler

#11   Deal Killers

#12   Delight Factors

#13   One Big Reason You Really Won't Get What You Bargained For

#14   The Law of "Unintended Consequences"

19

Dr. Karrass' Prescription for Success

The ideas covered in this book work. They are not theoretical. They've been tried and tested over the centuries by successful people everywhere, but they will be of no value unless you try them in future negotiations. If you practice on small negotiations, you'll develop the skills to handle the big ones as well.

I cannot guarantee that every approach suggested will work every time. I can, however, assure that your negotiating batting average will improve as you gain skill in using them. Putting these age-old techniques to work will allow you to make better agreements from now on - agreements which leave both parties more satisfied than ever.

There is always a zone of "not knowing" in every buyer-seller transaction, a range within which the final outcome may fall. This range may only be one or two percent when competition and market forces are active. In other situations - as in the settlement of a liability suit or in dealing for scarce goods or services - the outcome can vary by several hundred percent or more. In either case, the final outcome may reflect thousands or even millions of dollars in profit gained or lost at the negotiating table.

Bottom line profits and losses are involved in every buyer-seller negotiation. That's why the ability to negotiate is so important. Good negotiators are not born, they are trained. Nowhere in business does quality training pay off so quickly or so well as in learning negotiating skills.

With this in mind, I would like to conclude with a prescription for negotiating success - dos and don'ts that will help you in any bargaining situation, large or small.

 Negotiation is not a contest or a competition, Look for a better deal for both parties. It can always be found if the parties look for it together. *Win-win is the most po werfu l strategy in a negotiator's arsenal.*

 You have more power than you think. The other party has constraints and needs which you are not aware of but which put pressure on their position. In most negotiations you will be more aware of the pressures on yourself than those on the other party. Don't dwell on your own limits and pressures. Take the time to discover the pressures on them.

 Don't hope for the best. Do your planning and preparation before bargaining begins. At the very least, write down what you must have, what you would like to have and what issues are not very important to you. List these wants in order of priority. This minimal plan will prove helpful because it will force you into a negotiation with yourself. The key to bargaining success is good preparation. The negotiator who doesn't do so is hoping for the best.

Never fear to negotiate, no matter how great the differences between the parties may be. If the Palestinians and Israelis can reach agreement, you can. Patience, persistence and a win-win strategy can bring even the most distant sides together.

Negotiating with a team is better than doing it by yourself. If you are a team leader, be sure that everyone on your team is aware of the objectives and strategies to be pursued. See that the planning is well done and that positions are as logical and well documented as possible.

The effective team leader participates in setting team targets on each issue and secures the team's commitment to these goals. A well-coordinated team of competent people will be stronger than the person who negotiates alone.

Never enter an important negotiation without anticipating the other team's arguments and tactics. The "Devil's Advocate" approach pays dividends. Take the time to do it.

All facts, averages, statistics and other data submitted by the other party to support their position are self-serving. They are subject to challenge and negotiation. They are less credible than they appear. It pays to be skeptical. Things are not what they appear to be.

When deadlock occurs or appears imminent, you are likely to lose confidence and become anxious. Recognize that the other party may feel worse about the deadlock than you do. There are many good ways to get the negotiation back on track. The best way by far is to search for both-win solutions to bridge the gap. That will keep the talks moving toward agreement.

 Negotiate in depth. The opposing negotiators cannot say "yes" unless you help them to get a "yes" answer from people in their own organization. In that respect you are both on the same side.

 People negotiate to gain satisfaction. What they talk about at the table are issues such as dollars, goods, services and terms of doing business. What they don't talk about are personal issues that are important to them as individuals. Look for ways to give personal satisfaction and include these in your negotiating strategy. It will help get the "yes" answer you want.

 Good negotiators know how to walk away from the table and back again without losing face or bargaining power. If you practice walking away and coming back on small deals, you will do it more easily when the stakes are high.

 Negotiation involves conflict. People who have a strong need to be liked are apt to give too much away. If you are a sales manager, keep that in mind when you assign someone to do the negotiating on a big account.

 In negotiation, there is always a story. If you don't understand the other party's viewpoint, you won't be able to understand the final price. Listening is a concession which gives much and costs little. If you are disciplined enough to listen without interruption or criticism, you will get the story. You will also win respect from the other party for doing so.

 Power changes over time. It changes after an agreement is signed. It changes during performance. It changes after performance takes place. Power relationships are dynamic, not static. The effective negotiator recognizes this and builds the changing balance of power into the agreement.

 Set your targets higher. Be prepared to take the risks of deadlock that go with higher targets. Research indicates that those who aim higher do better.

 Time is money in negotiation. The more time you take, the more you will learn about the other side's needs, time limits, constraints and willingness to compromise or concede.

 Skilled negotiators do better than unskilled negotiators. The more you know about the strategies, tactics and countermeasures of negotiating, the more favorable your agreements will be. There is another payoff - you will be more comfortable with the bargaining process itself.

 Test the resolve of the other party, no matter how firm they appear to be during negotiation. You never know how much they will concede unless you ask for concessions and take the time to win them. That's because they may not be sure about how much they are willing to concede until the pressures of negotiating forces them to do so.

If you have pushed the other party too far, have the wisdom to renegotiate. At the very least, be sure you listen to their problems and have empathy for their position.

If you don't renegotiate after pushing the other side too far, they will renegotiate in hidden ways. They will try to get back at you by taking actions which may be worse for you than providing reasonable relief sooner.

A negotiation is not over:
1. when the parties agree,
2. when the memo of agreement is written, (iii) when the contract is written,
3. when performance takes place, or
4. when the product or service is delivered and paid for.

At each of these stages, differences between the parties are sure to emerge that require further negotiation. Even when the work is done and paid for, there remains the need to think about the next negotiation and how you will conduct it based on what you have learned previously.

• • • • •

In business as in life, you don't get what you deserve, you get what you negotiate. If you practice the techniques and strategies covered in this book you will be in a good position to make win-win deals in any negotiation and get the settlements you deserve.

Index

A

Acceptance time 279
Agree in principle: French culture 12-14
Agreements, win-win, tips 55-70
Alternatives, value of unchosen 252
Arab culture, making negotiating
    fun 14-15
Areas to Look for Win-Win
    Solutions, *Table* 70
Authority, cultural contrasts:
    French, German, Chinese,
    Japanese, Americans 316

B

Back-up support for price 157
Best and final offer 214
Bogey approach 217
Borderline and Dirty Tricks, *Table* 403
Borderline and dirty tricks 375-403
Breaking deadlocks 404-427
Breaking Deadlocks, *Table* 427
Building power, tips on 71-99
Building Negotiating Power, *Table* 99
Buyer and seller deadline tactics 276-279

C

Caucus, planning time 187-209
Cave-in at deadlines 42
Chinese culture 6-9, 267

Closers, psychological 443
Closing strategies and tactics 429-457
Closing Strategies, *Table* 458
Considered response, Japanese 9
Consistency of purpose, Chinese 8
Contrasts, needs and wants 233
Cost breakdowns 38
Cost, total 171
Creating win-win values 55-70
Cultures, learning from other 5-19

D

Deadlock, breaking 405-427
Deal killers 449
Deals, telephone 259-262; checklist 262
Decision making questions 207
Defending your selling price 165-185
Defending Your Selling Price, *Table* 185
Delight factors 452
Delivery, both-win 55, 60
Demand and offer tactics 213-255
Demand and Offer Tactics, *Table* 256
Devil in the details 379-382
Dirty tricks, *see* Borderline and
    dirty tricks
Discovering opponents' authority, tips
    314-316

E

Emotional intimidation 370

Entrepreneurial negotiation, for a house, 57; for a raise 67; for product to buy 62
Environmental intimidation 367-369
Escalation tactics 375-379
Expectations and aspirations 143-147

F

Fait Accompli 375, 382
Feiffer Cartoon, *Illustration* 406-407
Figure, finaglers 385
Financial limits 303
Flinch information 231
French culture 12-14
Fun in negotiation 14
Funny money 47-49

G

Gaining and Maintaining the Initiative, *Table* 349
Gaining and maintaining the initiative 321-349
Getting something in return, French 14,
Good cop-bad cop 388-389
Good negotiator traits 101-102
Guiding principles, history, logic rules, regulations, standards 332-338

H

Habit, power of 86
Hairy hand 336
Hard work theory 78
Hard-to-get principle 440
Haste makes mistakes 438
Heavenly approval, Japanese 10
Hidden motivators, Iceberg theory 73-75
Hitches, last minute 434
Hurry up and wait pressure tactics 267
Hurry up and wait, Chinese 267

I

Iceberg Theory, *Illustration* 74
Iceberg theory, hidden motivators 73-75
Information gathering questions 206
Interdependence, *Illustration* 89
Intersecting interests, bargaining power 89-91
Intimidation tactics 351-373
Intimidation tactics, *Table* 373
Inventory, win-win 70

J

Japanese culture 9-11

K

Knowledge and Information, bargaining power 81
Krunch 239

L

Last and final offer 214; *see also* Best and final offer
Legal Intimidation 352-356
Legitimacy, power of 86
Limited authority 300-306,
Long-term relationships 117-126

M

Maintaining the initiative 321-349,
Mediators, Japanese 417-419
Memorandum of agreement 431
Mid-East culture 14-15
Missing person authority 308
Money, funny 47-49

N

Needs and wants, contrasts 233
Negotiating Power, Building, *Table* 99
Negotiating contract changes 393-396

Negotiation, fun in 14
Negotiation, Winning in – Fourteen
    Rules, *Table*, 54
Negotiators, good, traits 106-110
Negotiator's Bill of Rights, *Illustration*,
323
Nibblers tactic 447
"No, no, no" 143

O

Off the record talks 441
Organizational depth moves 422-452

P

Part to whole move 413
Partnerships 125-135
Patience 275
Persuasion 339-343
Physical intimidation 367
Place to negotiate, best 27
Planning and preparation 201-208
Power bargaining, maintaining initiative
    321-349
Precision in words, Chinese 7
Prescription for success 459-464
Presley, Elvis' Ashtray 436
Pressure, maintaining initiative under
    321-349
Price, strategy defending 137-185
Principles, guiding 332
Psychological closers 443
Putting Together a Winning Team,
    Table 116
Pyramid of Planning, *Illustration* 199
Pyramid of planning 199-208

Q

QUANXI 6
Quick planning kit, tips on 188

R

Raising the stakes 359
Ready-fire-aim 137
Relative, negotiating with 254
Respectful silence, Japanese 9
Response, considered 7
Reverse auction 225
Risk-taking power of 83-86
Rules for winning, fourteen rules 27-53
Russian culture 143

S

Salami tactic 237
Salesperson's job 132-135
Seating, and conference room 338
Seeking heavenly approval 10
Seller deadlines 276-279
Setting targets 137-147
Sole-source, seller power limits 95
Spheres of mutual Interest
    and Interdependence, *Illustration* 89
Stakes, raising 359
Status intimidators 364

Strategies, closing 429-457
Success, prescription for 459-464
Sunk-cost principle 440

T

Tactics, closing,
    see Closing strategies and tactics
Tactics, time 257-291
Tactics, win-win,
    demand and offer 213-256
Taking on a firm price 155-161
Taking the high ground 331-336
Target Setting, *Table* 147
Targets 137-147
Telephone Checklist, *Table* 262
Telephone deals 259-264;
Ten Approaches From Abroad, *Table* 19

Ten power building tips 97-98
Testing a sellers asking price by buyer
        155-161;
Time pressure tactics, *see* Tactics,
        time pressure
Time Pressure Tactics, *Table* 291
Total cost 171
Traits, of a good negotiator 106-110

U

Unintended consequences 454

W

What-if tactic 248
Where to negotiate 27
White hat-black hat 388-396
Why negotiate if price is right? 25
Win-win negotiating 55-70
Winning, fourteen rules for 26-33
Winning in Negotiation - 14 Rules,
        Table 54
Winning the competitive negotiation 19-49
Words, differences in other cultures 16-18